WE MIGHT JUST
MAKE IT AFTER ALL

WE MIGHT JUST MAKE IT AFTER ALL

MY BEST FRIENDSHIP WITH
kate spade

ELYCE ARONS

GALLERY BOOKS

New York   Amsterdam/Antwerp   London
Toronto   Sydney/Melbourne   New Delhi

G

Gallery Books
An Imprint of Simon & Schuster, LLC
1230 Avenue of the Americas
New York, NY 10020

Some names and identifying characteristics have been changed, whether or not so noted in the text.

First Gallery Books hardcover edition June 2025

GALLERY BOOKS and colophon are registered trademarks of Simon & Schuster, LLC

Simon & Schuster strongly believes in freedom of expression and stands against censorship in all its forms. For more information, visit BooksBelong.com.

For information about special discounts for bulk purchases, please contact Simon & Schuster Special Sales at 1-866-506-1949 or business@simonandschuster.com.

The Simon & Schuster Speakers Bureau can bring authors to your live event. For more information or to book an event, contact the Simon & Schuster Speakers Bureau at 1-866-248-3049 or visit our website at www.simonspeakers.com.

Interior design by Karla Schweer
Illustrations by Lauren Klas

Manufactured in the United States of America

10 9 8 7 6 5 4 3 2 1

LCCN: 2024059758

ISBN 978-1-6680-6907-3
ISBN 978-1-6680-6909-7 (ebook)

If you're as honest and fair as you can be, not only in business but in life, things will work out. I hope that people remember me not just as a good businesswoman but as a great friend— and a heck of a lot of fun.

—Kate Spade, *Glamour*, December 2002

It has taken me more than seven years to write about my best friend, Katy, since her passing. I knew it would be important to do so before too many details slipped away. Most people who have asked me about her—very legitimately—want to know what happened. Why would someone with everything—family, friends, talent, fame—take her own life? I can tell you those of us closest to Katy knew she was battling depression in her later years, but none of us ever envisioned her taking that tragic step.

I'm writing now about an earlier period in our lives when there was no hint of what she would suffer later. We had our ups and downs like everyone, but we would always persevere. Katy and I met on our first day of college and were together almost every day afterward for nearly four decades. I wanted to tell that story about our time together—our college years and the founding of our company Kate Spade. It's really the story of a dear friendship. If you have ever had a best girlfriend who could finish your sentences, who made you laugh until your sides hurt, or who was the only person in the world you could talk to when your young heart was broken, you'll recognize our friendship.

PROLOGUE

On June 9, 2018, four days after my best friend of thirty-seven years took her own life, I had to go to her Park Avenue apartment to pick up some of my clothes from her closet. Katy and I had recently launched a new accessories company, Frances Valentine, and she had some pieces of mine that I needed at the office.

As soon as I walked in, I felt on edge. Ordinarily Katy's apartment was icebox cold in the summer, but the A/C had been turned off and the place was sweltering. Besides the oppressive heat, the air was stale and still. Katy usually left every light on 24/7 and kept her drapes tied open to let the sun in. I had never seen them closed. I warned her a few times that anyone passing by on the street could see into her beautiful third-floor apartment, but she didn't care. Since her death, paparazzi had been stationed outside the building, hoping to get a picture. For privacy, someone had closed the drapes and turned off the lights, leaving the apartment in unsettling darkness.

I headed for her bedroom, the room where it happened. I hadn't been there since that terrible day. I switched on the overhead light. The usual bright, colorful room was dim and disheveled, so uncharacteristic of the tidy space I knew. Discarded paperwork from the medics who responded to Katy's housekeeper's 911 call lay strewn across the floor. It was eerie to feel so freaked out in a place where I had spent so much carefree time.

I was still in disbelief that Katy was really gone. We'd pulled some very elaborate pranks over the years, always trying to one-up each other with every new stunt. We loved scaring people, mostly ourselves. It was one of the personality quirks we shared. I'd once faked my own death at our office, and it was as perfect as a prank could be. I could still hear her scream from a few offices away before I revealed my trick, and we both ended up doubled over laughing.

Being there alone in the stillness and gloom gave me an almost out-of-body sense as I was walked through the apartment.

As I put my hand on the closet door handle, I couldn't help but think Katy was going to jump out of the closet and scare the shit out of me. That would be so like her. The entire world believed Kate Spade was gone, but there was a part of me that fleetingly hoped her suicide was her most elaborate, epic prank yet.

The hairs at the back of my neck stood up as I held my breath and opened the closet door.

Hundreds of moths flew out in a black wave, coming right at me.

I shrieked, full–lung power, and stumbled backward. I kept shrieking as the moths circled the room around my head. *Katy must be watching this*, I thought. Any second, she was going to come up behind me, tap my shoulder, and say, "Gotcha!"

I yelled at the empty room, "If you're doing this, Katy, this time, it's not funny!" I put my hands on my legs as I bent over to catch my breath. It took me minutes to recover from that furnace blast of terror. Once my brain was functional again, I wiped the sweat off my face and realized how this had happened. Katy had never put mothballs in her closet because of the smell. Her assistant hadn't gone in her closet for a while—no one had—and moth colonies grow fast in the heat.

Katy hadn't planned this moth assault. She wasn't pulling a prank. She was really and truly gone. But if she were alive, and had heard my horror-movie-worthy scream, she would have thought it was the most hilarious thing in the world. She would have playacted that moment for our friends at a hundred parties in the future. While some in our circle would have said, "You guys are sick," the two of us would have been rolling on the floor.

I grabbed the garments I'd come for—now destroyed with moth holes—turned off the light and left her apartment for the final time. But the feeling that Katy was there, and that she was loving my terror remained. And one thing I was certain of: If she really were watching me from wherever she was, she would have been laughing her ass off.

CHAPTER 1

I looked over at my dad as he drove me the three hours from our cattle farm in Sedgwick, Kansas, to start my college career at the University of Kansas. He leaned back on the headrest of my red Cutlass Supreme while he steered with one hand, that signature cigar stub perched in the corner of his mouth on his handsome, sunburned face. He really did look a lot like Paul Newman, as all the Sedgwick ladies said. His favorite jazz station, the only jazz station accessible to our small town of 1,500 Kansans, played as it always did when Dad was around.

It was mid-August in 1981, and I was leaving everything I had ever known behind. We passed all the rows of our crops, alfalfa on my left, corn on my right, all stretching to the blue sky. Those rows we passed felt like years ticking off behind me as we drove east on the long, straight road toward the Kansas horizon. My heart was a little heavy—I still carry a longing for those early family days—but in my bones, I had a growing sense of excitement for the new adventure I was speeding toward. I had no way of knowing that later on that sunny summer afternoon I would meet the person who would change the trajectory of my life forever: Katy Brosnahan, who the world would someday know as Kate Spade.

* * *

With our passion for music, art and fashion, my family was a bit of an outlier compared to the general Sedgwick community. A fourth-generation farmer, my dad had fallen in love with Mom, an East Coast beauty who was a flight attendant when they met on a short flight my mother was working from Wichita to Kansas City. They got married in their early twenties in El Dorado, Kansas, on New Year's Day, and she moved to the Midwest. In addition to their farming day jobs, Dad was a musician who played piano as well as numerous other instruments, and Mom was an aspiring artist—she had a side career as an illustrator for retail stores in and around our nearest large city, Wichita. She subscribed to *Women's Wear Daily*, and my earliest memories involve running home from school and sneaking a peek at the pages featuring stylish women in their beautiful clothes before tending to my daily farm chores.

I was the youngest of the four Cox daughters. Holiday and Shon were the eldest, nine and eight years older than I, and I considered them glamorous grown-up teens at the time. Holiday was strikingly beautiful and had inherited my mother's interest in art. Shon had an incredible sense of humor, and in some ways was everybody's favorite. She has a remarkable singing voice, and even as a teen would wow the folks at the Plymouth Congregational Church when she sang in the choir. Years later, she would sing at my wedding and leave our guests virtually breathless. Willow was two years my senior, so most of my misadventures involved her. She was a whirlwind of energy and a horse fanatic—and would often get the two of us into all kinds of mischief.

Our 1,500-acre farm was small in comparison to our neighbors'. We raised mostly Angus cattle, grew a variety of crops including wheat, corn, soybeans, alfalfa and milo (some call this sorghum; it's used a lot as cattle feed). From around the age of six or seven years old we had daily chores. For my sisters and me, our primary job was to keep the animals fed, gather the eggs and keep things generally in order. My mom would say, "The animals don't know it's the weekend. They don't know it's your birthday. They don't know it's Christmas." The point was that our job was 365 days a year, no room for discussion. We were always home after school. Not that there was much of a neighborhood to play in, our nearest neighbor being three miles away. There were no playdates back in the late sixties and early seventies. We had each other; we had our animals; we had our chores.

Often on the weekends, we would have to drive the cattle from field to field. Dad would be on his tractor pulling a huge stack of alfalfa hay to lure the three hundred or so cattle in the right direction. Our team consisted of Willow on her quarter horse, Sweet Pea; me on Honey, my palomino; and my dog Bear, an enormous half German shepherd, half Catahoula, nipping at the heels of any cattle that were straggling. We generally had seasonal help for big drives, up to a dozen local hands who made their living working for farm families like ours. It was dirty, exhausting work, but in retrospect, those days introduced me to the value of a job well done. After the drive, my mother would make a huge dinner for anyone who could stay, usually fifteen or twenty people. My mother is a fantastic cook and would do the "farm to table" thing in a literal way.

The running of the farm and the business of the farm were a big part of our upbringing. At seven years old, each of us joined 4-H club.

Back then it was an organization primarily for teaching farm kids the business of farming and animal husbandry. Our annual project was raising cattle. My father would help me choose a calf, then walk me through the expenses of paying for the feed and maintenance of raising it. After a year we would enter the now fully grown steer in a regional competition. My very first steer I named Harry. For the show, I would have to wash him, fluff and brush his fur, shine his hooves with black shoe polish and style his tail with hair spray. Lastly, I would parade Harry around the arena much like a trainer at the Westminster dog show.

That first year, I won a blue ribbon, and afterward, they auctioned Harry off. I didn't really know what was happening, but my dad slapped him on the bottom and Harry ran up a ramp into a waiting semi. I suddenly understood where my steer was going. My dad explained that was the business we were in; it was our livelihood; it was how farms work to provide people with food for their family's table. I cried my eyes out in my best cowgirl outfit of Wrangler jeans, boots and my camel-colored cowboy hat. But in a few weeks, I received a check from the auction buyer for $1,200. From that, I paid back the cost of the feed, and all the other expenses of raising the steer. We put the balance of $400 in my account for the next year. My parents allowed me to take $20 of it to go out and buy whatever I wanted. Turns out almost everything I needed to know about business, I learned on a farm.

I have so many good memories from my childhood. Like on those dreamy days when spring began to show bright green wheat sprouts in our fields, Willow and I would wake up early before school and ride bareback through the sweet-smelling alfalfa fields with no halters on our horses. It was a pretty glorious way to be a kid. Like the stories in my favorite children's books, there was both magic and heartbreak in living on our farm. Those early days are the fabric that created the people we became. I feel lucky to have had them.

* * *

Dad and I pulled the Cutlass up to Gertrude Sellards Pearson Hall, which everyone called GSP, one of the two freshman girls' dorms at the University of Kansas. We found a small army of fraternity boys waiting on the sidewalk to help the incoming freshman girls haul their stuff to their rooms.

Dad frowned when he saw them, but I couldn't stop grinning. We got out of my car and unloaded my stuff—milk crates full of books, a Pier 1 Imports giant palm leaf and lamp, a wicker laundry basket filled with clothes and suitcases. Before the luggage hit the ground, a swarm of polite young male pledges grabbed my stuff and carried it toward the dorm.

"I think I should stick around for a while," grumbled Dad, eyeing the boys. Unlike most native Kansans, he was a bit suspicious when it came to strangers offering help. As the father of four daughters, he was particularly skeptical.

I gave him a reassuring hug. Reluctantly, and in retrospect, a bit teary-eyed, Dad got back in my car to drive home. I wasn't allowed to bring it to school until I could prove myself with good grades. I waved goodbye from the curb until he was out of sight and then spun around and ran up the stairs to my dorm. I know now that seeing the last of your children leaving for college is one of the hardest days in a parent's life. At that moment, I wasn't thinking about how my dad must have felt driving home without me.

On the top step, I took a minute to look around and get my bearings. Unlike the flat and open farm fields I grew up with, the University of Kansas was nestled into the rolling lush green hills that bordered the eastern part of our state. I felt like a character from the movie *Love Story* ensconced in the redbrick colonial buildings of our campus. The school was sprawling but organized like a small village. A fifteen-minute walk would bring us to downtown Lawrence, a quaint college town with great shopping and terrific barbecue and burger joints. As I stood in front of that door to my new home, I remember my heart pounding. Everywhere I turned, there were actually people walking around, not something I was used to seeing in Sedgwick.

I went inside to find my luggage already piled in the middle of my room. To one of the boys, I said, "Thanks for doing the heavy lifting."

He was cute.

"Happy to help," said Cute Boy, and he handed me a sheet of paper as he left.

It was an invitation to a party at his fraternity. I'd already heard about the KU tradition called Country Club Week, a solid week of parties between registration and the start of classes. The fraternity pledges (first-years) were on a mission to get freshman girls to come to their parties. It all sounded like a blast to me. I looked over the invite for a meet and greet that very night starring the omnipresent beer keg. In the next hour, I'd collect half a dozen invites to frat mixers for that week, all from freshman pledges, each one handsomer than the next! I remember thinking how in one day life had changed for me so quickly; I was the happiest I'd ever been.

My dormmates trickled in over the course of the day, and I was there to greet the gang. As it turned out, I was not the only Pier 1 Imports fan. I'd never seen so much wicker in my life. My roommate, Anne, was from North Carolina. Her style was hip and funky, head to toe in the Limited, the affordable high-fashion choice of the times—and I liked her on sight. I considered myself quite fashion-forward—I had just been on a trip with my mom and sisters to New York City. We shopped downtown in Greenwich Village at

Antique Boutique, where I bought a green crinkled jumpsuit, and at Unique Boutique, where I found a double-breasted jacket with Adam Ant–style shoulder pads. On that day, I was wearing the purple parachute pants and scrunched green leather pointy-toed boots that had earned me the gag honor of being named "Weirdest Dresser" at a high school party.

As more girls arrived and we introduced ourselves, we figured out that room assignments were in alphabetical order by last name. I was a Cox, so two doors down were Katy Brosnahan and her roommate, Robin Brown. They were both welcoming and friendly. They wore similar preppy popped-collar polo shirts, Weejun loafers and baggy cotton khaki shorts—I remember wondering if they planned to dress identically. I didn't realize at that time that they were the real McCoy, sporting preppy style early on, having actually attended private schools. That timeless American look was just gaining steam in the mass market. It was about to take the country by storm with the publication of Lisa Birnbach's witty *The Official Preppy Handbook*, outfits worn by fashion icons like Brooke Shields and Princess Di, and the coming explosion of brands like Ralph Lauren and J.Crew. I had a lot to learn.

* * *

When I first met Katy, who would become my lifelong best friend, there was no swelling background theme music, no lightning bolt, no fanfare. I kind of dismissed her as a potential friend, and I'm pretty sure she did the same to me. I thought she seemed like a nice person who was very polite, in our Midwestern way, so typical of most people at the university. She was pretty and petite with a slender hourglass figure. She had porcelain skin with a sprinkle of freckles across her upturned nose. Her hair was one of her most attractive features, thick and the color of shiny mahogany. She was endlessly experimenting with new updos, and eventually when we became close friends, she was always fussing with my hair as well.

It's funny, if I were handed a crystal ball in that moment and could have foreseen what the future would hold for both of us, it would have seemed unbelievable, like some impossibly crazy Hollywood production dreamed up by a team of screenwriters.

Once our rugs were unfurled and every mini-fridge was plugged in, we started getting ready for our first frat party. The college had distributed welcome bags to every freshman girl, which included Virginia Slims cigarettes (can you imagine that now?), Wella Balsam shampoo and conditioner, Crest toothpaste and Shower to Shower talcum powder. I sprinkled some of that powder under my arms and put on a clean, colorful top I had bought at Bloomingdale's in New York.

All the girls were lined up at bathroom mirrors with blow-dryers, curling irons, eye shadow and Charlie perfume. Favorites by Billy Joel and Fleetwood Mac, along with the Rolling Stones' new hit "Start Me Up," were blaring down our hallway.

Katy, the pretty, petite preppy, and I were next to each other at the mirror. She sniffed in my direction. "Oh my God, did you use that powder they gave us?" she asked.

"Um, yes."

"Don't you think it smells like a gas station bathroom?" She looked at me in the mirror we were sharing, held her nose and crossed her eyes.

I knew she was trying to be funny, but it did raise my hackles a bit. I never used that powder again.

The party was full of laughter and energy, with booming music and red Solo cups everywhere, and we danced until 4 a.m., ending the night at the doughnut shop. When we got back to the dorm, I mentioned to a bunch of the girls that I was heading to registration right when it opened the following morning—I figured that after our night of partying, everyone would be in recuperation mode and moving slowly.

I was pleasantly surprised when Katy said, "I'll go with you."

As we walked over to Ellsworth Hall together at 7:30 a.m., we chatted about the parties we had each gone to the night before. She was clearly tired and hungover, and I wondered why she wasn't still in bed. I had a guess, though. We neared the building, and I said, "I have to pick up my financial aid check before I register for classes."

Katy said, "I thought that was why you were coming so early. Me too, but let's not tell anyone."

Neither one of us wanted the others to know we were on financial aid. It wasn't that I was ashamed of it, but I didn't like having anything out there that would make people see me differently. I wanted to start college without any prejudgments of any kind, and Katy felt the same way. It was our first thing in common, and one that made each of us trust the other with a secret.

We arrived at the right place, and Katy got in the line for the A and B names. I got in the line for C and D names. She got her check, no problem, and waited for me before we headed over to registration for classes.

When it was my turn in line, I said my name: "Elyce Cox."

The friendly woman in a bright floral dress looked through her stack of envelopes and said, "Sorry, dear, nothing for Elyce Cox."

I spelled my name to her. She shook her head.

I said, "Okay, thank you, but can you please check again?"

"No, I'm sorry dear, there's nothing here for you," she said.

I got out of the line and walked three paces before choking back tears.

Katy put her hand on my shoulder and said, "Hey, what's wrong?"

"I can't go to school. They don't have my check, and I can't register for classes today without it." My mind sped toward the worst-case scenarios: packing up, leaving. I felt humiliated, totally frustrated . . . and then I realized, *I can't believe it! I gave her the wrong name!*

I ran back to the front of the line and said to the floral dress lady, "Sorry, can you look for the name *Barbara* Cox?" Barbara is my legal first name, but no one had ever called me anything but my middle name, Elyce, my whole life.

The woman was as relieved as I was as she handed me my check. Katy started laughing, and I joined in.

I said, "I really thought I wouldn't be able to register and go to school. I never have to use my legal name. I can't believe I forgot."

That episode became one of our running jokes, and in a way brought us a little closer. Katy saw me go from total terror to complete relief in a flash; she understood my panic and sympathized with me.

We both intended to major in journalism and signed up for a lot of the same classes. We started walking to classes together most days from GSP or home from class. One day, I asked her why she picked journalism as her major.

"This is gonna sound crazy," she explained, "but my favorite show growing up was *The Mary Tyler Moore Show*. I loved everything about Mary's life, how she worked at a TV news show and had her own apartment, everything."

I looked at her wide-eyed, not because I thought it was crazy, but because that show was the reason *I* was majoring in journalism, too. Every Saturday night growing up, my sisters and I were glued to the TV and teleported into Mary's world. She had made her own career in a male-dominated industry. She had her own place, dated whomever she wanted, wore fantastic clothes, ate whatever she liked, and hosted parties for her friends. She was likable and funny. Mary's was the life I'd fantasized about having since I was nine years old.

When I told her that, Katy and I stopped in our tracks and stared at each other. I'm sure millions of girls our age idolized Mary

Richards and wanted to grow up to have her life, but I'd never met another one before, besides my sisters. Katy and I stood there for a minute in front of Wescoe Hall in the center of campus, both of us so happily surprised that we had found another person who shared the identical dream of our future life.

* * *

We were both good students and serious about school, but there were so many great parties. The girls on our floor traveled in a pack from frat to frat, dancing, meeting guys and having a ball. One big gathering was at a lake on campus—so much beer, and not a ladies' room in sight.

I was standing with Katy and a few others and leaned over to whisper to her, "I have to go *so bad.*"

She whispered back, "Let's go behind some bushes."

Trees and shrubs surrounded the lake, but we wanted to go to a faraway dark place so no one would see us. Satisfied there was no one nearby, we squatted and did our business, giggling the whole time. We returned to our friends, relieved.

A couple of days later, I felt a burning sensation south of the border. My bottom and back of my thighs were alarmingly itchy. Katy found me in the dorm that night and said, "Elyce, something's going on with me. I have no idea what it is."

We went into her room and locked the door. She lowered her cuffed jeans and showed me a violent red rash in the same places I was itching like crazy. I recognized it right away. "You have poison ivy. I thought it was just me." We must have relieved ourselves on a huge patch of the stuff. Katy, the "city" girl, had never had a rash like this before, but I had, and I knew how stubborn poison ivy could be. Our case proved to be a bad one. We were so embarrassed to explain how we got it that we didn't tell anyone. For the next two weeks, we both tried not to scratch our bottoms in front of people, and it wasn't easy. Evenings we would take turns dabbing each other's backsides with cotton balls dipped in calamine lotion, which was humiliating, kind of funny and almost completely useless. By day I would catch her sneakily rubbing against a chair or doorframe and try not to crack up. But all we had to do was make eye contact and forget it—we'd both start laughing. Our friends thought we were crazy, but they never figured out what our big inside joke was.

There was a TV in the dorm living room, and twenty girls showed up every weekday afternoon to watch *All My Children* and *General Hospital.* We planned our class schedule around our soaps. For the full two hours, everybody had to be silent, except during commercials.

The *All My Children* villain, Erica Kane played by Susan Lucci, was a wealthy, conniving woman who always dressed to the nines like a real (we thought) sophisticated New Yorker. Katy loved Erica Kane's look, and said, "Someday, I'm going to be able to dress like that." They shared a petite frame, so Katy could see herself in Erica's strapless sequined gowns. But the dripping diamonds, big hair and face full of makeup? I was kind of shocked that Katy aspired to glitz and glamour. In some ways, her all-American preppy style was just a uniform she'd been wearing her whole life, but she fantasized about more. She'd had no real exposure to the wider world of fashion outside of the magazines she read. And aside from my few trips to New York City with my mom, neither had I. My fashion inspiration was also from magazines and from MTV, the crazy new video channel that had just launched. I loved the style of those '80s bands with the wild clothes and shoulder pads. We were not really sure what it was we wanted, but Katy and I both knew we aspired to more. We just didn't know at that time what form "more" would take.

Katy and I became "Little Sisters of Minerva" to Sigma Alpha Epsilon (SAE), basically female first-year affiliates to the fraternity, where all the pledges were our good friends. The signature party at their house was called Sleep-and-Eat (a little pun on the initials SAE). Everyone showed up in their pj's and drank trash can punch, which was Hawaiian Punch with every kind of alcohol you can imagine blended in, all served in a fresh and clean (we hoped) lined garbage can. It was traditional for the members to bring dates to these parties. Neither Katy nor I had a boyfriend, but it didn't matter. Guy friends would ask us just so we could go and have a terrific time. Usually, if I had a date and Katy didn't, my date would find a guy for Katy, and vice versa. So, for our first Sleep-and-Eat party, my date found one for her, a six-foot-two, two-hundred-pound gentle giant with a full beard. He also seemed to be one of the nicest guys we had met so far.

Katy and I both looked fetching in our pj's. I had on a lacy slip negligee over a T-shirt and shorts, and Katy wore a white mid-thigh-length negligee over a navy sweatshirt and shorts. Katy sometimes didn't eat dinner before we went to parties because she didn't like the dorm food. She liked to have fun at these parties—we all did—but that night, she had too much of a good time. Not that I was counting, but she downed several Solo cups of trash can punch on an empty stomach. Everyone at the party was dancing all night to Earth, Wind & Fire, the Bee Gees and the favorite single "Car Wash," which got the crowd on their feet. Around three in the morning, we were dancing to Kim Carnes's "Bette Davis Eyes" in the dim basement, when Katy slowly sank onto the floor that was covered in sticky spilled punch. Her date, Man Bear, leaned down and lifted her up with one hand and flung her over his shoulder as if she were a doll.

"I think Katy has had enough," he said. "We should take her home."

I left with them. He rode a Harley-Davidson. We managed to get Katy sandwiched between the two of us and motored back toward GSP in one piece. The roar of the bike and the wind revived her.

"Where are we going?" she shouted.

"Home," I yelled back.

"No!" she shouted. "Waffle House!"

And that was how we ended the evening—eating waffles at dawn wearing lingerie. Katy took a big bite and said, "Baby! That's good!" I came to understand then, and for all time, that whenever she was excited, she'd clench both fists, close her eyes and yell, "Baby!"

* * *

After some good quarterly grades, I was allowed to bring my car to campus. I was one of the few girls to have wheels, so I drove to a lot of our group outings. One of our friends worked at the local ice cream shop across town. Some of the girls wanted ice cream, so I volunteered to drive over there. Six of us piled into the red Cutlass, including Katy.

She said, "Cheryl's working today, and she'll give us all free ice cream!"

"Does Cheryl own the store?" I asked.

"No, weirdo. She's a student. She just works there," Katy said.

"Then how can she give us free ice cream? It's not hers to give."

Groans from everyone. Katy said, "Stop being such a Goody Two-shoes."

I admit, I was a little over-the-top with my "you always have to do the right thing" ideals. It was all part of my religious upbringing in a small community.

"You know what? Forget it. I can't drive you there knowing that you're stealing from the owner of the store!" I declared. That would make me complicit in something I felt was wrong.

Katy rolled her eyes, and everyone got out of the car. But the next time we went to that ice cream spot, our whole group made a point of paying for their cones.

A few weeks later, on a frigid November night, Katy and I went to the Mad Hatter, a favorite bar in town, along with a big group of girls. I left my pack of Virginia Slims in the Cutlass, and Katy offered to come with me to get them. The two of us wound up getting inside the car and smoking there. Good thing we'd brought our coats; it was freezing. Still, we opened the windows and blew our smoke outside. (While it's inconceivable for me to think about it today, most of our circle of friends smoked during our college days and into our late twenties. Newscasters would smoke on TV. We enjoyed smoking; it was a way of life. Now even a whiff of cigarette smoke as I'm walking down the street is gross to me. It's amazing how much things change.)

In the car that night, we talked about our families. I usually dodged questions about mine, other than answering the basics. I would tell people about our small town and what it was like growing up on a working farm. I knew just as much about Katy: She was the fifth of six kids in a big Irish family from Kansas City, Missouri, and she had gone to an all-girls Catholic high school.

That night, I was a little tipsy, and Katy looked at me with genuine curiosity, so I said, "I'm close with my family, but it's complicated." I hesitated for a moment. "We went through something when I was young, and it affected all of us. It made us closer, but we don't talk about it." Tears emerged, as they always did when I let myself go back there. Even today, when I think about those times, I get emotional.

Katy was curious but put her hand on my shoulder. "You don't have to say any more if it's hard for you."

"It's okay," I continued. "It was the saddest time for my family. When I was seven, my older sister, Holiday, got sick with a type of bone cancer. My parents took her all over the country to the best cancer clinics for chemo and radiation, but nothing worked. My other sisters, Shon and Willow, and I had to keep going without any news of what was happening. Willow and I had to live with my aunt and uncle for a time while my parents flew around with Holiday. After two years, Holiday passed away. She was just a teenager. It was so hard for us to lose our sister. It was so hard for my parents to lose their daughter. Everyone in Sedgwick knew what happened. They tried to help, but we kind of shut that down. It was a Protestant thing, I guess, like never involve other people in your personal business. Never cry in front of people. Don't be weak."

It was huge to share this story with someone outside my immediate family. I'd never talked to a relative stranger about Holiday before, but it felt safe with Katy. She hugged me and squeezed my hand while I cried. I had a box of Kleenex in the car, and she handed me tissue after tissue until I finished the story.

"I'm so sorry you had to go through that," she said. "Are your parents okay? I can't imagine losing a child."

"They're together. They're okay. We don't talk about it because it hurts too much."

"I was the same age when my family went through something really hard. It doesn't compare to yours . . ." Katy went on to tell me the story of her own family trials, how her parents' divorce had impacted their close family of six children. Her father and mother got separate places, and life for their family changed drastically. Though they weathered that storm, she carried that sadness with her along with the reluctance of talking about it with anyone. She started crying, and I was the hugger and Kleenex giver then. We'd been the same age when our lives changed, when our families were rearranged. The devastation was emotional and financial for both of our families. It was the biggest thing in our lives, the biggest thing we had in common. From the very start, we empathized with each other's internal sorrow, and it drew us together.

That conversation in the car went on for hours. We let all our childhood pain spill out and cried through a whole box of tissues. And it felt really *good*. In those days, especially in the Midwest, people didn't emotionally lean on one another. I was a private person, and as I'd learn over the years, Katy was extremely private herself.

I asked her not to tell anyone about Holiday. Since childhood, I was looked at by everyone outside our family as the girl whose sister died. Going to college was the first time I'd been free of other people's pity. Katy looked right at me, wiping away her tears and mine, and said, "I will never tell anyone what happened to you." From the tone of her voice and the look in her eyes, I knew she would keep my confidence forever—about my sister and anything else. Smiling, she added, "And I know you'd never tell anyone my secrets. You won't even steal an ice cream cone!" I could not have known it then, but that trust would last a lifetime.

CHAPTER 2

That spring semester, Katy and I had been ambivalent about rushing sororities. At the very last minute, we decided to go through the process and determine how we felt at the end of it. We ran into the Panhellenic Administration office to sign up, just as the doors were closing.

During rush, you'd travel around to different sororities and meet the members. You had to dress up—not too prim but not too casual. Almost everyone in our dorm was rushing, and we'd get ready together, borrowing each other's tops and pearls so we wouldn't be seen wearing the same outfit twice. We crammed into cars to arrive at parties together. Katy's brother, Earl, had loaned her his old car—a black Chevy with a cracked rearview mirror. She insisted on parking a few blocks from wherever we were going so the sorority girls didn't see her beat-up old car. We had to walk on slick and icy streets in pumps and risk falling and tearing someone else's skirt we had borrowed.

Katy was dead serious and stressed-out about rush. I came to realize that whatever Katy committed to, including rushing a sorority, she would focus on and strive to execute brilliantly. Of course, she got invited back to every single sorority. Katy pledged Kappa Kappa Gamma, and I pledged Chi Omega. For sophomore year, we lived at our respective sorority houses, but we were constantly in and out of each other's.

When you were invited to join a sorority, you had months to study its history, the songs, the members' names and other relevant information. Later you were tested, and if you passed the test there was an initiation ceremony and a big party. I felt like a princess that whole week. I enjoyed studying and learning about Chi O's traditions and generations of service to others. It was the first time I had been a part of a national organization that was so inspirational because of the commitment to service. Katy also appreciated the feeling of being part of something bigger than herself. It was so much more than we had ever thought it was going to be. Even now as an adult, I have so many friends and acquaintances because I'm a Chi Omega. At nineteen years old, I could not have foreseen how important those relationships with my sisters would be throughout my life.

* * *

When the school year ended, Katy flew to Arizona to stay with her sister Missy, a bright and vivacious flight attendant, and her husband Jon, a lawyer. They had a beautiful home in Paradise Valley outside Scottsdale, and Katy loved it there. The dry weather was great for her allergies, and she got to spend time with her beautiful new baby niece, Whitney. I went home and took a job at the

Wichita Country Club, a fancy business club downtown where the Koch brothers were members. I worked the lunch shift at the Men's Grill. Sorry, no women allowed (besides servers). If they needed more staff for an evening shift, I took it. I worked as many hours as I could; I needed to make as much money as possible for next year at school.

Since long-distance calls were too expensive for either of us, Katy and I wrote long letters to each other all summer long. Every time a letter from Katy arrived, I grabbed it out of the mailbox and ran up to my room to read it. I'd devour every word as she told me about her hostess job at a restaurant called Oscar Taylor's and described babysitting Whitney. Being apart was difficult, and the letters were such a joy—they made me feel still connected to Katy while we looked forward to seeing each other back at school.

One day, my Wichita Country Club manager, Mike, asked me to work an evening shift for "the Smith wedding." The uniform was a white tuxedo shirt, a bow tie and a really long polyester skirt with a slit halfway up my thigh. My role was to stand by the elevator with a tray. I was too young to serve alcohol legally, so I was responsible for taking people's used glasses and offering ashtrays for them to put out their cigarettes.

I realized within thirty minutes that the groom was a graduating senior from KU, and he was marrying Becky, a college acquaintance of mine, who had also just graduated. I barely knew them, so I wasn't upset that I was not invited, but I knew a lot of the guests from KU and was mortified to be serving them. I begged Mike to let me work in the kitchen, but he insisted I stand there at the elevator for the whole party and clean up my classmates' dirty glasses. I did my best to act like it didn't bother me.

The next morning, I told my mom how embarrassed I was by the situation.

She said, "Well, I think it's great. It builds character." She gave me the whole "That's the way life is" speech, refusing to see it from my perspective.

The only person who would understand how I felt was Katy. I called her long-distance to talk about it.

She agreed, "That's awful! I would have died. But it's over now, and in just a few weeks, we'll be together again. Baby!" It was the one time all summer we spoke by phone. It cost me a pretty penny just to hear her voice, but it was worth it.

Looking back, I know my mom was right, and it's what I would tell my own daughters. However, I wish I could give a giant hug and shout-out to all the kids who work to pay their way through college, or any kids who work to support themselves. Often it's life without a safety net, and it's not easy. But they should know, and I can tell them from my fairly extensive work experience, that they are the special ones. They will be the superstars. They're the ones who are never afraid to roll up their sleeves and make things happen.

One weekend, Katy came to the farm to meet my family and see where I had grown up. My parents had heard so much about this funny, amazing person I was spending all my time with, and they were looking forward to meeting her. My mom and dad and my very-hard-of-hearing eighty-five-year-old grandmother were all excited when we arrived, and they had a big feast of steak, baked potatoes, salad, vegetables and, of course, Mom's famous chocolate buttermilk cake waiting for us. Katy was her bubbly self at first, but then was uncharacteristically quiet the rest of the weekend.

As I was packing the car to leave, my mom asked, "Is this the same person you have been raving about for the last year? She is really polite but quiet as a mouse."

I explained to my mom that Katy can get really shy and she clams up when she is nervous, but inside I was bewildered, too.

When Katy and I were driving back, I asked her why she had been so quiet the entire weekend.

"I have to be honest with you," she said, "and I'm really sorry if it hurts your feelings, but I just couldn't take how mean your mom was to your grandmother! She constantly yelled at her about everything."

I actually had to pull off the road because I was laughing so hard. When I could finally catch my breath, I told her, "Katy, my grandmother can't hear unless you yell." It took us fifteen minutes to sit up straight after being doubled over with laughter.

Two weeks later, Katy invited me to Kansas City for the weekend to stay at her mom's place. I was a little nervous because Katy had always described her mother with reverence and awe. We drove into a beautiful tree-lined neighborhood to June Brosnahan's home. Although modest in size, it felt like an enormous, indoor garden. The living room was sunny with beautiful, richly colored prints on the sofa and chairs, and art on the walls. I admired a beautiful zebra vase with a live fern growing as the zebra's mane, which June graciously offered to give us. The surroundings immediately felt unique and authentic to Katy's mother's personality. June was warm and gracious when Katy introduced us, and as I got to know her, I appreciated her very colorful personality. She was really funny, and I now understood where Katy had gotten her wry sense of humor.

Katy left us in the living room alone to chat while she got ready to go out to lunch. I was trying to be on my best behavior with June. Her graciousness, her voice, vocabulary and flawless manners were no doubt meant to put me at ease, but I talked way too much out of nervousness. Thankfully June ended my babbling when she asked, "Katy, what on earth is taking you so long?"

From the other room, Katy replied, "Mom, I am almost done."

Her mother admonished, "Oh, Katy, you are never done, food is done. You are either finished or you are through."

After that, I remained quiet the whole weekend, fearing I would make some sort of verbal faux pas and June would think I was not very smart.

Meeting her family continued during spring break of our sophomore year when Katy and I were invited to Scottsdale to stay with her big sister, Missy, and her husband, Jon. Missy was a slightly older version of Katy, petite, with thick dark auburn hair. She was confident and quick to give advice in a good way. She and Jon rolled out the red carpet for us. They took us to fancy restaurants; chauffeured us around Scottsdale, Tempe and Phoenix to see the sights; gave us a tour of Arizona State University and showed us a nifty apartment complex near campus. As we took it all in, she asked, "Wouldn't it be great if you guys went here?"

Arizona was stunning and unlike anything I'd seen before. The warmth, sunshine, vegetation and lifestyle were completely different from Kansas. The idea of moving to this alien planet of the West intrigued me. Katy was ready for an adventure, too.

"What if we transferred?" she asked me in the guest room at Missy's. "If we did it together, it wouldn't be so scary. We could live together in that apartment complex Missy showed us."

I'd been transfixed by the apartment complex ever since we saw it. Missy, who was all about getting Katy to move to Arizona, had scoped out a place for us to live that she knew we would fall for. The complex had several dozen units on two levels that all overlooked a swimming pool. Most of the residents were students or recent grads. We could live in a real apartment, not a dorm or sorority house, like grown adults. We could be like Mary Richards and decorate the place in our style. We could host dinner parties for our friends, hang out by the pool all day when not in class. We could pop into our neighbors' for a cup of sugar.

In the guest room at Missy's, we were sharing a queen-size bed, wearing extra-large graphic T-shirts from an SAE party, and we talked long into the night about how great our life would be in Arizona.

Katy paused for a second. "Should we really do this? Is it nuts to switch colleges halfway through?"

I suddenly noticed that, for the first time since I'd known her, Katy wasn't constantly sniffing from allergies. Arizona agreed with her. She could breathe here. I made the decision for us and declared, "It is totally nuts, and we should totally do it."

"Really?" Katy asked, standing up on the bed.

"Let's do it!" I shouted.

"Baby!"

We started screaming and jumping up and down on the bed, with Katy yelling "Baby" over and over again.

The next day, I called my parents and told them about our new plan.

Mom asked, "Are you sure about this?" She was concerned. She didn't want me to move halfway across the country, and I didn't blame her.

I said to Mom, "I'm sure. Arizona is awesome, and I have Katy."

As shocked as my parents were by the idea, they didn't say no, although Mom told me later that she drank two martinis after we had hung up.

Straightaway, we applied for transfers and were accepted. Just like that, it was done. We returned to KU to finish sophomore year. It wasn't until we were back in our respective sororities that we realized what a big change this would be. The KKG and Chi O houses were like a family to us. We had shared so much with our sorority sisters, and now we were just leaving. Our friends and sisters were sad to hear it but promised to come and visit us for spring break the following year.

Katy and I both went home for the summer and worked to earn as much money as we could. In August 1983, a few days before our move-in date at the apartment complex, I loaded up my car and met Katy at a gas station in El Dorado, Kansas.

"Can you put one of my bags in your trunk?" she asked. "I can barely see out of my rear window."

"Mine's full." I popped open the trunk to show her.

"What are all these coolers?" she asked.

I blushed. "It's frozen beef from the farm." My parents insisted I bring a hundred pounds of Angus beef with me to Arizona, so we'd always have food.

Katy cracked up. "Okay, Jethro!" she said. For years to come, whenever I did anything that Katy thought was kind of "farmy" or "yee-haw" (her words), she would refer to me as "Jethro." It wasn't a nickname I loved, but eventually I wore it as a badge of honor.

We had our route mapped out with planned stops for gas, meals and an overnight stay. We jumped in our cars, revved them up and caravanned from Kansas to Arizona to start our brand-new life.

CHAPTER 3

For our cross-country caravan, Katy and I made our stops at a cheery-looking, budget-conscious motel and truck stop diners. The seventeen-hour drive passed quickly—I cranked the Cars, Elvis Costello and Joni Mitchell for company and kept my eye on Katy in her gray Mazda Sport the entire time. We drove through Oklahoma, Texas and New Mexico; the scenery was beautiful but desolate. If we lost each other on the road, I'd worry that we'd never see each other again. Luckily our cars didn't break down, and we were never more than a few car lengths apart.

With just a few miles left in our journey, we stopped for a look at our map outside of Tempe and to take stock of our new home. I remember thinking how vastly different this desert landscape was to the infinite flat green fields of my youth, or the rolling leafy hills of KU. In every direction, the land spread out in a rich, faded clay tone, dotted everywhere with varieties of multicolored cacti. Hazy mountains ringed the horizon. The air had a delicious scent that I learned to savor: a dry, slightly charred smell with a hint of a floral sweetness that came from the local creosote bushes.

We looked at the view, looked at each other, immediately grabbed hands and began jumping up and down like crazy people. "We made it! We made it!"

Minutes later, we pulled up to the Cedars, our hip new apartment complex. We'd already signed a lease on a sunny, furnished one-bedroom with twin beds. The freezer was just large enough for all my frozen beef, leaving no room for anything else. Within days of moving in, we went to a local fabric store and selected a large, colorful floral print for the entryway table. We found a complementary small, tan-and-forest-green geometric print fabric to wrap the living room sofa and chair. June Brosnahan's zebra vase with a fern made the trip from Kansas and sat on a windowsill. We really thought our decorating made the place unique and sophisticated. We threw in a couple of framed Picasso and Van Gogh posters and . . . voilà! Ready for *Architectural Digest*.

About a week before the start of classes, we were hanging out at the Cedars' pool, soaking up rays and the laid-back Western vibes. Katy listened to Sade; I sat back and appreciated the fact that she could breathe and was not sniffling. Our neighbors came by and introduced themselves. We started chatting with a couple of fellow ASU students, Lily and Chris, who were dating and who both happened to be from Kansas City. They knew a lot of the same people Katy grew up with. That coincidence sealed it for us: We were meant to be there.

Living in an apartment and not a dorm or sorority house made us feel like grown-ups, like our Mary Richards life had begun. One night that first week, I made one of Katy's favorite meals for dinner: fried chicken, mashed potatoes and peas. By the time she came home from errands, I'd set our little table with plates and napkins and put a platter of food in the middle.

She looked at our full table and said, "Elyce! Wow, I can't believe you did this."

Aside from the vague phrasing, she was being polite but not very enthusiastic. She was smiling, but not really.

"Okay, c'mon, what?" I asked.

"What, what?"

"I know you're not thrilled about our first dinner at our new home. Can you tell me why, please?"

Katy was quiet for a moment. "Well, I know you really worked hard to make this great for us, but I just don't want it to be like this every night. Staying in, lots of home-cooked meals, TV. You know. 'Gals Nights! Whoopee!'" She used air quotes for that last part.

"Okay, I get it. Very limited home cooking. No problem."

So the new rules were set, and we tucked into our fried-chicken dinner, which Katy enjoyed very much. We actually had a great time, but that exchange stands out in my memory because it was emblematic of one of the differences between us. I'm a homebody, likely as a result of a fairly solitary upbringing. Katy, on the other hand, though naturally a more reserved person than I am, always enjoyed being surrounded by people and being "in the mix."

Those types of differences in who we were became more pronounced now that our college friendship had become more mature. I'd like to think that some good stuff of mine rubbed off on Katy, but I can speak definitively about all the influence she had on me, particularly over time. I remember thinking back then that although I was brought up in a family where things like kindness and table manners were always taught and encouraged, there were other sets of rules to which I didn't have any exposure. Katy's family was brought up in a citified, mannerly way among other families at private schools and clubs. She knew social niceties I just hadn't been exposed to. I'm not sure she could have raised a steer, but then again, I don't think she would have wanted to.

* * *

Later that week, when we read about registration for classes, we realized we'd made a horrible miscalculation. Since ASU was a state school like KU had been, we assumed our tuition at both places would be basically the same. We were terribly mistaken. Because we weren't Arizona residents, our tuition was *quadruple* what we'd paid in Kansas. It might sound absurd that we didn't already know that, but we were so entranced by the sunshine and warmth of Arizona when we'd started the transfer process, we skipped over the fine print.

Plan A was to get jobs immediately. Katy and I put on our best businessy outfits—Katy in a navy skirt and cardigan sweater with pearls, and me in a camel-colored light summer suit with a silk blouse—and drove to a few strip malls all over Scottsdale. She dropped me off at one end, and she started at the other end. Going door-to-door, small office to small office, we asked for job applications and handed out our just-printed résumés. Each business we walked into had one, two or at most three people, and they looked at us like we were crazy. Most did not have an application to fill out. We had to come up with a new plan of attack. We were both getting nervous that this whole adventure we had joyfully undertaken was a huge mistake.

When Missy had us over for dinner that night, conversation was dominated by our job-search frustration.

She asked, "Why did you girls go looking for jobs at a strip mall? You should try the Biltmore Golf Club and try to get a job driving the beverage cart. It's really great money, and you're outside all day. You'll love it."

I had the experience at the Wichita Club, so I jumped on Missy's suggestion right away. The next morning, I went to the Biltmore Golf Club in Phoenix to apply for a job, any job. The hiring manager, Dick, told me, "I have nothing available now," but I kept calling two times a week until I wore him down. I'm pretty sure he hired me so that I would stop annoying him.

I learned that driving the beverage cart around the two eighteen-hole courses to serve Bloody Marys and Heinekens to thirsty golfers was a coveted role at the Biltmore. I'd need to prove myself worthy. Any new employee started at the hot dog stand, a steamy grill in a stuffy shed at the ninth hole of each course. It was a sweaty job, standing on concrete all day in my Biltmore logo polo shirt and pleated cotton shorts, and everything I wore ended up smelling like grilled meat. But I was determined to get that beverage-cart-driver job, so I showed up to work early, was as friendly as I could possibly be to everyone and stayed late to clean up. After a few months of slinging hot dogs, I got promoted to the beverage cart. Missy was right. It was the best job I'd ever had. I would drive around a beautifully manicured course, over hills and greens in a five-speed mini-truck with a white-and-red awning and a golf ball–proof windshield. As the "cold beverage with alcohol" delivery system, I was welcomed with open arms by all the happy club members and guests.

Missy was really bummed out that Katy had not gone right after that job at the Biltmore. But it really wasn't Katy's style to be so persistent. Relentlessly calling and begging for work would have been too embarrassing for her; Katy hated any kind of aggressiveness or confrontation. Around the same time I started my job at the Biltmore, she ended up finding a job at Johns & Co., a preppy clothing store that serviced the well-heeled men and women in Scottsdale and Paradise Valley, which was managed by Mike Carter, a buddy of Missy and Jon's. While my job's dress code was confined to the club uniform, she got to wear outfits of her choosing in keeping with the preppy feel of the store—navy, pink or kelly-green polo shirts, with a cable-knit sweater and either khakis, a skirt or shorts.

Katy and I signed up for Tuesday and Thursday day and night courses at school so we could be available to work the other five days a week (including weekends). Once again as journalism majors, we were in mostly the same classes. We both took notes, but to study for a test, I had to cram for hours while Katy could mostly skim the notes and ace it. It was a talent she always had. She could process a ton of information and retain it forever. To this day I'm still amazed thinking about it.

On nights when we didn't have classes, Katy and I would get in her car or mine and drive around, listening to Joni Mitchell's *Court and Spark* album over and over—the soundtrack of our wanderings was always soulful women who were like our goddesses: Joni Mitchell, Sade or Joan Armatrading. We usually took Katy's car, which had a better stereo (installed by her brother, Earl). We'd meander around the hills in Scottsdale peeking through the rocks and boulders at the million-dollar homes on Lincoln Drive, gazing at the purple-orange peaks of Camelback Mountain, Piestewa Peak and Shaw Butte. The landscape was like Mars to us, otherworldly and mysterious. At night, you could see every bright star in the night sky. If you looked down from the mountains, the yellow and red jewels of lights twinkled in the Phoenix Valley.

* * *

By far Katy's favorite thing about the new job was one of her coworkers. He was an ASU student named Andy Spade, whom she billed as a funny, handsome triathlete. She would come home from work and it was "Andy this" and "Andy that." Katy, a non-sporty person, would throw on shorts and sneakers, borrow a bike from a neighbor and hope to run into Andy on the local running trail, a few times even having me spritz her face and T-shirt with a water mister so she would look like she had just worked out.

Katy told me that Andy had a girlfriend, but she didn't seem to be put off by this. She said he hardly spoke about her, that it might not be very serious. She was patient in that way, looking at things in the long run.

Usually, I would pick Katy up at the store on my way home from the Biltmore after stopping at the nearby drive-through liquor store to buy two bottles of cold Heineken in brown bags for our drive home. One day, I parked out in front of Johns & Co. and went inside to meet Andy. He was a great-looking guy, thin as a blade, with the thickest, rich brownish-blond hair and a quirky smile. His affect was boyish and mischievous, like Dennis the Menace. I would come to learn that he was born in Michigan, moved to Arizona and then California after his parents' split, and finally landed back in Arizona. His style wandered, too, a little bit East Coast preppy mixed with SoCal skateboarder.

When their boss, Mike Carter, decided to leave Johns & Co. to open his own men's clothing store named Carter's, Katy and this funny-and-handsome Andy went with him. Mike had become a big brother to all of us, and when he was preparing for his new store, we all went to help him unpack boxes. His passion and knowledge of clothing and the great brands of that era really had a major impact on both of them. They learned everything about fabrics, thread counts, various kinds of wool for men's suiting and that timeless style that would soon become a global standard. It was the spark that would later ignite Katy and Andy's interest in the fashion business.

Katy, Andy and I became a tight platonic threesome and hung out together all the time. Our occasional fourth was Andy's brother

David Spade. (He was two years younger than me—so not dating material.) He was super funny just like Andy and already was part of an ASU comedy troupe called the Farce Side Comedy Hour. David also performed at stand-up clubs in Scottsdale, like Anderson's Fifth Estate. Katy, Andy and I went to see him whenever he performed. I especially liked David's comedy because he kept it clean, which I appreciated—no sex stuff, no swearing. The crowd always loved him even then, when he was eighteen. They would literally roar with laughter. Andy and David had a gift for storytelling and humor. With David especially, it was like his whole reason for being was to entertain onstage and off. Never before in my life had I been surrounded by people who got as much pleasure out of making others laugh as the Spade brothers. It made them so much fun to be around.

Of course, there was an elephant in the room that no one talked about much: Katy liked Andy, and Andy clearly had feelings for her, too. But they stayed just friends because Andy still had that girlfriend. Katy with her characteristic good sense was playing the long game with Andy and kept her emotional distance.

In the meantime, we were introduced to a group of thirtysomething men at parties thrown by Missy and Jon. Now that we were really living on our own, we had started relating as well to the older guys as we did to those our own age. Our attraction to older men included one of our journalism professors. Legal scholar/hot teacher David Bodney taught a class on journalistic ethics and First Amendment rights. We *both* had a huge crush on him and used to fight over our claim.

After every class, I'd say, "He likes me."

Katy would reply, "No, he likes *me*."

The competition was on. We dressed up for each class and always sat in the front row. We tried every trick to get his attention, raising our hand with an obvious question or answer, nodding in agreement with any point he was making. We would stop to thank him at the end of class for his amazing insights into First Amendment law. Nothing worked for either of us! Was this guy blind? We would come home from his class late on a Thursday night and usually have drinks with our neighbors Lily and Chris. They would make fun of us for fighting over our professor, who obviously had zero interest in either one of us. Though we moved on from our crush, the story didn't end there. Lily and Chris eventually broke up. After Katy and I graduated and left Arizona, we stayed in touch with Lily. She told us she had been very intrigued by our months of swooning over our professor, so she decided to fabricate an academic legal question and call to see if he would meet her. They met. They clicked. Flash forward a year, they married. Katy and I were both bridesmaids at their wedding in Kansas City. I should add to Lily's cred as a go-getter: Katy and I watched and cheered as she founded and built her super successful home design brand, Serena & Lily.

* * *

In the spring of our junior year, Andy casually mentioned that he and his girlfriend had broken up. While I immediately got excited for Katy, she approached the situation with her usual patience. She implied that she did not care too much. We all still went out together, but over the next few months they found time to be alone—the relationship just slowly progressed. But she made him work for it. If he called to hang out, she insisted he come up with a concrete plan or she'd say, "I'm busy." And whatever they did together, they always included me. They were dating, but we were still an "us." Beginning then, and over our many years of friendship when I was single, they never once made me feel like a third wheel.

The three of us had plans to go on a weekend trip to Sedona, a desert town with stunning vistas of red-rock buttes, gorgeous sandstone formations and spiral-shaped juniper trees. We were going to stay in a beautiful place called Junipine since it was offseason and the rates were lower. Andy asked, "Would it be okay if a buddy of mine came along?"

Oh shit. "Who is he?" I asked.

"My fraternity brother Scott. He's a really funny, great guy. He broke up with his girlfriend a month ago and needs company. Of course you'll have separate bedrooms."

"Okay, sure. Sounds great. If he is a friend of yours, it will be fun."

Katy lifted her little fists into the air. "Baby! So we'll go up in Andy's car, and you drive with Scott."

They were hard selling this. I felt a small flutter of hope in my heart that Scott might have potential. Katy would never push a guy on me who she didn't find worthy. She was very picky on my behalf to a fault.

Scott arrived to pick me up on Friday morning. I got in the car, nicely dressed, smiling hopefully. As billed, Scott was handsome. Unfortunately, he was not funny or even a little bit friendly. The guy hardly spoke the entire two-hour drive. I tried to make small talk, but he just nodded, stared ahead and looked uncomfortable. I thought he must be painfully shy or just sad about his breakup. I hoped he'd loosen up when he saw Andy.

When we pulled into the driveway of Junipine, Katy and Andy spilled out of our big cabin, both waving, saying, "Yay, you made it!"

Scott got out of the car and immediately ran into the pines and threw up.

Katy turned to me and, with her signature half smile and deadpan delivery, said, "Gee, Elyce, I guess you really wowed him with your personality."

I know it wasn't a funny moment, but it was one of those inappropriate times when she always tried to make me laugh. We learned he'd been drinking and doing lines of coke with his frat brothers the whole night before and hadn't slept at all when he came to pick me up. He was sick and in bed the whole weekend. We barely spoke, and I rode home on Sunday in Andy and Katy's car. I do give the guy a few points for showing up at all.

Later that spring, several of our KU sorority sisters made good on their promise to visit. They slept on the sofa and floor of our tiny apartment, and we soaked in the rays by the pool. Katy and I took two days off work to show them around the Tempe and Scottsdale area. We introduced them to the to the famous Tee Pee Mexican Food restaurant for stellar food and sipped margaritas while we caught up on KU gossip. What they enjoyed most was when we took them on one of our evening drives to a perch overlooking the city. They got to witness the magic of the desert and understood why we loved it there so much.

* * *

Arizona has a real driving culture, and we would spend hours a day in the car. We must have driven the length of Scottsdale Road a hundred times, going back and forth from our place to Missy's or the Biltmore. Every time, we noted the dozen adult video stores dotted on the side of the road. At twenty, I had still never seen a porn movie and neither had Katy. I'll admit I was curious but never enough to brave a stop at one of those grimy-looking places. I'm not sure there was a soap made for the deep clean that would require.

One night on the way to Missy's to house-sit and water her plants while she was out of town, Katy said, "Let's rent a porn video and watch it to see what it's like. We can return it on the ride home."

"But if I park in front of the store, people might spot my car!" The Cutlass was a bright red boat. It stuck out.

"Oh, come on, Jethro! No one will see. We'll be in and out in five minutes."

I agreed to do it but made sure my car was obscured by a pickup truck. We went into Skeeve Palace (our name for the joint), nervous, embarrassed and excited. We'd heard of *Debbie Does Dallas* and *Deep Throat*, but we had no idea how to select porn. This might take longer than five minutes. Naturally, we were the only women there, and every guy in the place was staring at us. Katy just grabbed a box off a rack, and we brought it up to the front counter.

The man behind it—around forty, long dirty-blond hair in a ponytail tied with a pink rubber band—grumbled at us, "The rental cost is two dollars, and you have to give me a credit card as a guarantee."

Katy said, "Okay, shoot, I left my wallet in the car."

"We'll use mine."

"If you don't return it in two days, your card will be charged for a replacement," croaked Ponytail as he put the video in a plastic bag. That was not going to happen.

We proceeded on to Missy's, got our popcorn ready and inserted the *Taboo II* video into the VHS player. We watched about ten minutes of it before we were both completely grossed out. I ejected the tape and, handling it very minimally, returned it to the bag.

"We're never doing that again!" I declared.

Katy nodded. "I don't get what the big deal is about porn. Yuck."

We drove home a few hours later feeling guilty and gross. As we approached Skeeve Palace, I said, "Let's drop off the tape."

Katy waved her hand at the place and shrugged off my suggestion, "Nah, let's do it tomorrow. It's late and that place will be crawling with creepy guys by now."

She had a point. So the next day, I tried again.

"Let's drive over there now."

The video sat on our kitchen table like a ticking time bomb about to go off.

Katy replied, "You go. I can't. I have a study group to meet, and I'm already late."

Wait. What? That was the first I'd heard of a study group. "You want me to go by myself? Hey! You just don't want to go back in there."

She smiled a bit as she denied it. Come to think of it, it was her idea to get the movie in the first place, and she had planned that I would be driving when she suggested it. Leaving her handbag in the car so I had to use my credit card was another brilliant move. And now I had to go back by myself, park the red Cutlass out front of the porn store and walk in there alone. I returned the tape, an uneventful experience outside of the skin-crawling intense stares of other customers. On that ride home, I just knew Katy was laughing her ass off. She was always a step ahead of me. I swore to myself I would get my revenge. I started fantasizing about ways I could get back at her, cackling as I came up with a few ideas. Game on! Pulling pranks on each other became a huge part of our relationship.

* * *

After our first year in Arizona, our lease was up and we each moved into our own separate apartments in Scottsdale. Now that she and Andy were official, sharing a one-bedroom with twin beds with me wasn't cutting it. I did not blame her, and it was time we each had our own places. Since Andy was a triathlete, he was careful about what he ate and drank, so now Katy was, too. She drank less, smoked less, ate well and exercised, all on her own for the first time. She seemed inspired by Andy, watching and supporting him at his triathlons. She took better care of herself by pure osmosis.

Andy Spade had a big influence on me in many ways, too. What

I appreciated most about him was his natural curiosity and enthusiasm. He opened up Katy's perspective, too, about art, movies and photography. If he happened to drive by an art fair, Andy would pull over and inspect the offerings, and nearly always walk away with a hidden gem, some eccentric collectable piece of art. His aesthetic was Wes Anderson before we knew about Wes Anderson—eclectic, with some off-kilter nostalgia thrown in.

My rental apartment was two blocks away from Katy's, a one-bedroom in a darling little cul-de-sac. Katy's younger sister, Eve, who had been at KU for her freshman and sophomore years, had just transferred to ASU for her junior year like us. Eve needed a place to stay, so she moved in with me. We had a ball together, and it gave Katy and Andy some solo time without feeling like they had to invite me to join. Katy's older brother, Earl, had just been accepted to graduate school at the prestigious Thunderbird School of Global Management in Phoenix. It made our get-togethers so much fun having a big part of the Brosnahan family living in town.

On Thanksgiving, Missy went into labor with her second child, a beautiful boy named Reese. In preparation for Thanksgiving, she'd bought a ton of food to host a big dinner for the entire family. Jon and Whitney went to the hospital to be with Missy and the new baby. Back at their house, Katy, Andy, Eve, David, Earl and I cooked a delicious classic Thanksgiving meal with the food Missy had bought. I was sad to not be with my own family for the holiday, but that year felt special because I would be with a chosen family, my dearest friends in the world.

Though we were all working, none of us had any money—we were in a continual state of broke. We finagled meals wherever we could. Missy and Jon belonged to the Village Tennis Club, and occasionally Katy and I would stop by to watch some tennis, split a tuna sandwich or a grilled cheese, and charge it to Missy and

Jon's account. Every time we were at their house, we'd eat bowls of cereal and "borrow" quarters out of Jon's change jar on the dresser to buy gas (it was 75 cents a gallon back then). Katy and I spent some of our earnings going out to bars and restaurants, but we were careful about it. We would go to the Cork 'N Cleaver once a month and share a surf and turf—a filet mignon and a lobster tail smothered in butter—and two glasses of the house cabernet. We would split the $21 bill, a fortune for us. We couldn't afford it, but that was our big splurge for the month. It was our ritual and reminder to treat ourselves for holding down full-time jobs and a full school schedule.

CHAPTER 4

Like all college seniors, Katy and I talked about the future and what we wanted to do with our lives. As we pored over fashion magazines and perused vintage shops, we considered the idea of how we might eventually land a career in fashion. We had watched Mike Carter successfully open his own clothing store, meet with apparel manufacturers, select the items to buy and market, and sell those to his customers. It planted a seed that perhaps we could someday have our own boutique with our own modern-vintage perspective. My focus had always been to move to New York after graduation and work at either a fashion magazine or in TV news. To complete my major, I took classes in broadcast journalism—pretending to report on stories and write up scripts for them—and imagined myself in a newsroom.

I landed an internship at the Phoenix NBC affiliate's local news show, working with Alan Rappoport for his "Four on Your Side" segments. My job was to read letters from viewers who had an issue with someone or were swindled in some way. I'd give the best letters to Alan, and we'd "gotcha" the offending parties on camera.

During my time on the show, we did a sting operation to prove that you could get an Arizona driver's license without showing an ID. I was asked by the producer of the show for evidence, so, the intrepid reporter that I was, I went to the Motor Vehicle Division and managed to score a license with just a library card. Three months later, I got a knock on my door and opened it up to find two FBI agents. They sat me down and proceeded to interrogate me with all kinds of intrusive questions about everything in my life. They scared the hell out of me! It took a while, but finally, I put two and two together: They were investigating Alan Rappoport's story and came down on me for getting that driver's license. I was almost in tears. "No. I was just an intern. . . . I did it for the story! I was asked to do it by the producers!" Eventually, they accepted that I was innocent and left. But the stress of being interrogated by the FBI didn't dissipate for days and turned me off a bit to TV news.

That experience, along with my growing appreciation for fashion, made my focus shift away from news toward magazines. If I could get a job in New York at a fashion magazine like *Vogue*, *Elle* or *Harper's Bazaar*, that would be amazing. My older sisters had a subscription to *Seventeen* and would occasionally come home with a copy of *Vogue* purchased from the local drugstore. I still remember the thrill of seeing those glossy covers and the fresh magazine smell when turning the pages.

Katy remained a journalism major throughout college, but she was never convinced she'd do anything specific with it. She floated the idea of opening a vintage clothing boutique of items that we'd source at thrift stores and flea markets. She really enjoyed her experience working at Carter's and now knew a lot about clothing. Meanwhile, Andy and his classmate Allen Hannawell started an advertising company called Spade/Hannawell, creating ads for local businesses. Even then we could see glimmers of the eccentric sense of humor that would someday make Andy a star in his field.

But in the meantime, before we pursued our postgrad dreams, Katy needed more hours than she was getting at Carter's. I'd hoped she would come work at the Biltmore with me and soon she did. Like me, she had to start at the ninth-hole snack stand to grill hot dogs for the likes of Bryant Gumbel, Alice Cooper and Glen Campbell (this unlikely trio often golfed together), and Leslie Nielsen from *Airplane*. Polyester-pants-loving Leslie was a prankster himself. He'd order two hot dogs, and when Katy served them to him, he'd say, "With the works," and squeeze the whoopee cushion he had hidden under his jacket. She was not at all amused.

I told her, "Just be patient and be really nice to everybody, and you'll soon get off the hot dog stand." I would sneak money into her tip jar because she wasn't very cheerful to people, which was really so unlike her. She just wasn't happy there and was not good at faking it.

"I know you're putting money in there," she insisted one day. "Nobody would leave me a twenty-dollar bill!"

"It wasn't me!" I wanted her to stay because I knew eventually she'd get on the beverage cart and her dedication would really pay off.

After a month and a half, she was still stuck in hot dog hell. One night at the end of her shift, she put the cash box under her arm and started walking to the main building. She'd gone no more than one hundred feet when there was an explosion and the interior of the hot dog stand was gone. It wasn't Katy's fault (there was a thorough investigation; it turned out to have been a gas leak), but we joked that she demolished the hot dog stand to get away from Leslie Nielsen and his whoopee cushion.

"You could have been killed!" I said.

"I hated that job anyway," Katy replied.

Her next job was at a motorcycle bar, a really tough place called Desperados—heavy on the leather, chains and tattoos. Katy was the only one in there wearing sneakers and pink polo shirts. Her brother, Earl, went to have a drink there one night, and as soon as he saw the clientele, he found his sister.

"Get your things," he told her. "We're leaving right *now*."

* * *

In the summer of 1984, Missy and Jon invited us to spend a week in San Diego, where they'd rented a beautiful little villa right on La Jolla Shores. I had never been to California before, and Katy and I excitedly drove the six-hour trip talking about how great it would be on the beach and the fancy dinners Missy and Jon would treat us to. We did have some babysitting duties for Katy's niece and nephew Whitney and Reese, but it was a small price to pay for an amazing vacation. I had never stayed in a place on the ocean before and had only been to East Coast beaches a handful of times in my life. Missy and Jon took us out for lobster at the fancyish Rusty Pelican, right on the water.

The following January, Katy and I decided to relive that dreamy vacation again by driving to La Jolla. We started out around eight that night with our overnight bags and a few bottles of red wine. We had about $250 between us for gas, food, lodging and anything else that might pop up.

When we arrived in La Jolla at two in the morning, we decided to drink one of the bottles of wine, put our seats back and just sleep in the car to save on the expense of a room. After driving around to find a quiet spot, we parked at a Residence Inn and woke up at five in the morning with a security guard rapping on the window.

"Hey, wake up, you two. You can't stay here!" he barked at us.

The two of us never wanted to be on the wrong side of anything, and it felt like we had broken the law. With tires screeching, we pulled out of the lot. We found a local diner full of boisterous construction workers and had some breakfast, then headed to the beach.

It might have been a good idea to check the forecast before leaving. It was foggy and rainy all day—not beach weather. After staying in the car watching the rain for a few hours before seeking dry land, we went back to the Residence Inn and got a room for $125 per night. We called Peter Pearlman, our friend from KU who had moved to San Diego for a job. We hung out in the room all day, bummed that the weather was so bad, and bided our time until we met up with Peter at the Rusty Pelican for drinks. We dressed in our best, arrived early and took photos of each other on the docks, by yachts and leaning against luxury cars.

We got a table in the bar (not enough money for dinner), and Peter showed up. After a couple of cocktails, reminiscing and having fun, a guy asked if he could buy us a round of drinks. We told him yes, and he joined us. Murray was in his late fifties and lived nearby, and we had a good time talking together. After another hour, Murray invited us all to his place. Since there were three of us, we decided it was safe to go. Murray walked us over to his forest-green Jaguar in the parking lot. (It was one of the cars Katy and I had taken photos in front of.)

He said, "One of you can ride with me, and the others can follow in your car." Since I was standing nearest, he put his hand on my waist. "Elyce, why don't you ride with me?"

A bit nervous, I got in and settled into the leather bucket seat, running my hand over the wood paneling.

Murray put the car in drive, checked the rearview to make sure Peter and Katy were behind, and placed his hand on my thigh. "I am so glad I met you guys. Can't wait to have some fun at my place!"

Well, I freaked out and jumped from the slowly moving car. "I'm riding with them!" I blurted, and ran over to Peter's car. He and Katy were looking at me like I was crazy. I hopped into the back seat and said, "We can't go. He wants to orgy!"

Katy and Peter looked at each other and burst out laughing. Katy asked, "Is orgy a verb?"

"He wants it to be!" I shouted.

Murray drove out of the driveway and took a right. We nudged out, took a left, drove in a circle and went right back to the Rusty Pelican. We ordered a few more drinks and processed our near accidental group sex experience.

Later, Peter was philosophical. "This place might be out of our league. I don't think that would have happened at Red Lobster."

* * *

It felt like a long haul to finally accumulate enough credits to graduate, but by December 1985, Katy and I had fulfilled our course requirements. We had achieved our goal of finishing our bachelor's degrees. We both were looking to our futures, uncertain but excited.

Andy had one more semester to complete before acquiring his degree. Katy wanted to stay together with him but knew that realizing her dream of seeing Europe was the right thing for her. She and I had both saved roughly what it would cost to travel for three months, providing we kept to a tight budget. We had talked a lot about going on that trip together, but as our college days came to an end, I knew that I would have to make a decision. I could either spend my finite savings on the trip with Katy or realize my own goal of moving to the Big Apple. I dreaded that discussion, but in the end, she was supportive and knew me well enough to know how long I had dreamed of living in New York City.

The great surprise was when she told me she was going to travel to Europe anyway. By herself.

"Alone?" I asked. "You?" She was a strong person but really didn't prefer to be solo for extended periods of time for any reason.

"I know," she explained. "I'm a little uptight about it. But this may be my only chance, so I'm going for it. I have some high school friends in London I'll visit. I also really want to see if Andy and I can keep it together when we're long-distance."

I know in today's terms, it does not seem like much of a big deal, but back then for a woman to travel alone for months with no plan was pretty unusual. Especially Katy.

Katy was staying with Missy before taking the trip to Europe. She was planning on returning to Arizona to figure out next steps for her career when she got back. Andy was staying in Arizona to run his two-person ad agency and finish his coursework. Katy and I avoided talking about the fact that we would be going our separate ways.

Logistically, we still had to clean out our apartments and get rid of all of our furniture. As usual, Missy knew what to do. "Just go down to the swap meet on Saturday and sell all your stuff there," she advised.

Great idea! We'd sell what we could and maybe pocket a decent amount. We invested in renting a U-Haul truck, looking to get the cheapest one they had. The only available vehicle was a massive truck that had a manual transmission and required double-clutching. We had the good idea to assure the rental guy that we had loads of experience driving a big truck so that would not present a problem. I'd handled tractors and could drive a stick. I had no idea what double-clutching was, but I managed to eventually get the truck to our apartments, stalling and jerking around the whole drive.

Andy helped us load up the U-Haul, which took hours longer than expected, and volunteered to drive to the swap meet.

"You know how to drive a big truck like this?" I asked.

He was confident. "Oh yeah, I can do it."

He was as bad at it as I was. We stalled on the road every hundred feet. By the time we got to the swap meet it was two in the afternoon and people were leaving. We'd paid to be there all day. We paid for the U-Haul. And now it was looking like we'd never get our money back, let alone make a profit.

I did manage to sell my sister's Italian racing bike for $20 and enough of our furniture to break even (barely). The one big item we failed to get rid of was a heavy, old-fashioned dining room table that Missy had given us. We couldn't return the U-Haul with the table in it.

It was just Katy and me by then. Since the process had taken quadruple the time we expected, Andy had left to go to work. As we were driving/stalling down Scottsdale Road, Katy shouted, "Wave goodbye to the Skeeve Palace!"

It was getting late and dark. We were just about done with the entire long day. We randomly pulled into a strip mall by the First Interstate Bank with Arizonan landscaping out front. There was just enough room next to the outside of the bank for our table to fit among the cacti, flowering bushes and decorative rocks. So Katy and I hefted the table out of the back of the U-Haul and donated it to the bank.

And then we U-Hauled our asses out of there.

CHAPTER 5

S oon came the joy-filled graduation day under a sapphire-blue Arizona sky. Katy and I both appreciated the experience of going to school there, but having arrived in our junior year and holding down full-time jobs, we didn't feel we needed the pomp and circumstance of the big event. We decided to skip the ceremony itself in favor of getting a quick start out of Dodge. My parents were a little upset when I told them I was skipping the graduation ceremony. I didn't want them to spend the money flying to Arizona, and I didn't want to miss any days of work to celebrate. I don't think they actually thought I had graduated until they saw my physical diploma arrive in the mail at the farm a few weeks later.

Our tight college gang was parting ways, unsure of where our paths would lead. We organized a final farewell dinner, which included the three of us, Andy's fraternity brother Walker, Lily and

Chris and a few others. We went to our favorite local Japanese restaurant and stayed up way too late partying and telling stories. The
owners knew us and were happy to let us hang out. I remember when
we were leaving, Andy had taken my sandals and somehow squeezed
his feet into them. He came out of the restaurant smiling and doing
a funny little shuffle behind us wearing my sandals. I still have the
photo evidence. We all hugged and kissed because we knew what the
next day was bringing; we were all leaving first thing in the morning
and going our separate ways. Katy and I clung to each other for a
few extra beats. I really didn't want to let go.

"I'll see you in New York on my way back, okay?" she said, smiling.

I knew her so well. She was holding on for dear life.

"Yes, yes, that's the plan!" I held back tears. I was barely keeping
it together.

We got into our cars and sped off on our separate ways. Our
four-year journey was coming to an end, and inside I knew there
was a chance that we may never be as close again.

The next morning, bright and early, I picked up Walker, who was
riding as far as Oklahoma with me, which was on my route back to
our farm in Kansas. The trip initially was uneventful if scenic, and
we were both slightly overwhelmed with the newfound gravity of
our open life before us. Oklahoma was pretty, with broad flat plains
leading into a green, low, hilly country. In a small town on those
charming hills, my faithful Cutlass gave a buck and a cough and just
decided to give up. Walker and I tried to make the best of it with a
few memorial toasts at the local diner, but the town, like many in
Oklahoma, was a dry one. We clinked our fountain glasses of grape
Fanta to the memory of that old car. Walker waved goodbye as he
stepped on the bus that would take him home. I did what most of the
smart gals do when they're in the weeds: I called my dad. He drove
the four hours in his pickup, chained the Cutlass to the back bumper,

turned around and hauled it home to points west of Wichita. We didn't fuss with details like brake lights in those days. Safety third!

I spent a week on the farm with my parents. Though they were sad to see me leave, I knew they felt comforted by the fact that I would be joining my sister Willow in New York. That week my mother threw a going-away party and invited all our family, friends and neighbors to see me off. Though I relished the time spent at home, I was ready when the day arrived to fly to New York.

Working out the bus schedule from JFK International Airport to Manhattan when I landed was a bit complicated. Most of what I remember from the early-evening bus ride that May was the hulks of four or five burned cars on the side of the expressway as we made our way toward Manhattan. *Hmm*, thought my twenty-two-year-old self. *This is going to be different.*

* * *

Manhattan in 1986 was a world of stark contrasts, a morning's stroll could expose you to both the most hard-scrabble examples of city life and the highest levels of wealth, and everything in between. It was all I had expected and much more.

The New York City financial businesses were producing vast mountains of wealth that inspired the Gordon Gekko "greed is good" *Wall Street* movie a few years later. Crime was an issue, though for the most part heavily concentrated in areas I learned to avoid. We had our share of vermin, rats and mice back home in our barn. But having grown up on a farm, I felt like people in the city made an unnecessarily big stink about those things. Aside from being gross, none of those critters were big enough to hurt you. Early on, a rat squeaked when it bumped into my shoe as I walked by the subway stop near my apartment. I barely noticed it, but I thought some of the people around me were going to have a heart attack.

Ed Koch was mayor at the time, known for his signature catch-phrase "How'm I doin'?" which he'd ask every New Yorker he met on the street. I remember thinking how it perfectly summed up the brassiness of the native city people I was meeting every day, how different everyone was from the polite Midwesterners I grew up with. Living among that vast sea of humanity, I felt completely free for the first time in my life.

Upon arrival, I knew only a few people in the city, and top of the list was my sister Willow. Willow was two years my senior, and as a young star ballerina had moved from Kansas to New York during high school to attend Joffrey Ballet School. A few years into the program, she had suffered a knee injury. While that had ended her ballet study, she began working on pivoting her dancing into an acting career. Willow lived in a studio apartment on the thirteenth floor of a rickety boardinghouse, the Hotel Lincoln Square, on West Seventy-Fifth Street and Amsterdam Avenue. The rent was reasonable, and unlike most of the boarders who had to share a hallway bathroom, Willow's bathroom was en suite.

On my first day, the airport bus dropped me at Port Authority, and I treated myself to a taxi to Willow's from the bus terminal, a pretty exciting adventure on its own. I remember trying to hail a cab, and I asked a woman, "Which way is uptown?" She smiled and pointed the way north. It took me a long time to flag down a cab on jam-packed Eighth Avenue. I finally hailed a taxi and headed due north the thirty blocks to Willow's.

My sister was waiting outside of her building for me, sitting on the stoop. She had a bunch of pink balloons tied to the front door and a sign she made showing the Statue of Liberty holding a bottle of wine instead of a torch. Lady Liberty had a little speech balloon that read, "Welcome Home!" It was really the best hello. The plan now was to live with Willow in her studio apartment to get settled.

I knew the space was going to be small, but it wasn't until I arrived that I saw the reality. It was about fifteen by twenty with no kitchen, roughly the size of the bedroom we shared at our farmhouse in Kansas. We did have a microwave, a hot pot, a mini-fridge and a toaster oven. We used the sink in the bathroom or the bathtub to wash dishes. That summer was particularly toasty, and since we had no air-conditioning, we'd leave the windows open, plug in noisy box fans, and give ourselves the occasional spritz with a water mister.

Not long before I arrived, Willow's best friend from high school, Shari, had moved to New York and was staying with her as well, sleeping on the couch; Willow and I shared a full-size bed and slept foot to head. Although three women in a studio the size of a shoebox was not ideal, I was so happy I was finally living in New York. My dream had come true, and I already felt as if my life had been altered in such an exciting way that it took my breath away.

Living on the Upper West Side of Manhattan and adjusting those first few weeks was an introduction into a whole new reality. The few blocks surrounding Willow's place were decidedly sketchy. That being the case, there were so many people constantly walking the streets that we didn't feel afraid, though we were cautious at night. By day it was like our block was inhabited by the staff of the United Nations. My favorite deli next door was run by Pakistani guys. The bodega on the corner of West Seventy-Fourth Street was owned and run by a Korean family, the Parks. One member of their large family was working there twenty-four hours a day. I knew the names of everyone at our local shops by the second week, and they knew mine.

Lesson one: In NYC back then (and still in local delis), a regular coffee was anything but regular. A "regular" meant a cup of semi-watery coffee with a lot of milk and a heaping spoon of sugar. Some people even go the next step and order a "light and sweet," though let's not even go there. Major moment on day one: I was served coffee for the very first time in the Aegean blue paper cup with Greek symbols and the phrase "We are happy to serve you." *I guess I've really arrived*, I thought. I was thrilled to be handed that cup that's been in every movie or TV show about New York City that I've ever seen.

I grew to love the Upper West Side during my steamy first summer in the city. Its proximity to Broadway and to the magnificent Lincoln Center complex made it a magnet for all types of people in the arts, like opera singers, ballet dancers, Broadway actors, classical musicians as well as TV actors and anchors who worked at the big network studios that were also in the neighborhood.

My first week there involved learning the lay of the land. I liked to stroll over to Riverside Park and walk by the Hudson River. Sometimes I'd go in the opposite direction and meander around the West Seventies and make my way to Central Park. At that time, the neighborhood was filled with modest and reasonably priced housing. Many folks in the performing arts could afford to live there. There was always music flowing from open windows as the residents practiced their instruments or sang opera that poured freely out of their walk-up buildings as I strolled by. Strawberry Fields, the beautiful open-air memorial to John Lennon in Central Park, had just been completed the year before, in 1985, across from the Dakota building where he had lived. I'd sit there with my eyes closed and listen to the music of the city, pretending to hear what John would have heard. The sound of truckers stepping on their brakes made a variety of musical tones; the clanging of trash cans and construction sounds were like a rhythm section. On top of those, the trees in the park were filled with birds that whistled and sang. It all sounded like an orchestra.

At twenty-four, Willow had been in the city a while by this time. She was a master at frugally living life to its fullest. I was like her young trainee. We would go to every free concert in various venues around the city. When it was time for the annual Shakespeare in the Park events that summer in the Delacorte Theater, we were the first in line for the free tickets. My first forays downtown were to join my fun-loving Chi Omega sorority sisters, Sandy and Susan, who had landed in New York the year before and already had jobs and social lives. Having that immediate tight connection made me appreciate my decision to join the sorority years back. We'd jump on the number 2 or 3 express train downtown to the reasonably priced Greenwich Village jazz bars. Not exactly white-glove-level cleanliness at all times, but you really didn't expect it, either.

I especially appreciated Willow's gang, who were so welcoming. Many of them were her work colleagues. Willow worked on her Broadway auditions by day and made money at night hostessing and serving at the uptown hot spot Cafe Central. It was a bar, restaurant and often random late-night dance party, and packed every night. With its redbrick walls, Italian marble tables and tons of beveled mirrors, Cafe Central was a favorite watering hole for the rich and famous as well as hordes of talented and up-and-coming West Siders. I couldn't even think of affording the drinks at Cafe Central, but I went there once a week to nurse a glass of vino Willow would buy me and to check out the famous faces and local characters drinking at the bar. On any given night, you might see Liza Minnelli, Cher, Andy Warhol, Kevin Spacey, Sean Penn, Christopher Walken or Matt Dillon. The tables were covered with white kraft paper and a rocks glass full of crayons for the customers to doodle with while they waited. Willow's close friend Christina still has a drawing by Francis Ford Coppola, and another server, Rhonda, was wise enough to rescue a doodle by Andy Warhol. For an aspiring actress like Willow, it was a good place to be. Her coworkers were a lot of fun, and they hung out together after the bar closed at two in the morning. Her besties were Christina, a server, and Christina's boyfriend, Bruno, a handsome heartthrob bartender.

With his boyish grin and tough-guy Jersey accent, everybody loved him. The year before, their whole group had thrown him a party to celebrate his signing as the lead on a TV pilot for a new show called *Moonlighting*, where he went by his real name, Bruce Willis.

Being surrounded by Willow and all her creative crew was inspirational. I started fantasizing of becoming a writer at a fashion or political publication. During my last semester at college, I had sent out résumés to every magazine and newspaper in the city but never got any response. An acquaintance who worked at *Elle* told me to try signing up with a specific temp agency called Career Blazers. It was often used by the big-league magazines of the day like those owned by Condé Nast, the company that published a dozen glossies including *Vogue*, *GQ*, *Mademoiselle*, and *Glamour*. If I were sent to Condé Nast as a temp and worked hard, I might get offered a full-time job.

"It happens all the time," my connection advised.

In my second week in New York, I went to the Career Blazers office, took a typing test and filled out some paperwork. Within the week I was hired for a temp gig at Citibank Visa in Midtown. I worked there for two weeks sending out promotional materials, and they offered me a full-time job in the marketing department. I ended up turning it down. I kept temping at various Midtown companies, holding out for the elusive Condé Nast dream opportunity.

Soon enough, I was offered a job at Ralph Lauren in the licensing department for a decent salary. While I was thinking about it, a company called Chroma Copy, which made large behind-the-counter beauty displays for Clinique, Bloomingdale's and other department stores, offered me a few thousand dollars more per year. I took the job with the higher salary instead of the Ralph offer, probably not the swiftest decision I've ever made, but at the time, it seemed to make sense given my lean bank account.

Every day I passed through the big triangular patch of pavement on the north side of Broadway and Seventy-Second that housed the subway entrance. It was called Needle Park due to its popularity with junkies and dealers. (*The Panic in Needle Park* was one of Al Pacino's first films.) I'd feel the crunch of crack vials under my shoes as I passed through, a daily reminder of the seamy side of the city of that era. Despite the grittiness, New York seemed magical to me. The energy. The mass of humanity. The street signs. How the traffic lights glowed on slick black streets after a storm. All the music of the city, the car horns and beeping garbage trucks, everyone in a hurry—walking and bustling by everywhere—the metal clang of storefront gates rolling up or down, men whistling and yelling "Taxi!" I enjoyed people-watching as I walked to work, knowing that each person was wrapped up in their own lives, their own stories. No one knew me. I could create my own story living in New York City.

CHAPTER 6

I knew early on that New York City was right for me, and I was there to stay. My salary at Chroma Copy was decent, but I would need more money long term if I was going to get my own place and be able to save anything. I started asking around for part-time jobs where I could work at night.

A block away from Willow's was the Beacon Theatre on Broadway and Seventy-Fifth Street, and underneath that was the China Club, one of the hottest clubs at the time. I had been there and heard that David Bowie, Iggy Pop, Stevie Nicks and other huge stars of the day would occasionally jump onstage and do a set. A lot of Cafe Central regulars went to the China Club after hours. Willow went occasionally and would come home with stories about dancing with Mikhail Baryshnikov or spinning around the floor with John Travolta. While it wasn't really a dance club, when it got late, people would often move tables and create a dance floor. Her coworker Christina also ran the coatroom at the China Club and offered to introduce me to the owners. I wanted *that* job! I could pay off my student loans at hyper speed, cover the rent and save a few bucks. So I applied to be a coat check girl at the China Club. I was hired as a cocktail waitress instead.

I'd waited tables my whole life and thought I knew what to expect. The issue wasn't the hours, which were definitely rough. I started at 11:00 p.m., sold drinks until 4:00 a.m. and woke up at 7:30 to get to Chroma Copy by 9:00. At the end of each shift, I was barely able to speak from screaming at customers to be heard over the music. Men would hold on to my waist or wrist while ordering a drink. Being casually groped was part of the job—the bosses told me I would get used to it. I really didn't, though, nor did I know of any waitresses who did. There was a lot of cocaine, and the customers barely tried to be discreet. They needed some added firepower to party and dance until four on a Monday (one of our most popular nights) and get to work the next day.

The China Club was the worst job I've ever had. The primary reason the job was so bad was the ownership—they made us wear aerobics-inspired leotards and constantly pushed all the servers to show more bum and cleavage. (My response was to wear crewneck sweaters on top of the leotards.) I stuck it out because the tips were so good. I'd managed to save up enough to look for an apartment. Our studio mate, Shari, was feeling the squeeze at Willow's, too, after three months of all of us crowded into a studio apartment. She had a demanding job as an analyst at Kidder, Peabody & Co., and when I mentioned wanting to look for an apartment, she immediately said, "I'll move with you!"

After a few weeks of looking, Shari got lucky and found a two-bedroom on the first floor of a skinny nondescript modern building with five stories on Fifty-Second Street between Ninth and Tenth Avenues. It was a loud, busy street in the heart of Hell's Kitchen, then a rough-around-the-edges neighborhood. I was excited to tell my family at home that I was living just a few blocks from where Sylvester Stallone grew up.

As soon as Shari and I moved in, so did a swarm of furry friends. Although the building had been recently, if cheaply, renovated, I soon learned that mice could eat through drywall. We definitely had a mouse issue and an ongoing problem with cockroaches. I became an expert on how to use boric acid to kill (or at least slow down) roaches and how steel wool pressed into drywall holes can keep the rodents out. I think everyone who moves to New York City as a wannabe eventually gets a crash course in the fine art of pest control. I learned that building management would never be overly concerned. Another tenant called our landlord to complain about a pretty severe mouse issue and he just grumbled, "Get a cat," and hung up the phone.

We had one piece of furniture, a square red sofa. When Merrill Lynch was renovating their offices, Shari told me that they were throwing out a barely used red fabric sofa. We pooled our money and paid for a man with a van to pick it up. It was kind of hard and uncomfortable, but it looked great. I got a futon. Everything else was furniture we bought secondhand that we stripped and refurbished, including a little nightstand that we used as a phone table (which I still have to this day). It's funny to look back and think we had special tables just to hold our landlines.

After paying my new rent and living expenses, I realized I would barely have enough to get by. I had my ear to the rail for some new roommates to help with rent, and fortuitously, one of Katy's Kansas City connections, Beth, decided to come to New York, and she moved in with us for a few months. Shortly after that, my hometown classmate Gayle called about moving in. She was working as a professional singer at the Tennessee Repertory Theatre with a stint at Opryland and, as soon as she heard I was looking, wanted to move to the city to give Broadway a try. Gayle was a kick-in-the-pants big personality. Where she went, fun followed. I was thrilled to have her. She moved in and immediately found a job waiting tables at the nearby popular faux-French brasserie Café 57.

Suddenly there were four of us splitting the rent, and both my social life and wardrobe took a turn for the better. For the first time I was able to meander around the colorful boutiques and the funky vintage shops in the Village. I'd make an occasional foray into the original Barneys on Seventh Avenue and Seventeenth Street where I would fantasize about what I would buy if I had the money.

Though everything felt like it was starting to go well, there was a bit of a cloud hanging over me. I didn't want to continue to work at the China Club but really needed the money. Ultimately, the long hours, coupled with the unsavory management, took their toll, and I decided it was time to quit.

Before I could gather my courage to do so, one of the owners called me into his office and told me, "I don't think it's working out."

I'd never been fired from a job in my life! I didn't get it. I sold more drinks than anyone. I asked, "Why?" and he really wouldn't give me a reason. I wasn't going to fight him on it. I assumed I was not the party-girl profile that they were looking for.

I knew I was going to need a second income very soon. That next day, as I sat in my apartment stewing about getting fired and stressing about finding a new waitressing job, the phone rang. It was my roommate Gayle's boss, the owner of the restaurant Café 57. I told him that she wasn't home.

He asked me in his heavy Greek accent, "Who's this? Are you blond?"

I said, "Um, yes?"

"Can you come to work today?" He didn't ask if I knew how to wait tables. He only asked if I was blond.

I started working at Café 57, thrilled with the skin-covering uniform of khaki skirts and blue oxford shirts, maroon ties and butcher aprons. It was a great job. The waitresses commandeered a central table to chat, eat, drink wine and keep an eye on our customers. Steve, the boss, let us get away with anything and always took our side.

*　*　*

It felt as if I was on the right path to all that I had envisioned for my life. But there was one thing missing, and as I fell into a good work and social life routine, it became more evident to me. I was starting to really miss my best friend. Katy had been sending a steady stream of postcards from all over Europe. She had made some new contacts in London and was traveling with them, having a ball. I was so happy for her, but now that the initial distraction of moving to the city had worn off, I was feeling her absence. She called every two weeks or so (collect), and I knew she was due back pretty soon, but she didn't have an exact date the last time she called. One Saturday in October, I was hanging out in the apartment, flipping through *New York* magazine, when the phone rang.

"Elyce, it's me." It was Katy.

"Where are you?" I asked. I was completely surprised. I could tell it was a local call because she didn't call collect.

"I'm at JFK." She sniffled. "I have five dollars to my name. I don't have a ticket back to Arizona. I don't even have enough money to take a taxi into the city. I have no idea what I'm going to do!" She sounded a little frantic.

"Get in a cab and come to my place," I said. "I'll pay the fare. And then we'll talk."

"What if you're not there when I get there?"

"I promise I'll sit on the stoop with my wallet until you get here."

Katy arrived an hour later, grungy from travel, carrying a massive green backpack almost the same size as she was. She was tanned and fit from her months away, and her curly hair was uncharacteristically wild. My heart leaped with joy seeing her step out of the taxi. We hugged, teary-eyed, and lugged her backpack into the crowded apartment. We were both so excited that the stories began to tumble out as we talked over each other. I took her to Lailai West, our local Chinese restaurant. Over kung pao chicken, I laid out a plan.

"This is what you're going to do. First thing Monday morning, you're going to the temp agency. You can make enough money temping to buy a plane ticket in a few weeks. Then you can go back to Arizona, if that's what you want to do."

"I still don't know what I want to do," she said.

"You don't need to know now. You can stay as long as you want until you figure it out." I was thrilled she was in New York with me, and giddy with the possibility that she'd fall for the city like I did and decide to stay permanently. We could figure out how to reel Andy east later.

Katy moved in, and then we were five. It made sense for her and her Kansas City friend Beth to take one bedroom. Gayle and Shari had the other. I slept on my futon in the living room and kept my clothes in a trunk that we used as a coffee table.

Katy went to Career Blazers the following Monday, and they called to tell her the next day she had an assignment. She was to report for duty at *Mademoiselle* magazine in the Condé Nast building on Madison Avenue. Katy scored my dream job on her second day in New York City. Yes, I was jealous! Katy and I joked about how she instantly got the career that we both wanted. I took solace in making more money than she did, and honestly, I was so proud of her and happy to have her there. *Mademoiselle*'s target reader was a young workingwoman in her twenties or thirties; it had an incredible literary legacy that included publishing Sylvia Plath, Joyce Carol Oates, and Truman Capote. Katy's temp job was in the fashion department, basically as an extra set of hands doing whatever needed to be done.

She was anxious about it. She decided to get dressed up in Beth's deep navy Adrienne Vittadini dress for her first day to make a good impression. Katy's intelligence and work ethic impressed her boss right away, and within weeks, *Mademoiselle* hired her full-time as an editorial assistant in the fashion department for $14,000 a year. It was a low salary and barely enough for her to cover her rent, living expenses and student loans. But the job came with tons of perks like free meals, car services, makeup, clothes and tickets to openings and clubs. Within months, she was going on photo shoots to the Caribbean and all over California. She would figure out her finances somehow.

The no-money thing was only a problem if we made it one. Financially, we struggled, but my memories of those days are some of the happiest times of my life. You don't need a fortune to stay entertained in New York. If it was warm outside, Katy and I went to Central Park to walk around or lay out in Sheep Meadow with a thousand other people. We went to every street fair in the city to stroll along, buy powdered-sugar zeppole, browse the stalls of discount jewelry, cheap dresses, handbags and six-packs of Hanes underwear that likely had "fallen off the back of a truck."

I remember it was at the Ninth Avenue Food Festival, one of those free street fairs, when I first showed my flair for being embarrassing in front of celebrities. I was walking with Katy along the bustling street, which was closed off to allow for festival foot traffic. I looked up and a handsome guy was coming straight toward me. I was sure I knew him, but I couldn't place him exactly. I spread my arms wide to fake it and gave him a giant hug.

"You!" I gushed, a big smile on my face. I knew that I knew this guy!

He looked back at me with wide eyes and kind of a tentative smile on his face. *Or was it fear?* Katy was behind me now and scrunching the back of my top as she pulled me away from the poor guy, who walked away looking confused.

"You don't know him," she scolded me. "That's Emilio Estevez!"

Ah, yes. I didn't know him personally, but I *had* just seen *The Breakfast Club* for the second time a few months ago on a rented Blockbuster video.

We also often went to free concerts and events around the city. Lincoln Center, only blocks from our apartment, would often have outdoor shows, and we went to all of them. Katy and I spent whole afternoons searching for small art pieces and vintage clothing at the fabulous Chelsea Flea on West Twenty-Fifth Street. At Christmas, we prowled indoor antiques markets and vintage stores for gifts and took some classic "us" photos with a Salvation Army Santa.

Some concerts were worth paying for. Katy and I *loved* Lou Reed, and we saved for weeks to buy tickets to his concert at Radio City Music Hall. No way were we missing that! We had a long-term love affair with Lou stretching back to our first year in college when we would blast "Walk on the Wild Side" as we were getting ready for almost every party or night out we ever had. It was kind of a theme song for us (and many other people) and came to represent one of those mysterious sides of New York City that drew us there in the first place. The night of the show, we donned our favorite downtown look—head-to-toe black sweaters, skirts, tights and boots—and we arrived, thrilled to be there. Along with the rest of the crowd, we patiently watched the opening act. As that band was finishing, the audience got a little rowdy and started booing, and kept it up until the openers left the stage. It made me feel terrible for them.

Katy and I got up to go to the bathroom and were pretty shaken by the rudeness of the crowd. In neighboring stalls, we talked about it. She said, "That was awful." From the bathroom, we could hear the boos getting louder and louder. "I don't think I can stay."

I said, "Why don't they just leave if they're not happy? Why are they booing?"

We exited the stalls and went to the sink to wash our hands. A young woman was standing there, leaning on the towel dispenser, looking our way. She asked us, "Were you just saying that everybody was booing?"

"Yeah, they still are. Listen," said Katy.

The woman smiled at us. "They're not booing. They're saying 'Lou, Lou, Louuu!'"

Of course they were. We were still a couple of newbies to the city.

The show was spectacular. By the end of the night, we were standing on our seats, and with everyone else in the theater we were screaming, "Lou Lou, Louuu!"

* * *

Throughout this period, while Andy remained in Arizona, he and Katy were still together romantically. They wrote letters and talked on the phone constantly. Their plan was to live together after Andy graduated. The question was New York, where Katy was, or San Francisco, where Andy wanted to be.

I wanted my best friends in New York. First, I worked on convincing Katy to stay. "Fashion and magazines are all based in New York," I explained. She didn't need much persuading. After all, she had a job at *Mademoiselle* that hundreds could only dream about. Who would just walk away from that?

Then Katy talked Andy into coming. She told him, "Advertising is based in New York!" Also true. "There's so much energy and opportunity here."

She did her part, but at the risk of sounding self-serving, my main objective in life was to have my closest friends with me. I hoped with all my heart that together they would fall head over heels in love with New York City, like I had, and stay.

Andy didn't take a lot of convincing, and before long, he arrived with a suitcase and his portfolio filled with his prior advertising work he'd created for local businesses while at Spade/Hannawell, the ad agency in Tempe he'd founded while still in college. Katy's roommate Beth had relocated back to Kansas City, so Andy seamlessly took her place. Soon, he and Katy moved out of West Fifty-Second Street and headed downtown into a fifth-floor walk-up apartment on Renwick Street in west SoHo. The artist Roy Lichtenstein had lived in the building and had painted all the baseboards in his signature primary color style. It was a unique thing about the place, and really its only redeeming feature. The apartment was so tiny, the bedroom was a closet, and the kitchen was in the entryway. The lock on the building's front door was ancient and needed a special key. The landlord had only one for the unit, and they couldn't find a locksmith able to make a spare. Katy and Andy had to figure out in the morning who was going to get home first that day. The second to arrive buzzed upstairs, and the first arriver would throw the key wrapped in a little pouch out of the window so the other could let themselves in.

Katy and Andy didn't need to adjust to living together at all, if anything it seemed they had not missed a step since college. They adored each other, and what they shared as a college romance blossomed into true love. Andy would joke about Katy being such a soft touch. "We don't have any money, why does she have to give a dollar to the homeless guy at the subway entrance seven days a week?" he complained. But we all knew how endearing that was to him.

Andy's dream career as an ad exec on Madison Avenue proved to be a tough road to take on his own. He was sending out letters and résumés to every agency without much luck, but his buoyant personality kept his optimism high. He would circle every job posting in *Adweek* and go to offices anywhere in the city to drop off his résumé and samples of his work. He needed to earn some money, so he took a job with me that Willow helped us find at a fancy caterer in Midtown. While he did okay there, he would be the first to admit that there was perhaps no one less suited to be a waiter than he. We were the only two workers there who were not aspiring actors, and though the hours were long, we had a pretty good time working side by side with all those big personalities. Like many transplants to the city, Andy and I had zero connections. Both of us were literally just throwing everything against the wall, hoping we would get lucky and something would stick.

Andy's breakthrough moment came in a random way that seemed straight out of a movie. Four months after he came to town, he worked with Willow and me at our catering gig. Andy was carrying his large zip-case portfolio through the Main Concourse of Grand Central Terminal on his way to drop his résumé at an office in Midtown when a well-dressed older gentleman stopped him and introduced himself.

"Excuse me, young man, can I ask you, what's inside your portfolio?"

Andy answered that he was a recent graduate and had moved here with some experience in the advertising business, and that he had samples of his work in the case.

"Well, that's fortunate for both of us," said the stranger. "I'm a recruiter for the advertising field. My name's Bob Maloney. Great to meet you. Can we take a look at your stuff?"

Bob took Andy to lunch at the Oyster Bar in the lower level of Grand Central. He must have been very impressed with his work because by the next day, he had secured Andy an interview with one of the big agencies of the era, Bozell Worldwide. Almost immediately Andy's whole world changed. He was hired for a copywriting job, and within months one of his first ads for a new sneaker brand called JUMP was on a massive billboard in Times Square. We all walked uptown to take pictures of it. It was the view of a player's feet suspended way up in the air with the basketball shoes prominent in the shot. Andy's copy read, "To get any higher is illegal."

Most of our early city adventures had been uptown or in Midtown. But Andy's new creative advertising crowd, along with his emerging passion for fine art, drew him to the downtown scene. Almost every day I would head south on the subway after work to hang out with them. Gayle and I soon moved into a three-bedroom walk-up in the East Village on Second Avenue between Fourth and Fifth Streets. The rent was much more affordable than uptown, and the handsome thirtysomething Irish brothers who managed the apartments were so kind to us, fixing every problem immediately and helping us anytime we needed a hand hauling things up the narrow stairwell.

Migrating to the East Village was the first time I was able to explore downtown Manhattan, a really different animal from what I had experienced living uptown those first few years. The neighborhoods in lower Manhattan each have a distinctive feel of their own, even more so up to the mid- and late 1980s. Our stomping grounds were the Village, SoHo and Tribeca, with an occasional romp into the Meatpacking District.

It's hard to believe how much these neighborhoods have changed with their current multimillion-dollar luxury brownstones and glistening apartment buildings. Today, downtown is definitely cleaner and safer, but certainly not better in all ways. Those downtown districts had always been a haven for the artistic class, and after the creative explosion of the late fifties and through the eighties, downtown Manhattan became one of the global epicenters of innovative thought, art and music. It's still a wonderful place, but I'm eternally happy that we got to see it then.

Our apartment was surprisingly clean, never felt grimy and was quite spacious compared to where we had lived before. We had south-facing windows, so the sun streamed in the morning and afternoon. And it was much closer to Katy and Andy in SoHo. Most of our gang now lived downtown. Our circle had expanded quite a bit by then with many new friends. Katy had met Eleni and Randall Gianopulos through some of her European travel buddies. This couple would become some of our closest friends. Scott Carlson and Steve Miller, both art directors at different agencies were funny and kindhearted additions to our merry band.

Our everyday local hangout spot was the Spring Lounge, a pub at the corner of Spring and Mulberry with wood paneling, a pressed-tin ceiling and cheap draft beer. Everyone called it the Shark Bar, because huge stuffed sharks hung over the bar and on the walls. No one was sure if they were real or used film props. The Ear Inn, another famous local bar and a favorite of ours, was on Katy and Andy's block, so super convenient. Much of the time, as we were all still short on funds, we hung out at my apartment, drinking, eating and playing endless games of charades. I hosted every holiday and big event, like Thanksgiving and the Super Bowl. My go-to was roasting a turkey and serving it on a bed of greens with bunches of grapes and soft rolls. Add a cheese plate, some dips and the table looked festive with little work and expense. All the guests thought it had been catered. For their contribution, my guests always brought the same thing: wine, beer and vodka.

Katy did not host often because her place was so small. But when she did have people over for dinner, she'd usually make her recipe that everybody loved: lasagna. I have to say, that girl made a great lasagna. It was a basic recipe for a beef lasagna, but Katy had put her full attention into cooking that one thing perfectly; juicy and tasty, with the edges slightly charred and crunchy. Once in a while, she'd buy a fully cooked rotisserie chicken at a store, warm it up in a pan with some potatoes and sprinkle some fresh chopped parsley on top, then pass it off as if she'd cooked it herself. No one knew the truth except me, and I wasn't talkin'.

One afternoon we were lounging around Katy's place, and deciding what we would have at our Oscar party at my place that night.

"I have an idea," I said. "Let's get some pot for the guys!"

Our group were not big smokers. Sometimes one of the guys would bring a joint over and whoever felt like it would partake.

"Yeah, okay, but how're we going to find some?" Katy asked.

We were competitive in weird ways. I knew I had her here, though. I had a six-month jump on her in the city, and whenever I could, I liked to show off that I knew a *little* bit more about things than she did.

"I know where. Don't worry. Let's head over to the park."

The two of us walked the ten minutes to Washington Square Park in the heart of the Village, then a good deal more run-down than the present day. We walked over to the west side of the park, where the dealers hung out among the guys playing speed chess. A thirtysomething guy in an army coat walked by us looking down while saying, "Dime bags, dime bags." It felt good that I was showing some leadership here. Katy was uncharacteristically a little quiet and I thought pretty impressed with me taking command on this excursion.

"I'll take a dime bag," I said to the guy.

"Ten bucks," he muttered.

"All I have is a twenty." I handed it to him.

"Okay, I'll be right back with the weed and the change," he said.

We both stood there for a minute in silence waiting for him. We kind of realized about the same time that he was never coming back with either the weed or the change, but I still stared forward quietly, hoping for the best. I could sense that Katy was looking at me. I darted my eyes her way for a second, and she was staring at me with her arms crossed, tapping her foot.

"Oh, big-shot pusher lady. Knows all the dealios here in town!" she said, smiling that mean little half smile.

"Okay, I know, that was dumb. I can't believe I fell for that!"

She went on with the jabs for a while, and she'd bring it up whenever I tried to show off after that for a long time. "Hey, pusher lady, where's your weed, girl?" That type of stuff. We didn't manage to score any pot for that party and recognized that we didn't really belong in that scene anyway. Those days we were still learning to navigate our way around the city and ultimately become lifelong New Yorkers. But even when we had settled in permanently, there always seemed to be something unexpected just around the corner.

CHAPTER 7

By late summer of 1987, I had left Chroma Copy and was working at Café 57 and the catering jobs. I knew I needed to get back to my goal to work in fashion and likely would have accepted any job just to get my foot in the door, so I started temping again. This time, I did get placed at *Mademoiselle*, in the fashion department, and I worked there for three months alongside Katy. Finally, after two years in New York City I was working at a fashion magazine. The reality wasn't quite as glamorous as I'd hoped. The senior editors were demanding and treated the assistants and junior editors like servants, the ugly side of creating beautiful pictures. None of them knew Katy and I were friends. Not that we kept it a secret, but we thought it was best that we didn't advertise it.

I was able to see with my own eyes what she did at work every day. Her job was to travel around New York to showrooms, shops and boutiques, and take Polaroids of each of the accessories she would choose for upcoming photo shoots. Katy was meticulous about how she organized the pictures and the items as they arrived for photo shoots. Her boss, senior fashion editor Suzanne Martine, a perfectly coiffed all-business type, was exacting about styling. Katy had to stay until seven, eight or nine o'clock to meet Suzanne's standards. But if she stayed that late, she'd get a car service voucher for a ride home in a black Lincoln Town Car. If she worked through lunch, the magazine paid for it. If she worked through dinner, same thing. If she wanted, Katy could have fed herself entirely on the magazine's dime from places in the neighborhood like Mangia or Burke & Burke. A lot of her colleagues did.

I was helping her organize the accessories for a forthcoming photo shoot in LA late one Friday night in the glass-walled conference room. We had an assortment of colorful jewelry, scarves, belts and handbags. From Craft Caravan we had bright red bead necklaces, Robert Lee Morris provided thick silver cuffs and bangles, Echo had brightly printed silk scarves and Carlos Falchi–designed bold handbags in leather that Katy had selected. Suzanne was taking all of it to Los Angeles for a photo shoot that next day.

"It has to be perfect," Katy said to me. She was checking and rechecking the items laid out on the enormous oak table. We had to document and pack it all up meticulously.

"It'll be fine," I tried to assure her.

Katy said, "For Suzanne, 'fine' isn't good enough."

"When do you think we'll be finished?" I asked. It was Friday evening, and we had plans to meet Andy and Walker, our college friend who had recently moved to the city, at El Sombrero for margaritas.

Suzanne came into the conference room, and Katy's guard immediately went up. She braced for criticism as her boss checked the jewelry, belts, hats and purses lined up on the table. While Katy waited for permission to breathe, Suzanne said, "Everything looks good. Pack it up for the flight tomorrow. I had a change in plans and won't be able to go. So, Katy, you'll be in charge."

Whoa, this was big. I watched Katy react to the news. The emotions rolled across her face: excited, nervous, proud, terrified.

"Thank you," she said. "I won't let you down."

"I hope so." Suzanne turned to me. "Elyce, are you free to go this weekend, too? You can be Katy's assistant."

"Yes, of course," I replied, keeping my composure.

As soon as Suzanne left the room, Katy and I silent-screamed and waved our fists around in the air. Not only was she getting to head up her first fashion shoot, but I was going to go with her for a weekend in California, all-expenses-paid.

Saturday morning, a few hours before our flight, we went back to Condé Nast to do a final check. As we were tagging and zipping up wardrobe bags, an assistant from the photo department came into the fashion closet and muttered, "They told me to give this to you." She looked bored and dropped two giant brown paper bags on the center table. I looked inside to find dozens of film canisters for the shoot. *Very important. Must not leave behind.*

We rushed to get all the bags and boxes into the trunk of the Town Car and then sped to JFK. At the ticket counter, Katy was methodical about getting receipts for every parcel we checked. Only upon sitting down on the plane, in business class, a first for both of us, were we able to look at each other and squeal with delight. The whole flight, the two of us chatted away, toasting ourselves with the free champagne. The hours passed like minutes.

Deplaning was as smooth as the silk dresses we'd transported from New York. None of the garment bags went missing; we found the driver easily and he helped us carry everything to the waiting luxury sedan. The job was a lot of schlepping, but I was starting to see the fun of it, too. We made it to our fancy LA hotel and collapsed on Katy's king-size bed.

"We did it," she declared.

Just as we were reveling in the logistical accomplishment, the phone on the nightstand rang. Katy answered it and mouthed to me, "It's Robert Erdmann." She held the phone so I could hear his end of the call.

Robert Erdmann was the photographer on the shoot. He'd shot covers for *Vogue* and was kind of intimidating because he was such a big deal. Robert was telling Katy he had some concerns about the shoot location because it was threatening to rain in Los Angeles, something that rarely happened. "I'm worried about the light," he said.

"Okay," agreed Katy.

"You have the film, right?"

As soon as he spoke the words, my heart dropped to my knees. I was picturing those two brown paper bags on the table in the fashion closet, *right where I left them*. I signaled to Katy that I had forgotten them.

Katy's mouthed to me, *OH MY GOD!* To Erdmann, she confessed, "Slight problem."

It was now Saturday evening. Katy and I took out the yellow pages and called every photo shop in the greater Los Angeles area, but they were all closed. I felt *horrible*.

"It's totally my fault," I said.

Katy took it better than I expected.

"Elyce, it'll be okay. Let's not panic yet," she said. Katy could be a ball of nerves, but if I freaked out, which wasn't very often, she always calmed me down.

Before I suggested breaking and entering a photo store, Erdmann's assistant called and said, "Robert thinks we have enough film left over from the last shoot to cover this one."

Hearing this news was like a reprieve from the governor if I were on death row. The stakes felt really high to make this shoot go well. Katy wanted so badly for it to be a success, and it was my job, and my desire, to make that happen for her.

But we had a new problem. Erdmann kept on about the "bad light." His assistant, James, informed us, "Robert thinks we should fly to Palm Springs and do the shoot there."

Whatever the photographer wants, the photographer gets. This was the era of the supermodel and the star photographer—the era of bottomless budgets, when glossy magazines controlled the billion-dollar fashion industry. This last-minute change of plans was going to cost the magazine a fortune.

Katy's nerves were clearly fraying. She kept saying, "Tell me this is all going to work out, it's going to be okay."

It was my turn to calm her down. Plus, we both knew going over budget by $10,000 or $20,000 on a photo shoot happened all the time.

I worked with the Condé Nast travel office and chartered a tiny airplane to fly into the desert. This forty-five-minute flight was absolutely harrowing. As we flew over the mountains, the wind created a tunnel effect that sucked the plane down—and sent my stomach with it. Everyone on board—Katy, Robert, James, another photo assistant, three models, two hair and makeup artists, and me—had their heads between their knees. By some miracle, we landed in one piece. I would have kissed the ground if I wasn't trying so hard to make a good impression.

The light in the desert *was* golden and magical.

I said to Katy, "This is better, right?"

She said, "It better be better. We only have half a day to get it right."

We needed a rental car to find a good location and transport a ton of stuff, all our bags, plus Robert's equipment. We chose a brand-

new fancy minivan. Katy assured me, "It's okay. Si will get it." She
meant Samuel Irving (S.I.) Newhouse, the owner of Condé Nast,
who everyone called "Si." I used my driver's license and my personal
credit card at Avis because Katy's was expired. What could go wrong?

We drove to meet the location van, our base of operations, and
started to set up the clothes and accessories so Katy could style the
two models. Meanwhile, Robert and James took the rented van to
scout a location for the shoot. Katy's taste was perfection. The shoot
was to present spring apparel and accessories. The models were
expertly styled in a sporty knit green dress from Norma Kamali,
and another slim-fitting two-piece Lycra suit by Azzedine Alaïa
selected by Suzanne. All would be accessorized with Katy's selec-
tions of bags, jewelry and shoes. The glam squad did their hair and
makeup. Although the style at the time was big hair, Katy directed
the stylist to go sleek, glossy and straight. Make up was simple and
natural with only a bold pink lip color. I helped however I could,
but I mostly just stood by and watched how naturally Katy put
everything together.

An hour went by. Then another. The sun was high and hot. Robert
and James should have been back by now with the van. After three
hours, we saw the wavy mirage-like image of Robert and his assistant
riding up the road in a cab toward us. They stepped out of the car,
looking like they survived a sandstorm.

"What happened?" asked Katy, aghast.

Robert said, "We got stuck in a dune and had to taxi back."

"Where's the van now?" I dared to ask.

After Robert guzzled some water, he gestured toward the open
desert, "Back there somewhere."

What? "So how are we going to find it?" It was rented in *my*
name. Neither GPS nor LoJack existed back then. Was I going to
be responsible for this?

He shrugged. "I have no idea." This guy did not care one bit that he'd lost an entire car, or that we had to fly to Palm Springs at a moment's notice.

Katy urged him to get the shoot going. Robert found a suitable location within walking distance of our base of operations. The actual shoot took only a couple of hours, and Katy never lost her focus. When we got back to our hotel in LA, we were crazy with exhaustion and relief.

Katy said, "We lost a van!"

"Yeah, we did."

"And those poor models! I thought they were going to melt."

I laughed and agreed, "They barely made it!"

"The photos will be good, don't you think?"

"Of course! You did a great job. And we didn't crash into those mountains." Surviving our adventure had left us both giddy.

We flew home on Monday morning, with all the garments *and* the film, which I did not let out of my sight. A day later, Avis found the van in the desert, and it'd been completely stripped. I was not held responsible, thank God. It took a lot of paperwork to get it sorted out, but I was relieved when all the corporate folks didn't bat an eyelash about it.

The photo department processed the film, and Katy was eager to see the images, as was I. We gave blood, sweat and tears to get those pictures, but it would all be worth it if they were gorgeous. When they were ready, Suzanne went to the art department to look at the photos along with Katy (I lurked nearby in earshot).

"They're all too bright," sighed Suzanne. "You can't see the detail in the clothes. We can't use them." Amy Levin Cooper, the editor in chief, soon agreed, much to our chagrin.

In the end, the quest for sunshine doomed the shoot, and Katy's first fashion feature was killed. She was incredibly disappointed, but she kept her composure. I could tell she was doing her best to hold it all in until we left the office for a cigarette break. And then she burst into tears.

"I know you're upset, but this is just the first of a lot of shoots you'll run," I said. "You did your job. The models looked beautiful. Things that went wrong were out of your control. You know this happens all the time. Half the shoots don't make it to the magazine."

"All of that is true. I don't think bad lighting is my fault, but it's still on me."

Katy's frustration wasn't about the fact that the photos would never be published or that unforeseen events ruined her effort. It was more that she hated the idea that her bosses likely thought she'd failed to do her job with the utmost professionalism. I know from working there that the editors moved on right away and never gave it a second thought. Many shoots never made it into the magazine. Though Katy was upset for days at the outcome of that assignment, she eventually was too busy to worry about it. Ultimately, the idea of moving on from a less than ideal work experience would be good training for the future.

CHAPTER 8

While there were no immediate openings at *Mademoiselle*, Katy's editor, Suzanne, kindly connected me with the preppy fashion company JG Hook, where I was hired as an assistant to the director of public relations in October 1988. My main responsibility was writing press releases for new apparel collections and calling editors to make appointments to come in and see the new pieces. My boss was a professional and good at her job, but absolutely nuts. We shared an office, so she would watch me working all day. A perfectionist, she made me do tasks over and over until they were exactly how she wanted them. She didn't believe in Wite-Out (used to correct mistakes on typewritten letters), so if she decided to change a word, I had to retype the whole thing. Every night, she made a big pan of sautéed onions and garlic and brought it to work. She didn't eat anything else. The smell oozed out of her pores, and our whole office reeked of garlic. People in the neighboring offices left notes under our door complaining about the smell, but she just told me, "Fuck 'em."

But I began to make connections in the industry with my role of calling editors to come and see the new collections and sending them pieces for photo shoots. Even though my boss was kooky, I learned a lot at that job, especially the discipline of getting things right, whether it be correspondence or styling layered outfits.

I had my first New York boyfriend, too, that year. Matt was a redheaded, Irish American, good-looking twenty-five-year-old contractor, and was a roommate of Willow's boyfriend. I met Willow and her date at the Plaza Hotel's classic Oak Room for drinks, and Matt showed up, too. After they left to see a movie, Matt and I talked for hours and then walked through Central Park. It started lightly snowing, the flakes illuminated by the full moon. It was a beautiful, storybook night.

Matt and I had a good time together and good chemistry. While he worked long hours renovating people's apartments, always juggling multiple jobs, we spent all of our free time together.

Matt got a job to dig a new well at a client's second home in Martha's Vineyard. The house was a cozy five-bedroom shingled beach house, with expensive, comfortable furnishings and a chef's kitchen. The goal was to do the work during the spring so the house would be ready come summer. Matt had to go to the Vineyard in February to assess what work needed to be done. The client, a wealthy banker, told him to stay in the house for the weekend, and to bring guests if he wanted.

We invited Katy and Andy and Eleni and Randall. The plan was for Matt and me to arrive on Thursday, while the others would fly up on Friday night. I realized that this would be the ultimate opportunity to pull a prank, so we sold this weekend hard. "It's a great place, right next to Jackie Kennedy's compound!" When Matt and I got to the house, we rounded up sleeping bags and a lantern and brought them out to a little shed on the outskirts of the property. The shed was not insulated. It was freezing and had a cement floor. Tools hung from hooks.

As we saw the lights of our friend's rental car in the distance, we turned off the house lights and ran down to the front gate. They pulled up and we acted all upset. "We can't get into the house!" I said. "But don't worry! We set up sleeping bags in the shed for us. We can sleep in there together." We showed them the shed. They were pretty shocked.

Andy said, "We're not sleeping in there!"

Randall chimed in, "Let's just break a window to get into the big house."

"There's an alarm," said Matt. "The police will come."

Andy told him, "Call your client! There must be a way in."

"The client's out of the country."

It went on like this for thirty minutes as we all sat around the one lantern in the freezing shed with a bottle of wine. No one talked much, I could tell they were bummed out that the whole weekend was going to be a frozen mess. The hard part was keeping a straight face. When the wine was finished, I said, "We better go to the house and get another bottle."

Katy and Andy blinked at me a few times until they got it, and then everyone started chuckling.

Katy said, "Good one!"

We ended up having an amazing weekend by the fireplace, drinking, making roast chicken and playing charades.

Matt and I broke up a few months after that weekend. We each knew it was never going to be anything serious. We were both too young for a hardcore relationship and had our own dreams to pursue.

He moved to Puerto Rico to start a roofing company, married a flight attendant and is very happy.

* * *

By 1989, David Spade, the last of the Arizona gang, arrived in New York and jumped right onto the comedy circuit. He opened at Caroline's comedy club for Dennis Miller, and soon after, got a job at *Saturday Night Live* as a writer. He invited us to sit in the audience at dress rehearsals and live shows, and we were able to attend the legendary after-parties with wall-to-wall celebrities. These parties were unbelievable. For security reasons they would wait until the last minute to announce the location, and when he heard, David would let Andy know where to meet him. The spots were generally the newest or hippest swanky restaurant or nightclub downtown, mostly places we had absolutely no business being in.

One in particular I remember was at the Odeon, on West Broadway. Aerosmith was the musical guest on the show that night. The three of us went there, and though we didn't know anyone except for David, we had a blast with each other, hobnobbing with all the stars and musical guests. Katy and I entertained ourselves with a little game we played. Photos were generally frowned upon, so the two of us would stage fake photos of each other near famous people, that we would each shoot with imaginary cameras that we would pretend to be holding. We'd keep just far enough away so the celebs wouldn't notice us. We did that all the time—a little juvenile, but we thought it was hilarious. I would lean on the bar near Aerosmith, then toss my head back and smile as if Steven Tyler had shared something funny just with me. Katy would watch me and laugh and snap her imaginary photo with her "air" camera. Katy was busted once when she was standing next to Alec Baldwin. She had her head leaning on her chin and was acting serious, as if she was listening intently

Eight-year-old me and
my first steer, Harry, at the
Harvey County Fair, 1970.

My family in
1972, clockwise
from top left:
sisters Shon
and Holiday,
dad Dana, mom
Louise, sister
Willow, and me.

Bear and me,
Kansas, 1976.

My mom, Louise
Cox, circa 1979.

My dad, Dana Cox,
circa 1979.

High school graduation,
spring 1981.

Gertrude Sellards Pearson (GSP) hallmates Sophia, Anne, Robin and Katy at University of Kansas sorority rush in January 1982.

Me and Katy at the "Sleep and Eat" fraternity party in fall 1981.

Me and Katy at the University of Kansas, fall 1981.

With the
beverage cart
at the Biltmore
Country Club
in Phoenix,
circa 1983.

Katy and I hit Mexico
during ASU spring
break, 1984.

Katy in La
Jolla, 1984.

Katy at John's & Co.
in Phoenix, 1984.

Katy and Andy
in Arizona,
1984.

Andy and Katy
on our Flagstaff–
Sedona road trip,
December 1984.

Andy Spade and
me in Sedona, 1984.

David Spade, me
and Andy Spade at
Missy Brosnahan's
house in Phoenix,
Thanksgiving, 1985.

Employees of Carter's, from
left: Charles Alexander,
Mike Cook, Mike Carter,
Katy Brosnahan, Andy
Spade and our friend/
neighbor Lily Kanter, 1984.
Mike Carter

Andy, Katy and
Walker in our college
apartment, 1985.

Me and Katy
preparing
to leave
Arizona,
spring 1986.

Our last dinner
in Arizona, at our
favorite Japanese
restaurant,
May 1986.

Me and Katy
outside our
first New York
apartment on
West Fifty-
Second Street in
the fall of 1986.

Katy in New
York, 1986.

In our Hell's
Kitchen apartment,
fall 1986.

Flanking Santa
Claus at the Sixth
Avenue Flea Market,
December 1986.

Andy and Katy in our West Fifty-Second Street apartment, Christmas 1986.

Katy and Andy skateboarding in Central Park, 1987.
Tiff Pemberton

Andy and Katy in spring 1987.
Tiff Pemberton

Maude Gabriel, me and Katy at the *Mademoiselle* Christmas Party in 1989.

With Gayle, Andy and Katy at Café 57, 1988.

Walker, Katy, Andy and me at Kate and Andy's apartment, December 1988.

Katy and I flank
our friend Eleni at
her wedding in San
Francisco, 1991.

My sister Willow in
New York in 1992.

At left, with Girbaud colleagues
on a business trip to Paris, 1992.

Katy making her
signature lasagna in
her Upper West Side
apartment, 1992.

Celebrating Katy's thirtieth birthday downtown, with a homemade chocolate cake. The top was shaped like a handbag. December 1992.

Surrounded by George and Katy celebrating my birthday in March 1993.

Katy at the Amagansett
beach house, 1993.

David Spade, Andy Spade
and Katy in May 1993.

Andy and Katy in Amagansett, 1993.

Katy at our first Accessories Circuit show, Javits Center, New York, 1993.

Katy at her wedding
party in 1994.

Katy showing off
her wedding hat.

to something Alec was saying. While we were snickering as I took the pretend photo, Alec turned and looked at her like she was a nut. We both scurried away like little bugs, totally embarrassed, but we cracked each other up talking about it later. The thing was, we couldn't believe we were there at all. If only our twenty-two-year-old selves could see our twenty-seven-year-old selves. I don't think there was a way we could have possibly imagined ourselves at those type of parties with all those famous faces.

* * *

Katy was promoted at *Mademoiselle*, first to accessories editor and later to fashion editor. With each promotion, we took the opportunity to celebrate with drinks and dinner at one of our favorite East Village haunts—either Ghandi, a BYOB Indian restaurant, or Cucina Di Pesce, a small, lively Italian place.

When she became a senior editor in 1990, she was thrilled to have her own assistant, the position she had started in at the magazine just four years earlier.

Soon after, she and Andy moved to Prince Street, to a studio with an exposed-brick wall. It was very expensive and had a real old New York vibe. We used to roast marshmallows in the fireplace.

By early 1990 I was looking to move on from JG Hook. I liked the company and the people, but I was not passionate about the style, and in addition it was a mature business with many lifer-type employees. I didn't feel like there was a lot of room for growth, so I started looking around. I applied to a want ad in *Women's Wear Daily* and was hired as the PR manager at Marithé François Girbaud, a cutting-edge French company, which was the hottest denim brand at the time. Our office was on Seventh Avenue in the center of the fashion district. The Girbaud showroom was crackling with energy and had eclectic loud music playing constantly though the office;

everything from David Bowie to Édith Piaf. The PR room was packed with samples coming in and out for editorial shoots regularly. I loved my new job, and my salary ballooned to what seemed like a fortune to me then.

After working nonstop for years, Katy, Andy and I had pocket money for the first time, and we spent it all at restaurants and bars downtown. Our lives, like most of our contemporaries in the early nineties, were about going out and commiserating about the work-week over cocktails and wine.

Raoul's, on Prince Street, was one of our regular hangs. Opened by the Raoul brothers in the midseventies, in the then-sparse res-taurant scene in SoHo, it was a dark, romantic outpost with deep red banquettes. The walls were covered with work from mostly local artists, including one scandalous reclining-nude photo that covered an entire wall; the model was rumored to be "Fergie," Sarah Ferguson, the former Duchess of York who was a friend of the photographer, Martin Schreiber. Raoul's had fabulous classic French cuisine with a modern twist, the menus written on individual slate chalkboards, all in French and changing daily. To venture up the spiral staircase to the second-floor dining room you would pass a full-time fortune teller sitting at her table ready to read your cards. All in all, a great experience on any night. One of the first times we went to Raoul's, Rob Jones, the maître d', descended the spiral staircase as his drag persona, Dusty. Whatever music was playing stopped, and Dusty Springfield's song "You Don't Have to Say You Love Me" came on loudly. Dusty, with her feather boa, stepped onto the bar, made it her stage for an impromptu weekly drag show, and lip-synced while the entire restaurant stood and cheered. *This is why I love living in New York,* I thought.

We haunted our favorite bars and restaurants, like Café Noir, Felix and the Raccoon Lodge. Nick & Eddie's was the place for roast chicken, mashed potatoes and spinach. El Teddy's on West Broadway was one of our go-tos on any night for its great margaritas and never-ending party vibe. We were not really into the club scene, which was dominated by three or four biggies like the Palladium, Area and Limelight. We would go occasionally, but those clubs were huge and crowded. Our favorite dance spot was a small local place in Tribeca, just a few blocks from Katy and Andy's apartment. You'd have to make your way down a dark alley to find Madame Rosa's behind a steel door. No sign. We'd go midweek, dressed in the signature look of the time in all black or oversized paper-bag-waist jeans and a black sweater or jacket, and black lace-up ankle boots. Often, downtown dignitaries like the artist Jean-Michel Basquiat would jump onstage and DJ. One week, we planned to go every night the club was open because we heard from the bartender that Prince and the Revolution were coming in. *Purple Rain* had come out a few years before, and Katy and I were both huge fans. We gave up after a few nights, and of course that was when they came. No Prince, but we heard his beautiful drummer Sheila E. and the band were there dancing with the crowd all night.

* * *

In February 1991, after I had been working at the jeans company for about a year, I received surprising news. The headquarters of Girbaud's North American parent company, VF Corporation, were in Greensboro, North Carolina, and a few key New York–based staffers were being asked to relocate there. They offered me a big raise and a new title to go with it. It was tempting to move for a bigger job, title and salary. But it was a tough decision—by that time New York had been my home for six years. The thought of being separated from Katy and Andy physically hurt. But I decided to make the move. Of course my family all agreed it was a great chance for advancement.

I thought it made sense to take the big career opportunity, and it was leading me south.

I'd convinced everyone to come to New York, and now I was leaving it. It felt like the end of an era. But when I look back, I think of that as the golden period of our friendship, with youthful happiness and personal growth for both of us. Even our struggles were a source of hilarity when we went through them together.

The day before I left for North Carolina, Katy wrote me a long letter. Here's a part of it:

Dear Elyce,

Here it is, 2:00 AM, and my eyes are swollen shut from crying at the thought of you leaving for North Carolina. . . . There are so many things I feel that I have failed to tell you in the ten years I've known you and I've decided it was about time, starting with the most important thing: You were the first person in my life to really show me how it feels to be truly loved.

You've shown me so many things I had never before seen in anyone, like unconditional love and trust. You have always been there for me, Elyce, and in so many more ways than you will ever know. You used to say that it was you who needed me, but I think we both know that it has always been I who truly looked up to you and have needed you much more. It is just more difficult for me to admit. I have always been envious of your honesty, kindness, and ability to make so many people feel good about themselves, of which I have been the lucky recipient for all of these years. People have always warmed up to you, and I hope you know just how wonderful you are.

You and Andy are the only two people in my life that allow me to be me and still feel as loved as I do by both of you. And I have never trusted anyone as I do the two of you and know that means so much to me. I am so proud of you for all that you have accomplished in your new job, though I have been less inclined to tell you because it now represents the biggest threat: you leaving. I don't think I am really sure how this will affect me, but I'm trying to hang in there because I have no choice. I am going to miss you so much. I feel so privileged to be your best friend. Andy is probably most nervous about your move, not only because of how much he will miss you, but because of how he will have to listen to me talk about it.

I love you, Elyce, so much, and I hope you will always remain my dearest and most cherished friend for life.

Love, Katy

I sobbed when I read it then. I have this letter, and after all these years, I still sob when I read it now.

CHAPTER 9

While living in Manhattan had always been my dream, the draw of an exciting position with a company I admired was a huge opportunity for me. In addition to a big raise, I would have considerably more responsibility than I'd had thus far in my career. As one of the few marketing execs, I'd be working with inspiring transplanted New Yorkers with similar backgrounds to mine. I knew I couldn't pass up the offer, but as I packed to move, I thought, *What am I doing? Why am I leaving? What if I get stuck down there?* On a molecular level, I knew that New York was where I belonged. I made a deal with myself that I'd stay in the south for two years, and then I'd figure out a way to move back north.

Once I arrived in Greensboro, I was glad that I'd taken the risk. The city was appealing, with a population then of about 200,000. What it lacked in size, it made up for with Southern charm. It's a garden city, with lush green parks and scattered thickets of beautiful tulip trees and mossy beeches. At the time, it was made up of mostly low-rise structures with a sprawling residential area. The downtown historic district was delightful with one-of-a-kind shops and dotted with galleries and restaurants. The company helped me find a large furnished apartment. Since there was no real public transportation option, I bought myself a car, a used, boxy, butterscotch-colored Volvo four-door sedan, with a four-on-the-floor manual transmission, always trying to keep those tractor-driving skills well honed. I had to admit, much as I had grown to crave the energy and bustle of New York, the air in North Carolina was clean and fresh, each inhale scented with magnolia and dogwood blossoms. I *really* missed my friends, but the ease by which I folded into my new life compared to the everyday challenges of New York City threw me off a little. I had to get used to the friendly smiling strangers, the clean air and the spacious apartment.

Surprisingly, I found myself too busy to be homesick about being away from Katy and everyone in New York. As soon as I arrived in North Carolina, I had to hit the road for promotional events. Girbaud by this time had grown into a major international brand with their signature stonewashed and baggy-fit jeans. They were in the process of a significant expansion across the US. I knew I was lucky to have the job and that experience. I genuinely liked the clothes, and especially at that age it was exciting to watch all the artists on MTV wearing our jeans. It made me feel like I was part of the cultural mainstream. When not on the road I was busy in the Greensboro corporate office planning future events, booking venues, selecting musical groups to perform and organizing the staffing for each location.

I started traveling extensively around the United States to plan and execute these events, mainly on college campuses. Our top locations included Austin for University of Texas (UT), Dallas for Southern Methodist University (SMU), and New Orleans for Tulane and Louisiana State University (LSU), among many others. I was able to live in New Orleans for two or three weeks at a time in a company rental and leaned right into the Big Easy, the ever-present music, the lifestyle, the beignets and the chicory coffee. Tulane was a beautiful campus. We had a great reception at both LSU and Loyola, too. I oversaw a five-person team, all of us in our twenties and early thirties. Our strategy was to engage college students by doing promotional events on campus that would draw a big crowd. We would find fashion majors or leaders of fashion clubs with our pitch: "We'll help you put on a major event on campus. We'll provide outfits for you to style, hair and makeup people, and live entertainment. All you have to do is get permission from the college and host the event."

Colleges were strict about allowing companies to come on-site and run promotions. By having students host our events, we avoided a lot of red tape. It was a novel approach back then and highly effective. The student hosts were excited to gain some real experience working on a professional-level fashion show, with great music and free clothes, plus, they were able to add a line to their résumés. Some of them later became interns at Girbaud after they graduated. It was a win-win. The attendees loved these events and came in droves for the free music, products and fun.

We eventually sponsored larger events, including a free music festival at the bandshell in Central Park in the summer of 1993. I researched and hired the local bands, all of them outfitted head-to-toe in Girbaud. I hired MCs as well to banter between acts and introduce the bands—and, of course, to model our clothes. A young Dave Chappelle was one of our first MCs. He was great, although he showed up an hour late, forcing me to go out onstage and apologize for the delay. I stupidly tried to placate the crowd with a fascinating info session about Girbaud. I bombed in a big way.

Overall, these experiences were my introduction to the importance of living in a brand through the eyes of our customers, galvanizing the present buyers and opening the tent wide to new people. I learned the importance of fusing a brand with its own energy and personality. Those were formative years and overall a great learning experience.

For every long weekend or holiday, I used airline points to fly the ninety minutes to New York and spend time with Katy and Andy and all of our crew. After living in the studio on Prince Street, Katy and Andy had moved to a large one-bedroom apartment on West Ninety-Second Street. On those nonwork trips, I usually stayed with them, sleeping on their green velvet sofa. It felt like old times. They always greeted me with hugs and kisses and plenty of reunited excitement. I needed it. I never thought that they'd stopped caring about me, but it was still a relief to know that New York and my best friends hadn't moved on without me. I still belonged, both in the city and with Katy and Andy.

On one flight to New York from North Carolina, the plane was forced to circle for a while before landing. I looked out the window at the grid of skyscrapers and imagined all the people below riding in taxis to parties, putting on makeup before dates, making eye contact over martini glasses in bars. Millions of them.

New York is the land of single people, I thought. The culture of the city was to explore, mingle, meet everyone and taste everything. In North Carolina at that time, the culture was more to pair off and settle down in one's early twenties. The contrast, like my dating life, was stark. Just seeing the city lights—and knowing that Manhattan was teeming with single men—filled my lonely heart with joy. Whenever I flew back, as soon as the plane landed, I had the feeling I was back where I was supposed to be.

On one long weekend, about a year after I moved to North Carolina, Andy invited Katy and me to a gathering with his advertising
friends at a bar downtown. I started talking to a handsome copywriter
named George. His look, in a word: *disheveled*. His burned-out
chambray button-front shirt was half-untucked, and his jeans were
frayed, but in a really awkward way as if they had been snagged on
some barbed wire. His shiny dark curls were a few weeks overdue for
a trim. His smiling brown eyes and olive skin did a lot to compensate
for those sartorial shortcomings, though.

In the first five minutes of talking, he told me about his big Greek
family back in Chicago, where he grew up. He explained in a sincere
way that his nonchalant look was his rejection of what he considered
the era's obsession with wearing designer clothing to seek status. "I
don't want anyone to like me because of what I wear," he explained
sincerely. "If they like me, they like me."

I can fix this, I thought.

George and I fell into a long-distance relationship, not ideal when
you are just getting to know someone. We made it work, though. I
came to New York often, and he flew down to North Carolina, too.
The more I got to know him, the more I liked him. George was so
funny and creative, constantly spouting new ideas for ads or random
concepts. One of my favorites was a Monopoly-type board game
but with Mafia characters who could kill each other and take over
territories. Aside from the humor, he was also very warmhearted and
a really good person.

* * *

Maybe more than most people, New Yorkers identify themselves
with their jobs. If you're living there, you have to fight to stay, both
in big and little ways, almost daily. Most people who are not born
in the city have come for their work, and jobs at glamorous places

are generally very competitive. Those who worked at Condé Nast in the nineties were at the top of their profession, and they worked hard and fought to be there.

Katy enjoyed the cachet and identity of being an editor at *Mademoiselle* for five years. But eventually working at the magazine was taking its toll on her, impacting her sense of self and making her grow progressively less happy. We spoke almost every day throughout my time in North Carolina. One of us would call the other, usually late at night after work. I was so happy to have those moments with her. Though my job was exciting, my social life consisted of mostly hanging out with colleagues after work. Katy, for her part, sounded increasingly spent by laboring the ten hours a day to grind out fashion editorial, issue after issue, year after year. She no longer saw being a fashion editor as her long-term career.

"Andy thinks I should quit and take some time until I figure out my next move," she said.

We talked about this prospect many times. I thought Katy was looking to me for affirmation that it was a good idea to leave the magazine. At that time, I encouraged her *not* to quit without lining up something else first. For myself, being jobless would have been tense, likely because I had money and security anxiety that went back to childhood. To combat her job fatigue, I gave her practical advice about going outside and taking long walks instead—advice that, in hindsight, was useless.

My grandma's type of wisdom—"Get some exercise. Eat an apple. Put on some lipstick, you'll feel better!"—did nothing to lift Katy's spirits or give her any insight into what to do with her life. It can be daunting to figure out your path at twenty-nine, Katy's age then. She had abundant talent and a Midwestern work ethic; she could have easily gone to another magazine or taken a job at a fashion brand. She could also go in a completely different direction. In the early nineties, there was so much opportunity in New York City. It was like going to a Greek diner hungry, paging through the huge menu, and asking yourself, "Do I want the lobster thermidor or the pancakes?" With so many options, it was difficult to choose a path.

Ultimately, Katy made the only choice she could, given how stressed-out and unhappy she'd become. In the spring of 1993, she decided to quit *Mademoiselle* after five years. She gave them a month's notice to find her replacement, but the moment she made the decision and let them know, it was like a great weight was lifted off her shoulders. I distinctly remember our call that evening. I came home to my phone ringing (landline of course), picked up, and her greeting to me was, "I did it!" I could tell by her buoyancy and the change in her tone that she had made the right move.

While she took a breather, she worked a few short-term gigs freelancing as a fashion stylist. She landed one memorable job through our friend Marybeth Schmitt, a top stylist in the fashion department at *Allure*, Condé Nast's beauty magazine. Marybeth wanted to take a vacation to Paris with her boyfriend, but the only way she could go was by hiring her own replacement on a big shoot with the magazine's legendary creative director Polly Mellen and A-list photographer Steven Meisel. Polly had a reputation for being really tough and very particular, but she was absolutely brilliant at creating gorgeous fashion spreads. Katy initially said no, but Marybeth begged her to reconsider. Marybeth had worked with Katy since Marybeth was a fashion publicist, and she knew that Katy had a great eye for vintage styles. The theme of this feature was "Beauty Through the Decades." Even though the photos would focus on the models' faces, each model would be styled top to bottom in decade-appropriate looks from the forties to the nineties. The story was totally in Katy's wheelhouse, and Marybeth was desperate to spend the time in Paris. Katy agreed to take the job with one condition: She didn't want to go to the Condé Nast building. She'd only just left the company, and possibly running into her former colleagues in the lobby or elevators would have been uncomfortable. To source and select styles, Katy did not have to be physically present at the office anyway.

Polly was demanding, and she wanted to see *everything*. Katy had to scour the marketplace and send Polaroids of every belt, pair of earrings, top, pant and shoe to her. Katy threw herself into the job. She meticulously organized the merchandise, hundreds of items, at her apartment. The night before the shoot at a studio downtown, Katy packed and labeled everything. An assistant was scheduled to pick it all up the next morning.

At 7:00 a.m., Katy's phone rang. Groggily, she answered, "Hello?"

The voice on the other end said, "This is Polly Mellen. Do you know who I am?"

It was the first time the two had spoken directly. Hearing her testy tone, Katy started to get scared. "Yes, hello," she said.

"*Where are you?*"

"I'm in my apartment waiting for someone to—"

Polly scolded her, "*WHERE ARE YOU?*"

"I'm sorry, I'm not—"

"GET DOWN HERE, NOW!" Then she hung up the phone.

Katy was so stunned, she sat there frozen. Andy had heard the call and settled her down somewhat. For Marybeth's sake, Katy knew she had to make sure everything went off flawlessly with Polly. She got dressed in her typical outfit at that time, a pair of Andy's jeans cinched paper-bag style with one of his belts, a button-down white shirt and loafers, then hauled all the merch to the street. Back in her *Mademoiselle* days, a driver and Town Car would have been parked at the curb, waiting for her. This time, she had to hail a cab herself and load up bag after bag, box after box, into the back seat and trunk.

As soon as she arrived at the studio, Polly immediately wanted to see what she had brought. Katy provided a dozen options for every look, but she wanted more. When it came time to choose from the mass of belts Katy had laid out, Polly rejected them all, pointed at Katy's waist and commanded, "Give me that one."

"What one?"

"*The belt you're wearing! Give it to me!*"

That belt was holding up her (Andy's) pants. She handed it over anyway. When Polly sent Katy back out into the market of accessories showrooms to find a particular pair of sunglasses, she was too rattled to grab one of the other belts. She ran around New York with her big pants slipping down, trying to hold them up with one hand and sorting through stylish sunglasses with the other.

It wasn't funny while it was happening, but Katy laughed about it a lot later and liked to tell that story, although she never told it in front of Marybeth. Ten years later, when Marybeth mentioned to an editor that she briefly worked for Polly Mellen at *Allure*, the woman said, "Kate Spade used to tell the funniest story about that." That's how Marybeth found out what really happened at that shoot. She told me recently, "When I got back from Paris, Katy thanked me for the job and told me it all went really well." Katy spared her the truth: that it had been a miserable experience. I smiled when Marybeth told me that.

Of course she didn't tell you, I thought. *It would have made you feel bad.* It's one of those private little insights that a woman knows about her closest friend.

CHAPTER 10

After a few years on the Upper West Side, Katy and Andy moved back downtown to a loft on Warren Street in Tribeca in 1992. The shiny Tribeca of today was still mostly loft buildings and warehouses back then, some structures still housing their original working factories for storage or manufacturing. Many of the loft spaces were raw and empty with exposed ducts, original wood-plank floors, eighteen-foot ceilings and industrial cage elevators. Most had no walls or kitchens. Andy told me that when they first went to see the two-thousand-square-foot loft on Warren Street, he opened a closet door and found a rat skeleton. He threw a newspaper over it so Katy wouldn't see it; she would never have let him lease the place otherwise. They decided to leave the space open and had a carpenter buddy build a kitchen on an eight-inch platform so it felt separate. Their bed was opposite the kitchen in the center of the loft, against the wall, built up on a high platform. One end of the space was filled with a long desk and the other end served as the living room area. The green velvet sofa made the trip from the former apartment along with two club chairs and a handmade heavy wooden table designed by an artist friend out of old wood floor planks. There were no curtains as the windows were so tall. It felt huge and empty but was so much like a blank canvas it was ideal for Andy to display his ever-growing art collection.

The collection had become a minor issue between the two. After their initial move downtown, Andy had let his curiosity from the flea market days blossom into a full-blown obsession with all kinds of art. Mostly he collected paintings. Some of his favorites at the time were Rene Ricard, Lowell Boyers, Hugo Guinness, James Nares and Robert Hawkins. Living amid a sea of galleries, Andy would meander through the streets of SoHo and the East Village, speaking to all the gallerists and meeting the artists. Paintings, sculpture, street art—his interest was broad, and he started buying pieces he liked. Katy, though encouraging of his interest and also sincerely liking much of what he bought, had to put her foot down. They had run out of wall space, and their storage area in the building's basement was full to the ceiling. He agreed to stop collecting, and there was a lull in the tide for a while, except for an occasional small piece. One day, Katy went to have lunch with Andy at his agency office. She had not been to visit in a long time. She walked in and assumed there was a big shoot going on because his office was full of objects of all kinds—paintings, sculptures, furniture, some stacked on one another.

Katy asked Steve Miller, Andy's director, partner and officemate, "Steve, what's going on today? Why is there so much stuff in here? Are these props for a shoot?"

He looked back at her and asked, "What do you mean? That's Andy's art collection." When Katy was telling me the story she pretended to be annoyed. Of course I could see the pride on her face; Andy's passion and appreciation of art was something she adored about him.

While Katy was working out her career move, Andy's star was ascending in the advertising world at the cutting-edge agency Kirshenbaum + Bond, where they were pioneering new ideas in advertising. The firm created sidewalk signs, pop-ups, loads of novel directions that they referred to as guerilla marketing. With clients like Target, Snapple, BMW and Kenneth Cole, K + B was the agency on everybody's radar. Andy really felt like his level of forward thinking and creativity had found a home.

Meanwhile, Katy was treading water to some extent. Andy could tell she needed to focus her high energy and attention on one thing. He thought Katy should make use of her years of experience as a market editor in accessories. They spoke at length to help her identify and focus on what was missing in the broad category of fashion accessories.

She thought about an ongoing source of frustration for her at the magazine: Katy often could not find just the right handbag that would be correct for a particular fashion shoot. She complained about it repeatedly. On the high end of the spectrum, there were leather handbags with complex designs, mostly unstructured, and embellished with luxury hardware. Those handbags were beautiful and expensive, and viewed on their own were really works of art. When styling an outfit, she tried to create a balance using luxury bags with the other elements of a shoot, and often found it a challenge. On the other end of the spectrum were ultra-chic minimalist evening bags of various shapes. Also art pieces, they were usually micro-thin or tiny, not designed for carrying much, and made sense for only a few shoots.

A solution started brewing in her mind. It was not an *aha!* moment, more of a studied thought process that rested upon Katy's greatest strength, her real superpower: her ability to edit. Only those of us who worked closely with her had seen it, but when we were in full swing years later it became more evident. We would look at a hundred permutations of the same shape of an item, or dozens of another in different colors. She would scan them, then think about it. Then she'd start another scan and pull out those that she didn't think would work. I think I have a good eye; I have at least a pretty good sense of what will work. But Katy's instincts were exceptional. She would view an entire category or specific line, then in a contemplative way would think about them—not for a long time, just a few minutes. She would then home in on half a dozen items she knew intuitively would sell. They always did. After a while we never even argued with her; we learned she was *that good* at spotting the winners.

Katy used this same process to develop her first handbags. First she considered all the bag shapes she had seen over her years at *Mademoiselle* and others she grew up with in the sixties and seventies. Katy liked the simplicity of basic geometric design, and that clean shape would have more internal surface area to hold more things. Ideas started to gel in her mind, and she got more excited about the possibilities.

* * *

One evening in June 1992, Katy called me in Greensboro. Andy was on the line, too. They'd just returned home from dinner at a favorite neighborhood spot. And they had big news.

Andy said, "Elyce! We think we're ready to go into the handbag business!"

In frequent phone calls over the previous month, I had been following along with Katy as she talked about the ideal handbags, and perhaps even designing them herself. Over the years, we had a thousand fantasy conversations about starting a business together, everything from a vintage clothing store to a catering company to a travel agency. This time felt different. Katy had the bandwidth now that she wasn't working. And Andy was involved in the discussion, which had never happened before. I was intrigued, but still a little skeptical.

They laid out what they were thinking—the style, the shapes— and asked my opinion on the price point. Andy thought the bags should be chic but accessible for women just like us who had a high taste level and loved beautiful things, but did not have the income to afford luxury brands.

I was interested right away. "I'd want one of those bags."

"Really, do you think it's a good idea?" Katy asked cautiously. "Tell the truth." She was a relatively careful and conservative thinker, while Andy was audacious and courageous about taking risks. This was the yin and yang of their relationship, the thing that made it work.

I really did like the idea. Objectively, there was no reason that we couldn't start a handbag company from scratch—apart from the lack of capital, the absence of know-how in manufacturing, zero experience in finance and a hundred other things I didn't know about yet. Fortunately, we had no clue about all those challenges. We focused on what we could bring to the table to make the idea work. Katy had an incredible eye, an excellent work ethic and knew what was missing in the handbag market. Andy's lifetime interest in art and new ideas resonated within everything he did in business, and he'd bring branding genius to the table. I'd spent years in the sales and marketing department of a small company and helped it grow into a large one. Our individual strengths added up to an impressive whole.

Andy offered to pay all the start-up costs out of his advertising salary. There was no reason not to go for it, except for Katy's worry about losing all of Andy's money. She was quiet for a second, then asked, "Well, Jethro, whaddya say? Will you move back to the city and start this business with me?"

There was a moment of silence on the call.

The month prior, I was up for a review. I met with my boss, a generally congenial guy, in his office. I was working mostly seven days a week, traveling a lot. My events had grown larger and more complicated over the last year, and it was challenging to keep all the plates spinning. Despite the long hours and hard work, I liked it there and thought that I'd have a future with the company. My boss had some basic complimentary things to say at my review, but he felt we needed to "wait a bit" before increasing my salary. In a slightly patronizing tone, he explained that management perceived me to be a "party girl," and that I needed to fix that before we discussed any future compensation or promotion.

I was so shocked that I was speechless. Working weeks on end, literally with no days off, and putting on a successful run of great events, only to get the "constructive criticism" that I should try not to be such a "party girl"? He couldn't have been referring to my social life in North Carolina. That was a null set. I ran those huge events and made sure everyone was having a great time. I guess somehow that was interpreted as "party girl" behavior. I never drank while working—it would have been impossible to keep everything organized. Those comments felt humiliating after all the effort I had put into the job. A deeper lesson stuck with me as I left that meeting. As long as I worked for someone else, particularly in the male-dominated corporate world, I'd always have to put up with bullshit from some jerk in a suit.

Katy was waiting for an answer.

I pulled the phone closer to my cheek and said, "I'm in."

CHAPTER 11

The plan for the launch of our fledgling company was that I would wrap everything up with Girbaud and work through the few months remaining time on my lease in Greensboro. Katy would start full-time right away on the project designing the bags and lining up manufacturers. I would collaborate with her on weekends in person when I was able to be in New York, or over the phone from Greensboro. Andy would stay on with his advertising firm and provide the financing for the business for as long as possible.

After three months had passed, fortuitously, a position for the head of communications opened up at Girbaud's New York office. I applied for it and was able to move back and still make a living while Katy was preparing our first samples. Going home to New York City with our plan in mind was thrilling. I loaded Butterscotch to the roof with all of my apartment stuff and drove north on I-95. I'm sure I looked ridiculous with an entire apartment's worth of clutter crammed into the boxy Volvo. I remember having to catch my breath on that drive when I saw the nighttime Manhattan skyline twinkling with a million possibilities. Flying through the Lincoln Tunnel from New Jersey to Manhattan, I was happy to have made the nine-hour trip in one day. I parked the loaded car in a garage and met Katy and Andy in Midtown at the Royalton Hotel bar to celebrate.

Katy had been busy working out how to get things started. She had been an insider in the business for years now, and immediately turned to people she knew for advice. She spoke to designers, fashion business owners and loads of people adjacent to the fashion world like other editors, marketing people and executives at the brands with whom she had come up in the industry.

The number one item on the agenda was designing and making samples. In her loft, Katy started cutting out geometric shapes from construction paper, which she then taped together as three-dimensional representations of her first boxy horizontal bags. To create an actual handbag sample, she needed to source materials, find a patternmaker and hire a manufacturer. The patternmaker would use Katy's physical 3D samples to produce accurate blueprints from which a manufacturer could work to make the finished product. In the early phase, she intended to use unexpected fabrics and prints rather than leather. Katy and Andy had gained a lot of knowledge and real feel for textiles working at Carter's in Arizona.

Katy found a patternmaker in the classified ads in the back of *Women's Wear Daily*. That was easy. Her initial inspiration was to create a collection of burlap bags. She called burlap suppliers and gave them a rough estimate of how much fabric she needed. When they scoffed at her tiny yardage quote, she took to the yellow pages, where she could look up a category of items that she would need and identify a local business and their phone number. She found a company that sold burlap potato sacks and was happy to ship to her. For another handbag she wanted to use heavy duty nylon that was being used for industrial products. She called around and ultimately sourced bolts of thick nylon from DuPont.

* * *

As luck would have it, I soon heard about an apartment on East Fourth Street and the Bowery on the Lower East Side. I knew the area. Phebe's Tavern, a great bar and meeting place, was on that corner and I'd been there a few times. The legendary punk club CBGBs was a few blocks away.

The guy who had connected me with me the place told me, "If I were you, I'd go look at it today. You've got to jump on it really fast."

I had my coat on before he finished the sentence.

I arrived at the apartment with a cashier's check for the first and last month's rent, plus a security deposit, just in case. As soon as I saw the 1,100-square-foot one-bed one-bath, I knew it had to be mine. It had a sunken living room—just like Mary Richards's apartment—floor-to-ceiling windows that faced the street, and a little terrace in the back. It was also a great deal. I signed the lease that day and found a monthly parking lot to tuck away Butterscotch.

* * *

Summer 1993 rolled around. We had always spent our summers in sticky New York City. Many friends our age were renting their first summer share houses that year, and a friend of Eleni's told her about a four-bedroom place she found in Amagansett, a beachfront village adjacent to East Hampton, Long Island.

Katy, Andy, Eleni, Randall and I cobbled together enough money to join in. The house was clean, spacious and ours for the whole summer. Amagansett was (and still is) a beautiful place with gorgeous broad sandy beaches and silvery shingled summer cottages.

Since summer shares were expensive, it was common to fill up bedrooms and offset costs with people you didn't know. Sometimes, by the end of the summer, you would have new best friends. I was excited to meet the couple who had organized the house, Pamela Bell and Alex Simotas. That first Friday evening in June (and every Friday evening until the end of August), Katy, Andy, George and I piled into the Volvo and joined the stop-and-go snarled traffic to the Hamptons. It took forever, but singing along with R.E.M. and the Fine Young Cannibals made the hours fly by.

As soon as we arrived, we unloaded our suitcases and all ran through the house to claim our rooms. Eleni, Randall and the new couple were already there. We met Alex, the husband, whose family was Greek (like Randall and Eleni's). He was a doctor at the Hospital for Special Surgery, slightly older than the rest of us, and very handsome.

While chatting with him, Katy and I pulled out our packs of Marlboro Lights and lit up, the first smoke in the new house. All of a sudden, a female voice we didn't recognize—Alex's wife, Pamela—piped up from another room.

"Who's smoking?" she yelled.

Really? Katy and I looked at each other. Was this Pamela going to give us a hard time about smoking in the house all summer?

The kitchen door swung open and in walked a young Kate Winslet look-alike with honey-colored hair and sky-blue eyes. She stared at us. We both looked a little guilty, sitting there on the sofa holding our burning cigs. She pointed straight at us.

Uh-oh, I thought.

"Can I have one of those?" she said, flashing one of the loveliest smiles that still makes my day every time I see her. That's how we met our partner Pamela.

Sitting down with us, Pamela told us about her career as an entrepreneur. She'd launched her first business in college and had an impressive success during the first Gulf War in 1990 selling American flag–themed hair accessories to retail stores. The way she described her experience, it was clear she was a get-things-done kind of person. She'd recently sold that business for what seemed like a ton of money to us at the time. Now she was actively trying to get pregnant while casually looking around for a new business venture to sink her teeth into.

Of course, Katy and I told her about the handbag company.

Over the next few weeks, Katy was conferring more and more with Pamela on the fine points of manufacturing, inventory, production runs and other items. As we grew to know her, she soon became the go-to person to ask about the nuts and bolts of starting a company. It seemed like the universe had deposited exactly the right person into our laps at exactly the right time.

Pamela agreed to come on full-time as a partner to help Katy with the setup. Ultimately the partnership agreement between the four of us was equal voting and equal pay with an eventual equity split of 30 percent to each Katy and Andy, and 20 percent each to Pamela and me. I worked for Girbaud by day and our company on nights and weekends, preparing potential customer mailing lists and line sheets while they got the samples ready.

Pamela and Katy hit the ground running on production. There were snafus, as was to be expected, but Pamela was instrumental in guiding production and explaining the manufacturing process to Katy. For example, Katy prepaid a patternmaker and requested that the patterns be ready on a certain date. When Katy showed up to collect them, the maker hadn't met the deadline and had nothing for her. Katy was dismayed that someone didn't do what they were supposed to do. The real issue was that her level of expectation of excellence had been forged at one of the top magazine companies in the country. In Katy's training ground, there had never been room for excuses or missed deadlines. It was surprising for her to see how the rest of the world worked.

Pamela found a new pattern-maker, Luis, who introduced us to a local manufacturer in the Garment District, Hernan Alvarez. Katy, Pamela and I went to see Hernan at his factory, Veje Leather Corp. (named for his children: Veronica, Evelyn, Jeffrey, Erica) on West Twenty-Ninth Street between Seventh and Eighth Avenues. After some cajoling, he agreed to make us some sample bags, though he seemed a bit suspicious of us. Hernan is from Ecuador and a very traditional and conservative gentleman. He has a fastidious style, wears pressed pleated trousers, starched collars and a meticulously trimmed mustache. We showed up for our first meeting in ripped jeans and T-shirts—being on trend—and he looked at us a little funny. Eventually, Hernan became our primary manufacturer, and one of the most important figures in the early days of our business. After his initial blip of doubt, he supported us right from the start. I asked him once what he thought of us when we first met. He told me, "I thought you ladies were kind of crazy, but you were so nice that I wanted to help you."

Despite the struggle to get things made, Katy and Pamela amassed dozens of sample bags by the end of the summer, and those were impressive and beautiful. It was almost a shock so see how far they had come with the finished product.

Our first bags were essentially organized into a series of five styles. Three of those five were variations on the original concept Katy had envisioned—takes on the rectangular design she had been working on from the start, both a small version and a larger version, vertical and horizontal. In addition there were two more styles they had worked up: a sleek messenger bag and a backpack, each of those tied in structure and essence to the clean geometric contours of the rectangular line. The bags were finished with several materials varying per category. We had a unique, thick nylon with a smooth satin feel and finish for the rectangular tote bags. They were simple and beautiful in black, chocolate or navy blue. We offered some of those same shapes in either pink or yellow linen, very stylish and cute as hell.

After all of our discussions and planning, I expected something really good. But when Pamela and Katy came through the door with those first bags, I was feeling *big* excitement about the company for the first time. I got it. This might actually work.

It was time to name the baby. We expected Andy Spade, our copywriter/branding guy partner, to do his thing and have the final word on that. His idea was to combine Katy Brosnahan's first name with his last name—Katy became "Kate" because Andy liked the rhythm of two one-syllable words together. We put together some logos that read "Kate Spade New York." Right away, we all loved the feel and look of the brand, and the person the name evoked. "Kate Spade" could be your best girlfriend from high school, a famous Broadway star or a female British spy. Katy liked it a lot, too, but from the start, her shyness made her cautious. "Don't expect me to *be* Kate Spade!" she said when we first agreed on the name, and many times after that.

Once the name was settled, Katy and Andy decided to call June, Katy's mom, and fill her in on the big news about the company. Katy recounted all the details, the idea, our team, Pamela coming on board and lastly, our shiny new brand name, Kate Spade.

"Does this mean you're finally getting married?" asked June.

Of course, June's thinking raced right to where every mother's first concern would be.

After all of those years of college-girl fantasy discussions, we were actually starting something. One warm, breezy night late that summer the four of us were together on the roof of Katy and Andy's building, staring at the lights sparkling in the Manhattan skyline as we looked uptown. We popped a bottle of champagne and, smiling, made multiple toasts to our new venture. We had no way of knowing what the future held for us, but we were young, we had our idea and we had one another.

CHAPTER 12

It was high time to introduce our handbags to the world. We knew that the best way to do that was to show our line in September at the upcoming trade show—the biannual three-day Accessories Circuit show at the Jacob Javits Convention Center. The Accessories Circuit show was like a car show or a boat show but for jewelry, hats, bags, shoes, belts, sunglasses and hair accessories. Thousands of vendors set up booths to show off their collections mainly for buyers at department stores and boutiques, as well as fashion press. Katy used to go to the shows every year as a fashion editor just to see what was out there and to spot trends. She had strong connections from her editor days, and we quickly navigated through the requisite paperwork and preparation. To rent a booth at this accessories trade show, we had to scrape together the $2,500 fee, and we'd barely made the cutoff deadline to enter. Now Kate Spade's debut as a brand was scheduled.

The show was a huge opportunity for us. If a buyer from Saks Fifth Avenue, Neiman Marcus, or any other large or small accounts walked by the booth and thought her customers would like our bags, she could either place an order immediately or take the information and send us a purchase order in the next few weeks via mail or fax. They could buy a dozen or a hundred or a thousand of them wholesale to sell at their retail stores. This one event could put our fledgling business on the map.

The last weekend of the summer at the beach house, Pamela, Katy and I were preparing for the upcoming accessories show. Katy was anxious that the investment wouldn't pay off. Andy had been footing the bills thus far, and now we all had agreed to put in our share of the expenses. Katy had always worked to pay her own way and having to depend on her boyfriend felt awkward. Along with Andy's money, she'd already invested many months of her time into the company.

We inspected each sample bag for any imperfections and collated info sheets with specs and pricing for each design. Andy had developed a logo with the help of some of his art director contacts. His thinking was that the logo should reflect the simplicity of the design, a consistent differentiation between our new brand and the big logo luxury brands of the time, like Gucci and Louis Vuitton. He spent weeks looking at a thousand layouts for the right label. Andy eventually chose a font called New Baskerville, lowercase and italicized for our brand name, coupled with a bold statement of where we called home, signaling a particular attitude. Our new logo "*kate spade* NEW YORK" was born. He had it printed in chocolate brown on men's shirt labels, minimalist yet quietly striking. They were sewn onto the inside lining of the bags, as per Katy's instructions to the manufacturer.

At the beach house, Katy stared at the black nylon tote, and said, "Something's missing."

"It looks beautiful to me," I said.

"It doesn't have any hardware or ornaments. We need somewhere for the eye to go."

"What are you thinking?" asked Pamela.

Katy had some of the logo shirt labels with her, and she positioned one right under the lip on the top of the bag, on the *outside*. "A label, right here," she said.

"The show starts in two days," Pamela said. "We can't get the manufacturer to sew them that fast."

"We can do it," I said. "Ourselves, right now."

For the next three hours, we sewed tiny shirt labels on those bags, punching through the lining and the outer material for each tiny stitch. It was hard to get them right as each stitch had to be perfect, and our fingers were bleeding by the end of it. But the labels on the outside of the bag looked fantastic. That one small decision transformed an idea into a brand.

Day one of the Accessories Circuit show, a Saturday, was for setting up. Katy and I wheeled a suitcase full of sample bags and decorations through the gloomy streets of Hell's Kitchen. Our destination was the great glass behemoth Javits Center, perched on the western edge of Manhattan, looming over the Hudson River and spanning three square city blocks. I felt overwhelmed by the sheer size of the place, and the number of other vendors who were filing in. There were thousands of us, and only a handful of buyers from big department stores.

We found our assigned booth after much exploration, and it was in a truly terrible location toward the back, adjacent to a hot dog stand.

"Oh no!" said Katy.

"What?"

"Not a hot dog stand. That's a bad omen."

I joked, "Well, just don't blow it up." But Katy was in no mood for kidding around—she was so anxious she didn't even smile.

The booth itself was very plain and sterile, just a square on the floor and some metal poles for hanging signage. But Katy had a plan to make it stand out. We'd have to do the sprucing ourselves, though, because of union rules, which were clearly posted at every booth—if we asked the Javits Center workers for any help or borrowed their tools, they would charge a fortune, and we didn't have a penny to spare. We came prepared with all the materials we needed. We draped white muslin from the metal poles to create the illusion of walls and tied the corners in knots. What really set our booth apart was Katy's little kelly-green chipped wood table. She placed it near the entrance and put a vase of zinnias on top. No one else used fresh flowers to decorate their booths back then. Just having the splash of color against the elegant white muslin drew the eye. Behind the table and flowers, we arranged our colorful, flirty, fun bags in three groups: burlap, nylon, and patterned fabric.

The setup took an entire day, but Katy and I were satisfied with how our booth looked, and we started to feel cautiously optimistic about day two, when buyers would see the designs for the first time and, hopefully, place big orders for their retail stores. Wearing my cheerleader hat, I tried to keep Katy's hopes high, but, even so, she was nervous that we'd fail. Both of us were aware of the stakes. If the company flamed out at its first accessories show, Katy might lose her enthusiasm and move on to something else. I knew how much women would love the bags—they really were something very different than anything else out there.

Our least expensive bag was $45 wholesale, $120 retail. The most expensive was $95 wholesale, $250 retail. Compared to Chanel and YSL, our bags were accessible luxury. At that time, handbags weren't at the top of most clothing designers' lists. Prada had nylon European-style bags, but that was about it. No one was doing well-constructed, chic, aspirational bags aimed at women who were just starting out in life. Katy had created a whole new category that could be huge. My hopes were high.

On day two, we stood around our booth, hoping, praying, that we'd get a big order or three right off the bat. Our "line sheets" with my hand-drawn sketches of available shapes and the prices sat in a stack on the kelly-green table. Bigger operations used photos, but we weren't equipped for that yet.

After an hour on our feet, smiling as people walked by but did not stop to talk to us, it was getting harder to stay positive. We hadn't placed a single order all morning. "We've got everything riding on this," said Katy.

"Something is going to happen," I predicted. "You'll see. We're going to get some orders."

Just then, a young man slowed to a stop in front of our booth. "What's this?" he asked. "Just handbags?" He introduced himself as the owner/buyer for the specialty store Intermix.

Katy squared off her shoulders and said, "We're a new handbag brand. I'm Katy Brosnahan. This is Elyce Cox. The brand is called Kate Spade. I was a fashion editor at *Mademoiselle*, and I was always frustrated that I couldn't find the handbag designs I wanted to feature in the magazine. So I designed these myself."

The buyer said, "Great story. Let me take a closer look. I love the burlap!" He placed an order.

"One down," I said.

"It's ten bags," she sighed.

Several other specialty buyers stopped by and were really enthusiastic about the handbags, immediately placing orders, filling out the purchase forms in triplicate and leaving us a copy. "It's happening," I said. "I can feel it."

"Maybe. I'm going crazy just standing here. I'm going to do a lap and say hi to some people," said Katy. She knew a lot of the vendors from her time as an editor. I watched her walk into the throngs. Hopefully chitchatting with some fashion folks would perk her up. Things *were* going well, I thought. They could be better, sure, but I really had a feeling that something good was happening.

Katy had been gone for about three minutes when two fabulously chic women came up to the booth. I smiled and took a deep breath, "Hello. How are you? I'm Elyce, and this is our brand, Kate Spade."

They shook my hand and introduced themselves. I instantly forgot their names when I heard they were buyers for Barneys New York, the high-end department store with their flagship location on Seventh Avenue. In Katy's fantasy, she'd have a boutique in Barneys and sell exclusively there. Smiling with false bravado and my fingers crossed, I showed the Barneys buyers the whole collection and went over our line sheet carefully.

One said, "I love it all."

"Thank you!"

The other said, "We'll let you know. Have a good show."

I was on cloud nine as they walked away. Just as their heather gray cashmere blazers faded into the crowd, Katy reappeared. I told her, "Barneys just came! They loved everything!"

She looked stricken. "No way. Oh my God."

"This is *good* news."

"I walk away for a minute, and that's when Barneys comes!"

Toward the end of the day, Katy saw an old colleague of hers at another booth and said, "I have to go say hi. It'll just be one second."

Sure enough, as soon as she was gone, the buyer for Charivari, a top New York City boutique, came up to the booth. Same thing, I showed her the line, and she said, "Those little labels are so unique! I can see these bags in all of our stores. I'll be in touch." She took the line sheet and moved on.

Katy returned, and then her face fell when she saw me beaming. "Not again!"

"Charivari was just here."

"I'm like the magic touch, but only when I leave," she lamented.

By the end of the day, we had orders from several specialty stores and the promise of orders from two big ones. We'd sold over $2,500 worth of bags. I was happy about that and left for the night with aching feet and a positive outlook.

On day three, we dismantled the booth and got all our stuff into a cab. I was feeling really good about the whole experience. As we taxied downtown to Katy's loft on Warren Street to drop off everything, she was fidgeting. I could tell she was worried about something.

"What's wrong?" I asked.

"We didn't make enough to pay for the show," she said, factoring in the cost of labor and materials.

"But some orders haven't come in yet. This is just a start. It's the first show. What did you expect?"

"I don't know. Ten thousand in orders."

It took two weeks to convince Katy that the show wasn't a disaster—and that only happened because the Barneys and Charivari orders both came in, with each totaling around $3,500.

I asked, "So now do you consider it a success?"

She did, but grudgingly.

We schlepped to those trade shows twice a year for years to come. After a while, I started to dread them. The Javits Center was dusty and overwhelming. I went home every night utterly exhausted with throbbing feet and aching legs. But now, I look back and remember those shows fondly. No one would have ever found us otherwise.

And yes, it was tiring and nerve-racking. But we were able to meet people we would be in business with for years.

I'm still on that accessories circuit (now called "Coterie") today and see a lot of the same people. We set up our booth for Frances Valentine with colorful vintage rugs, a cute table and fresh flowers. Just as before, we steam and place all the pieces in our collection meticulously on display. I still smile at everyone who walks by, and I often think of those many years of being there with my friend, and of all the faces that smiled back at us.

CHAPTER 13

By January 1994, after a few months at Girbaud's New York office, I felt it was time to finally join Katy and Pamela full-time in the office and devote all of my attention to our fledging business. I made my goodbyes to the team on a Friday, and was off to start our new adventure the following Monday. Katy and Andy's loft on Warren Street became the de facto office for the company. George had the first version of the Macintosh personal computer that looked like a cinder block, and he donated it to the cause. I started using that for all the official Kate Spade correspondence but stuck with the old faithful typewriter for purchase orders and invoices.

During my tenure at Girbaud, I watched the company grow to $200 million in revenue in just two short years. I wanted to see that happen for Kate Spade. After a decade of working for other people,

I'd made a long mental list of things I'd do differently if I were in charge. Our company would be scrappy and fiscally responsible—no needless extravagance or bloated budgets. We would try to hire only kind, polite people. We'd hire and promote women. The workplace culture would be inclusive and fun.

Soon after the accessories show, Katy, Pamela and I met at Pamela's apartment on the Upper East Side. The point of the meeting was to decide how the three of us were going to divide labor and responsibilities going forward. We drank tea and nibbled on biscuits, and chatted about bag handles and zipper pulls. I became a bit frustrated that the conversation was mired in tiny details instead of discussing the big picture. I challenged them: "C'mon, how are we going to turn Kate Spade into a two-hundred-million-dollar company in the next five years?"

They both just stared at me in disbelief.

"I didn't quit my job to sit here and have a tea party," I proclaimed. "I want to get stuff done. Let's go! Let's get to work!"

I think that was the turning point when Pamela decided she had a serious problem with me. I know I came off as much too aggressive, but I really meant it. I pushed everyone to work at a fast pace with intensity. I showed up at Katy and Andy's apartment at eight thirty every morning, ready to go. They were not early risers and didn't appreciate my pulling them out of bed. I tried to be gracious about it and always brought coffee. Pamela and I had gotten along so well in the summer house, but by the time we were working together in the loft, our relationship had deteriorated. Most of our arguments were over different ways to do the same thing. For example, Pamela had her own hands-on method of keeping inventory, involving scraps of paper marked up with big colored Sharpies. It worked well for her but only she could decipher it. I preferred to keep a typed chart that we could update regularly. She thought my way was a slow, unnecessary step at our level. This simple disagreement devolved into multiple heated arguments. Now I've learned, when you have a group of partners, everyone's responsibility must be very clearly delineated. It helps if your partners bring different skill sets to the table. That structure takes advantage of each member's strengths— and it keeps partners from killing each other. We suffered from that new-business syndrome of everyone being in charge of everything. We were second-guessing one another. I was already on Pamela's naughty list for being so pushy. We locked horns constantly about everything from how to balance the checkbook to when we should pay suppliers. Katy was always in the middle acting as the referee.

I could feel myself about to blow within minutes of getting into an argument with Pamela. Before that happened, I would wave my hand at her and say things like, "Get out. Bye now. Bye-bye," and point at the elevator door. She wasn't going to be talked to that way and would storm out the door. Katy, the peacemaker, would always run after her. I'd say, "Go ahead! Go after the baby! Bye, baby, bye now!" I even pronounced "baby" like Meryl Streep's Australian character in the movie *A Cry in the Dark*, ("The dingo took my bay-bee!") just to further annoy Pamela. Even though I felt frustrated that the useless squabbling was hindering our progress, I can't believe I spoke to her like that—I can honestly say I had never acted that way to anyone else in my life. I'm so embarrassed when I think back on it.

I'd watch through the front windows every time Katy consoled Pamela on the sidewalk in front of the building. I'd be standing there alone with piles of paperwork and so much stuff to do, and after a few minutes, I would feel awful for being such a pill. As soon as Pamela and Katy came back up to the fifth floor, I would apologize. This pattern happened in one form or another too often during our early months. We were all tense about getting the company going and filling orders. Pamela and I just could not seem to get along. Apart from that, I recognized that we both were competing on some level for Katy's friendship. There was some inherent conflict in our long-standing duo learning how to grow into a trio.

It only got worse when Pamela got pregnant and suddenly loathed the smell of cigarette smoke. In hindsight, I can't blame her. Years later when I was pregnant, I hated it, too. She would stay on her end of the loft, and I'd smoke out the window at the other end. It was very rude of me, and I do feel bad that I was so stubborn. But going down to the street to have a cigarette break would have felt like a surrender. There were times when the loft wasn't big enough for the two of us.

The Warren Street loft/office was soon crammed with bags of zippers, bolts of fabrics and boxes of sample bags. The building had an old, slow cage elevator, with an accordion door seemingly designed to pinch your fingers, that opened directly into each floor's apartment. The elevator car would stay on one floor until someone else rang for it, then you'd have to bring it back down in person. It was such a pain for us because we had UPS dropping off deliveries throughout the day. If the elevator was sitting on someone else's floor and we couldn't get a hold of them, we were stuck babysitting boxes on the street for fear that our stuff would get stolen.

We finally figured out the best way to divide the workload. Pamela handled manufacturing and acted like a kind of detective who sniffed out problems and came up with solutions. Katy worked on design, kept the peace and was the silent last word on creative decisions. I handled the sales and the financial side of the business, as well as overseeing the marketing and PR effort. We hired a part-time intern named Anna, a recent college grad, to do clerical work. We all still did a little of everything, but now we had our own areas of responsibility and some structure.

None of us made salaries. Andy and Katy paid the rent on Warren Street with Andy's advertising income, and we took turns paying the company bills out of our personal funds. One Friday, Pamela would pay the contractor. The next week, I'd cover the manufacturing costs. Then Andy would write a check for shipping. I kept track of who put in what and made sure that our contributions were reimbursed when we were paid by customers. After expenses were paid, every dollar that came in went immediately back into the business. We'd pay the vendor, pick up the goods from the contractor and then ship out to retailers. Our process was streamlined. That was the advantage of having all our manufacturing in New York.

I stayed focused on knocking off my long list of daily tasks and felt secure in the knowledge that we were working toward something great. Unlike Katy and Pamela, I didn't have a partner to help cover my personal and business expenses. I had the most to lose financially if our company went nowhere. But I saw how people reacted to the bags and had every faith that gradually emptying my 401(k) for living expenses and covering company bills was a risk worth taking. Any doubts I had were chased away by little signs of hope that arrived every day. A new boutique placed an order, and then would call back three days later to reorder. One of Katy's former colleagues in fashion editorial would call to ask for, say, a red patent leather handbag for their fall issue, and we'd design it and have it made practically overnight. We were lean and fleet and could get things done. The adrenaline rush of hitting those small deliverables was like a drug and kept us going.

* * *

Five months pregnant, Pamela had an appointment for a routine sonogram, but she was in the middle of a task and didn't want to go. She kept saying, "I'm fine! I'm not going to leave you guys." She was as deeply committed as I was. I wouldn't have wanted to leave, either. In the end, intern Anna convinced her to keep the appointment, promising to do Pamela's work while she was out.

During that sonogram, Pamela learned that her pregnancy had fairly severe (though not life-threatening) complications. For the last four months of it, she had to be on bed rest at home. I felt concerned for her, of course. But losing her on-site at that crucial stage of building the business worried me terribly. As the one in charge of production, she had to go to factories and check orders for quality and quantity, a massive list of tasks she could not do from bed.

Around that time, Andy took an advertising job in Los Angeles. Katy went to visit him for two weeks and then decided to stay for longer to decompress. I encouraged her to take as much time as she needed. I felt that being together with Andy without the pressure of the business would benefit her greatly. Summer was our slow season anyway, and I thought I could go it alone, with Anna's help.

The Warren Street loft had no air-conditioning and was like an oven. And contrary to my sales projection, we were getting busier, not slower. I had to organize the production at the factories, check inventories and make sure everything was ready to ship out, and ultimately oversee the actual shipments. I had too much to do on my own, including FedExing fabric swatches to Los Angeles for Katy's approval.

Pamela, like a champion, worked the phones and handled everything she could from bed uptown, much more than I thought she'd be able to. I was so thankful for her strong work ethic and iron will with the manufacturers. I picked up her slack but didn't know the nuances of what needed to be done, so she and I were on the phone together all day long. Without Katy there to smooth things over, we had no choice but to cooperate. Once we lowered our guards, Pamela and I started to get along really well. It didn't happen overnight, but we gradually softened toward each other and the mutual respect began to grow. That period solidified our work relationship and developed into a dear friendship that I cherish to this day.

Katy and Andy returned from Los Angeles and were astonished to see how well Pamela and I were getting along.

"Well, look at you two," Katy said, "I'm glad I left."

But I was so glad she was back.

Pamela went into labor in October at New York Hospital. We kept calling her room to check on her; her labor was taking a long time. At one point I realized I needed some fabric to finish an order that was scheduled to go to the factory by the end of the day. Katy and I tore the place apart trying to find the damn bolt, but we couldn't locate it anywhere. Only one person could tell me exactly where to find it, and she was currently breathing through contractions.

I picked up the phone. Katy read my mind and forcefully said, "Don't do it."

I knew Pamela. She was a trooper. I'd just call to check in again, and sneak in my tiny question. Her husband, Alex, picked up and passed the phone to Pamela. Katy watched me, eyes and mouth wide open.

"Elyce?" asked Pamela.

"Pamela, we're so excited! You have to call us the second you possibly can after the baby arrives."

"Okay," she said, a little puzzled.

There was no easy way to do this. "By the way, do you know where the bolt of bold-print fabric is that we need to ship to Hernan's today? Sorry to ask you!"

"Are you crazy?! I'm in labor!"

"I know, I know," I said. "I'm so sorry! Dumb question!"

"Wait, wait," Pamela said. "Try under the stairway in the hall. Next to the liner material."

It was right there. Like I said, Pamela was a trooper.

That same special day, baby Elenore came into our world. Katy, Andy, Anna and I went to the hospital straight from the office bearing flowers and gifts. The first Kate Spade baby had arrived, and we were all thrilled for Pamela and Alex. Seeing their happy little family and the joy that was so abundant in that room, I felt a sudden curiosity and true desire to experience that myself. I knew I would have to wait for the timing to be right, and to be sure I was with the right person. For the first time, I knew for sure I wanted a family someday. But for now, we had a business to build.

It was never really practical to work out of Katy and Andy's loft, and now even less so. Aside from the extreme disruption of Katy and Andy's living space, we were just getting too busy to accommodate all the orders that were starting to roll in. It was a big decision to move, and signaled the first time we would really have to put ourselves financially on the line to sign a lease with a big monthly rent and a security deposit. It felt like stepping off a cliff and not knowing what was below.

An opportunity presented itself when Pamela was meeting with Hernan at his production facility on West Twenty-Ninth Street, where we were doing most of our manufacturing. He mentioned that a space in the building had become available—we jumped on it right away and moved in within a month. It gave us more room, and actually saved us some shipping cost and time being so close to our primary manufacturer. The building was in the fur district, so there was always fur fuzz flying through the air, feather-like. Fur dust coated every surface. The space was grungy and dingy, so we painted everything—the floors, ceiling, walls, pipes—white. We didn't have desks, so we worked in Hernan's studio a lot of the time. One day, we were walking back to the office from a fabric appointment and saw half a dozen metal *Mad Men*–style desks lined up on the curb. Someone was throwing them away. We ran back to our building, borrowed hand trucks, loaded four of the desks and hauled them back to our office. They were each the size of a small cruise ship and weighed a ton, so it took us all day. The rest of our furniture was thrown together from found objects and used office cabinets. Our architect-carpenter neighbor, Scott, built showroom-style shelves for the handbags. Most of it was free, but it looked professional.

Pamela's friend donated a used scuffed-up fax machine. We had only one phone line, and whenever it rang, one of us would answer, "Kate Spade, may I help you?" If we heard the beeps and buzzes that come from another machine, that meant a fax was coming our way, so we'd unplug the cord from the phone and put it into our fax machine. Hopefully it would start spitting out sheets of shiny paper that curled into rolls as they hit the floor. This was our system for receiving orders, and they were coming in, slowly but surely.

One day that fall, Pamela brought little Elenore to the office for the workday. I was dealing with an order that came with the labels sewn in the wrong place. Katy was working on specs for a new design. We heard the phone ring and did the dance with unplugging and replugging in the fax machine. The thing would rattle and shimmy while it was printing, and then let loose a curl of paper that floated to the floor.

I was closest, so I picked it up. "It's an order from Saks," I said.

"How much?" they asked.

I had to show it to them or they'd never believe it. It was for $20,000—by far, our biggest order to date. When Katy and Pamela saw the number, they both screamed. The three of us started hooting and jumping around the loft.

"Baby, baby!" shouted Katy, dancing around in a circle.

Baby Elenore slept through the whole thing.

The order was especially exciting because it was so unexpected. Saks buyers had come to a mini version of the Javits accessories show that took place at the Plaza Hotel a month earlier. They didn't place an order at the show, and as time passed, we stopped hoping for anything.

As soon as our excitement died down, reality set in. We'd never had such a huge order, and now we had to buy more material and get it to our contractor and make more bags as soon as possible. We'd be going full tilt for over a year already, some money was beginning to roll in. But now it was time to roll up our sleeves and *really* get to work.

* * *

We all looked forward to those days when Pamela would bring little Elenore to the office. She was such a serene baby; her presence would lend a feeling of calm to our otherwise frenetic workdays. She also provided the inspiration for one of our all-time best sellers, our Baby Bag. Pamela was complaining to Katy about the baby bags full of stuff she would have to schlep around whenever she brought Elenore anywhere. Not only were those cheaply constructed, but they always had some cartoonish motif—often pink unicorns or rainbows. "It's not like the baby is enjoying that design, she's an infant!" Pamela would lament. In addition, she would always still have to carry her handbag. She had the idea of utilizing our largest horizontal designed bag, the H120, and began to use that as her all-in-one, combining a handbag with a tote for baby items. In that bag, she'd pack an oversize changing pad which she handmade at first and included some smaller nylon pouches to carry extra items she would need for Elenore. It would also contain the contents of her usual handbag. Now she would only have one bag to carry with Elenore, and it looked terrific.

She proposed an idea to Katy: "Let's make a Kate Spade bag for moms. All our customers either have kids or many will eventually have babies!" Katy's response was lukewarm at first. She thought it was slightly off-brand, and she was hesitant to stray from our path that was working so well. She finally acquiesced after some prodding from the both of us. Pamela sketched it out and asked our manufacturer to send some samples. The nifty product of her idea was a revved up H120 with large pockets both on the outside and internally, an extra-large padded nylon changing pad that rolled up and tied and a waterproof wipeable lining. We displayed the samples at our next market, and the buyers loved them. Months later when all those bags arrived at their respective retail stores, they essentially exploded off the shelves. A mom could now leave the house with her baby and carry just one all-in-one bag, and she would look uber-stylish. The Baby Bag remained one of our best sellers for years; we offered it in the original black and navy nylon, and later printed fabric and Harris Tweed. And as for our original source of inspiration? Adorable Elenore's photo graced the tag of the Baby Bag as the Kate Spade baby for a decade.

* * *

After ten years as a couple, Katy and Andy finally got married in 1994. A small, intimate ceremony took place at Eleni and Randall's apartment on the Upper East Side. They did a stellar job setting the scene in their already stylish apartment and served homemade beautiful appetizers along with champagne in crystal glasses. The only attendees were family and "like family" friends. Andy and Katy didn't want a big splashy affair. But what the day lacked in extravagance, it made up for in heart.

Katy wore a silver top and jacket twin set, a long Heidi Weisel skirt and a white marabou feather hat that was reminiscent of Grace

Kelly. On Katy, the hat was chic and elegant. She looked beautiful and beamed with joy. Her sister Eve was the maid of honor; David Spade was Andy's best man. The ceremony itself lasted all of five minutes. We toasted the couple with champagne and had a joyous night celebrating with dinner at La Lunchonette in Chelsea, one of our favorite restaurants.

I was happy, too. Seeing them exchange vows made me feel secure for them, like my two best friends weren't going anywhere. They were obviously committed, living together, being in business together, sharing a checking account. But having that piece of paper solidified their bond. It was real and legal now.

Two weeks later, the newlyweds hosted a reception at their loft on Warren Street. That never would have been possible had we not moved our whole operation—and the wall of boxes and bolts of material—to Twenty-Ninth Street by then. Now the entire spacious loft was available for party guests to mingle and celebrate the couple. Katy was luminous in a Cynthia Rowley dress with a tulle train. She put tiny votive candles everywhere, on every flat surface, including one on each step of the staircase that led up to the building's roof. Otherwise, the lights were dim, and all of those flickering candles cast flattering golden pink light, making everyone look beautiful.

People climbed halfway up the staircase to make toasts so they could be seen by the crowd. I made a corny one about how the company name was now legitimate because Katy's married name was Kate Spade. When Katy and Andy went up to make their toast, the tulle hem of her gown came too close to one of the votive candles and, with a whoosh, went up in flames. There was a brief moment of chaos when everyone screamed and threw their drinks on her train. Katy really thought it was hilarious and she thought it was "lucky" to have her guests douse her in alcohol at her wedding celebration. She laughed. We all did. She was always so gracious. She made sure that nothing would spoil that wonderful day for her or our friends.

People's feelings were always more important to her than objects, even something as cherished as Katy's dress from her wedding party. I remember asking her afterward if she was secretly heartbroken about her dress being destroyed.

She actually gave me a funny look, like "How can you even be asking me that?" and replied, "C'mon, Elyce, I loved that dress. But it's just a *thing*."

CHAPTER 14

As scruffy as our new West Twenty-Ninth Street office was, the new white coat of paint and all the extra space gave us a chance to stretch our wings and be more productive. The building was mostly a garment manufacturing facility, which is typically made up of full floors with a large open area, and some rooms built out as offices. The floors were made of scratched-up wide wood planks with no finish. Katy's office in the back had a small window with a view of the building's dark air shaft. It was our only window that safely opened and closed, so that particular window frame held our spiffy new AC unit I purchased at Crazy Eddie's in the Village. In the front offices and showroom we had some tall, old factory windows that you could open with some difficulty but were best left closed. They were divided light style with the square panes held in place by rickety frames. Though we scrubbed the inside, the exterior of the window was permanently coated in a thin layer of grime, so when you looked out at the cityscape it was like watching a grainy old movie. I know it all sounds pretty grim, but we filled the place with lighting and lots of arguing (mostly pretty good-natured by then), so my memories of that time seem as bright as the spotlights that we hung.

Katy's office had the most space, so we stored prototype bags, boxes and big bolts of fabric on wooden pallets in there. Most of the bolts were huge and very heavy, seven or eight feet tall, leaning precariously against the walls. Occasionally, we'd hear a "boom" and run into the office to find a bolt had crashed onto the floor. One of us would always say, "Someone's going to get hurt in there!" but we never did anything about it.

We were too busy to worry as we had a steady stream of orders coming in, each one seemed larger than the last. A big purchase order came in from Mark Shale, a high-end Chicago-based department store chain. With stock and production concerns in mind, Pamela and I made the executive decision to pack up the 120 handbags for this order as soon as they were made and hold them in inventory in boxes in Katy's office. Otherwise, we might use those to fill other small orders and be left with some shipping delays when the time came to send out to the Mark Shale stores. Generally, we had been working on "just in time" inventory to keep cash flow healthy, but as the business was growing, that strategy was becoming untenable.

Of course we knew it was wrong, but we immediately started poaching out of that inventory for other orders, planning on replacing them in time for the Shale shipment. The night before the shipment was ready to go to Chicago, Katy called me at home and started scolding me, "I can't believe you and Pamela really screwed up the Shale order," she said.

"What are you talking about? It's packed and ready to go," I huffed back.

"Well, the handles on the new bags are a different color than the ones you packed originally. So the order has two different handle colors."

Oops. We knew it was a bad idea to start dipping into that inventory. It was mostly my fault, as I was overseeing sales and I'd missed that. But I was irked by her tone. We went back and forth on the phone about the mismatched handles until we were both furious with each other. Exasperated, I said, "I'll fix it tomorrow!"

"It ships tomorrow!"

That set off round two of a big fight, the kind only best friends can have occasionally without fear of losing their friendship. I knew that a lot of our squabbling was really a by-product of the pressure we were both under with the new volume and our shared desire to get things right. But it did not merit her being so snippy with me.

"I'm going over there right now to fix it. Will that make you happy?" I yelled, and like a furious teen, slammed down the phone.

I cooled off right away since Katy was right. She did, however, deserve to be punished a bit for being so rude to me. As I've thought so many times through the years with her, *Game on, grouchy!* I quietly snickered as my plan began to take shape.

At six the next morning, I took a cab to the office before anyone else would be there. I went into Katy's office and stuffed the pair of jeans I'd been wearing that week with packing paper and threw them on the floor, so they looked like legs. I tucked the legs into my trademark high suede boots, and arranged my white faux fur coat where a torso would go above the pants and boots. Then, I pulled several of the massive bolts of fabric down to fall on top of my makeshift scarecrow. The pièce de résistance of the tableau was a lit flashlight that I dropped on the floor nearby. Hopefully the flashlight would still have some juice in a few hours, even better if it was sputtering on and off. I stepped back to behold my work. It really looked as if I'd gone into the dark office holding the flashlight and had been brutally crushed by those unstable huge bolts of cloth. I turned off the lights and went to wait in one of Hernan's offices down the hall for people to show up for work. I heard a few people slowly starting to trickle in, but I just sat quietly in Hernan's office, like a spider waiting for its snippy little prey.

When Katy came in around nine, a few people intercepted her on the way to her office to ask, "Have you seen Elyce? She's not here yet." I always arrived first at seven thirty and unlocked the main office door for everyone else to come in. Some folks had noticed that I was uncharacteristically not there.

"Where is she?" Katy asked as she walked past Pamela's desk on the way to her office. "Do you know if she took care of that Mark Shale order?"

Pamela—who had no idea what I'd done—said, "No clue. When I got here at eight, Hernan had to let me in. I haven't seen Elyce since yesterday, and she hasn't called in."

"Huh, that's weird," said Katy.

Katy went back into her office, flipped on the lights . . . and let loose a bloodcurdling scream when she saw my lifeless crushed "body." I could hear her all the way down in Hernan's office, and without guilt I can say that the paint-peeling screech was like music to my ears.

This prank was a goodie. When I appeared in her office doorway a minute later, I found her wide-eyed and clutching her heart.

"Gotcha," I crowed.

At first she was mad as a hornet, while our colleagues howled for minutes. To her credit, Katy quickly admired the artfulness of the plan, and soon she started laughing as well. When she caught her breath, she said, "Good one. I guess I deserved that." Together we sorted out the handbag handle crisis while rehashing her moment of terror. We kept reliving that hilarious moment all morning until tears were in our eyes. By the end of the day, the order shipped in full and on time.

* * *

February 1995 was the middle of a long, frigid New York winter with record snowfall. As freezing as it was in Manhattan, it was even colder in Chicago. The first week of that month, Katy and I flew to the Windy City to make a personal appearance at Mark Shale's flagship store for a grand debut of Kate Spade bags. We'd done similar events at Neiman Marcus and Saks in New York, and shoppers had swarmed. The morning of the Mark Shale event, we walked into the department store on Michigan Avenue right on time, expecting to see signage or a big display announcing it. Nothing. There wasn't even someone at the entrance to greet us. We had to chase down a salesperson and ask her to call the special-events director, a woman who took a long time to make her way down to the lobby to introduce herself. "I have your table set up downstairs," she said. We followed her to the basement level, where a card table with a white cloth had been set up in a corner near the elevators with a few of our bags on top of it.

It didn't look at all promising. We sat down and waited for shoppers to come over. Whenever the elevator doors pinged, we'd look up hopefully. No one stopped at our table. Not one person asked us to sign a bag. If someone did glance in our direction, they looked away quickly, like they were embarrassed for us. Katy and I perched there for more than three hours and didn't sell a single bag, though some people asked us for directions to various departments. We'd flown all that way, in negative-degree weather, to sit and stare at each other. Though both of us were rather deflated, by the time we left the store, we were joking about it. We'd been taking giant leaps forward for months now. This was just a small step back. It made us recognize that as popular as we were in New York, we had a lot of work to do before we became a national brand.

That night in Chicago, we got together for dinner with Katy's older brother, Earl, who lived in a nearby suburb. As the only son and second-oldest kid in their family, he was always her calm in the storm. He was with his charming wife, Carol, and their two oldest kids, Rachel and Alec. They all asked how our splashy event went at Mark Shale.

Katy put a good face on it, saying, "It wasn't what we were expecting."

We did really enjoy that time with Earl and Carol. Earl was like family to me. We had remained close since our college days, and Carol was a dear person who I knew well from all the time spent with the Brosnahans. After that dreary day in the department store basement, it was comforting to be around people we cared about. Their kids were both adorable, chatting away and enjoying spending time with their beloved Aunt Katy. At that moment, Katy and I would have been so surprised if we had been able to peer into the distant future and see that her little niece would one day move to New York City to pursue her dream of an acting career. Someday, that precocious kid Rachel Brosnahan would be grown up, and millions of her fans would be thrilled to watch her accept multiple Emmy Awards and Golden Globes for her dynamic starring role in *The Marvelous Mrs. Maisel.*

* * *

Back in Manhattan, Katy's Chicago funk had lingered a bit. As always, Andy was trying to cheer her up and make her happy. They took a walk one night after dinner in the Village and passed a pet store. A tiny pure white Maltese puppy pressed his black nose in the window and wagged his tail when Katy stopped out front.

She said, "He's so adorable! Can we go in?"

Andy said, "No, no, absolutely not."

Half an hour later, they headed back to their Warren Street loft with the two-pound Maltese puppy they named Henry. Katy was smitten. It was love at first sight. Andy, a little less so. He'd grown up with German shepherds. He joked that Henry wasn't masculine enough for him to be seen with. Katy said, "Oh, get over it. *You* think you're too macho to walk this dog down the street?"

He said, "Yes, I do."

"That's ridiculous, I know you're kidding."

He definitely was not.

Katy started bringing Henry everywhere, carrying him in a small canvas bag with his little puppy dog face popping out of the top. The entire office doted on him. He immediately adopted me and spent time each day on my lap while I typed and talked on the phone. Katy had the idea that Henry needed a little canine buddy to pal around with. A few weeks later, she arrived at the office with a female Yorkshire terrier puppy, handed her to me and said, "I have a present for you!"

The Yorkie had a shiny black coat, a tiny pink tongue, and was small enough to fit in two cupped hands. I thought a more adorable creature had never existed. I held her against my chest and realized that this dog was the best thing that had ever happened to me. I named her Edna at the request of my boyfriend, George. Henry and Edna romped together in the office thereafter, looking like the world's cutest salt and pepper shakers.

Boyfriend George was not a fan of "girlie" toy dog breeds, either. He called Edna "Ed," to try to make her marginally more masculine. Andy, who'd come around to appreciating Henry, told George, "It's gonna be okay. My stepfather was a Marine. He built the Apache helicopter. And he has two little Yorkies and a shih tzu."

George complained, "*I don't care about your stepfather.* When I walk Ed, I feel like an idiot."

Honestly, if I were forced to choose between puppy Edna and boyfriend George, it would not have been a difficult decision, and George would have been terribly disappointed.

* * *

By early 1995, the company was getting a lot of requests for media interviews from magazines like *Glamour, Elle* and *Marie Claire.* I was the one with PR experience, so I fielded requests and oversaw all our press at that time. Katy was starting to become the public face of the company, given her role as our designer, coupled with her name being on the letterhead. She was reluctant about being the object of attention, and anxious and reticent about interviews. They made her uncomfortable.

People magazine came to the office to do a story about us on one muggy day that June. We thought the reporter, Nancy Jo Sales, would want to do the interview by our bag display in the showroom. She insisted on doing it in Katy's office, the room with the view of the grungy air shaft and the loud air conditioner. What the reporter didn't know was that the floor around Katy's desk was covered with Wee-Wee Pads and newspapers. Henry never "went" outside, and Edna sometimes had bowel incontinence. They were good dogs in that they used the pads and paper, but accidents did happen.

Yes, Katy and I realized letting our dogs go on the floor or on papers was weird and gross. But they were ours, and we loved them. Our staff understood. Or, more likely, they were just good at pretending. But I didn't think that this reporter would be charmed by having to step over Wee-Wee Pads to do the interview.

"I think you'll be more comfortable in the showroom," I explained to her. "The bags are displayed there, and you'll have more room."

But the writer insisted, "I prefer to do the interview in Katy's office. It's more private." We felt like we couldn't say no to her.

When Katy and Nancy Jo first entered the office, the newspapers and pads were clean. Whew. I offered to get Nancy Jo some iced tea, and then went to our galley kitchen to prepare drinks and put some cookies on a plate. As I returned with the tray, Katy came bolting down the hallway toward me, her face frantic.

"Edna just had diarrhea on the newspapers right next to Nancy Jo Sales!" she cried.

"Oh my God!"

We rushed back into her office. I put the tray of drinks on the desk, rushed out to get cleaning supplies, and started cleaning up after Edna with paper towels and ammonia spray, the only cleanser I had. It smelled horrible, like a toxic gas attack. The look on Nancy Jo's face was pure horror. Katy and I were mortified, but as we caught each other's eye, I had to desperately try not to make us both start laughing.

After the interview, the *People* photographer wanted to shoot Katy on the roof, staged among vases full of zinnias.

"I'm not doing that," she argued. "I don't want to seem like a cutesy girl with a handbag company. It has to have more sophistication." Katy understood the brand better than anyone. The bags were colorful with an element of whimsy. But Kate Spade was a fashion design company, and Katy herself was by this point a seasoned New York City businesswoman, and she wanted to be acknowledged as that. When she pushed back, the editor threatened to pull the story.

I ran interference, and we reached a compromise. Katy posed with one vase of flowers, though she wasn't thrilled with the image.

The article, ultimately, was a triumph and read like a love letter to Katy and to Kate Spade. It was tremendous for the company. We wanted to have our brand recognized throughout the country, and that issue of *People* could be found in many homes and in every salon and doctor's waiting room in America.

In the end we were very appreciative of the gracious *People* writer Nancy Jo Sales—she didn't hold Edna's tummy trouble against us.

* * *

Despite her reticence to be in the spotlight, Katy very much enjoyed interacting with our customers, particularly in a smaller, more intimate setting like a department store retail event. Women of all ages—sisters, friend groups, mother and daughters, grandmother and granddaughters—would make a day of it and line up for hours just to meet Katy and have their handbags signed. In those moments, we always made certain there were plenty of silver and gold fine-point Sharpies on hand for Katy to sign her name in the interior lining of the bags. As the designer, she loved all the firsthand customer comments and took the overwhelmingly positive input to heart. She was truly grateful to these women who would come to see her. More than once, we had to physically pull her away from speaking to our customers so she didn't miss a plane or an important meeting. Each woman would tell her own story of first spotting one of our bags in a shop window and just knowing she had to have it. One anecdote in particular we would hear over and over again from women just like us: She would be just starting out in her career and save for months until she could walk into that department store and purchase her first designer piece—a Kate Spade bag—with her own money she had earned.

Katy had what seemed to be an infinite ability to hear the stories from our customers, and variations of those were repeated again and again for years across the country. She was very present when talking to those women, and we discussed that on many occasions traveling to those events together. Rather than her basking in the glory of her accomplishments with the glowing praise from those moments, she related to each person directly by virtue of her own life experience. We both had spent years with enough to only pay for the basics. When we were finally able to afford to buy ourselves some special things, they took on a different meaning for us. They represented a new phase of life where we could work hard on our own and reward ourselves for a job well done. At its core those moments were a transition to our independence as women, and those purchases became a symbol of that independence. That was what our Kate Spade bags were about to those women. Many customers over the years would tell us that they still had their first Kate Spade bag they ever bought. We knew it was more than an object to them; it was a reminder of a special moment in their life.

We came to realize our bags were a rite of passage for generations of women. Our little bags meant to a woman that she had arrived, she could make it on her own. Katy listened to those stories and drew inspiration and a feeling of connection to each person she spoke with. I know that's why over the years her persona has resonated so deeply with people. She was genuinely moved that her work meant so much to them, and her sincerity rang true.

CHAPTER 15

By year two of Kate Spade, we were earning enough to feel comfortable about paying our bills and giving ourselves a subsistence salary—and we still had a little left over at the end of the month. One hundred percent of our profit was reinvested in the company. We weren't in the position yet to take normal salaries, so I had to live off my savings. But that summer, we had set enough money aside to rent a Hamptons beach house in the village of Bridgehampton. The usual suspects and some new squad members filled up the bedrooms: Katy and Andy, Eleni and Randall, George and me, Marybeth, our neighbor Talmage and a few others.

George and I had reached a critical point in our relationship, as people in our thirties who had been together for three years. In New York City, as elsewhere, buying real estate with someone is a far bigger commitment than getting married. It was a huge step when George and I put down a deposit on a two-bedroom apartment in Gramercy Park. We rode a wave of excitement through the mortgage application, building inspection, co-op approval process. The day before our closing, George and I looked at each other and came to the same conclusion at the same moment: *This doesn't feel right.* We'd been moving forward, chugging along, without pausing to ask ourselves, "Is this really what we want?" Getting so close to signing a thirty-year mortgage forced us to admit that, as close as we were and as much as we respected each other, we were not meant to be together.

At the eleventh hour, I called our attorney and told him, "We're not going to go through with buying the apartment after all." We lost half of our deposit. George was chivalrous enough to handle that because he knew I was low on funds. (I paid him back with interest ten years later.)

We knew the breakup was right, but that didn't make it easy. Of course I was upset. The next day was Friday, so I went out to our share house in Bridgehampton with Katy and the gang while George stayed in the city. I was glad to be heading to the beach with my housemates.

Ironically, that weekend was my turn to sleep in the beach house's massive bedroom suite. George and I had been looking forward to it. Now it would be just Edna and me in the king-size bed.

I didn't have time to dwell on it: We were throwing a big party that night and I had margaritas to mix. We danced around the pool and drank until two. No matter how late I stayed up or how hungover I was, I always rose at six to water the flowers, make coffee, get the newspapers and take Edna for a walk. On Saturday, as usual, I woke at dawn. But when I tried to get out of bed, I couldn't move. I was paralyzed with agonizing back pain. I couldn't even roll myself off the bed to crawl to the bathroom or let Edna out. No one in the other bedrooms could hear me calling for help for over an hour.

When Katy finally came in and saw me frozen and weeping, she just kept saying, "Oh my God! Oh my God!" She seemed like an angel from heaven there to save me, and Edna, too, with a quick walk. She tried to help me sit up, but even the smallest movement took my breath away.

We called Pamela's husband, Alex, a sports doctor. He said, "Take four Advil and come see me in an hour."

I didn't think I could get out of bed, much less get in a car and drive to their place in Amagansett. But with the Advil and Katy's help, we made it, and he examined me. My back was in full spasm. He said, "What might have set it off?"

"I have no idea."

"Wait a minute, didn't you and George break up this week?" he asked. "It's probably stress-induced."

That made sense. My back had gone out during anxious and stressful times in the past. Pulling out of the apartment and ending the relationship were affecting me more profoundly than I'd realized. For the next month, I had to wear a back brace most of the time. The upside was I went from being bent sideways to having the upright posture of a ballerina whenever I wore the thing.

I healed up by August and enjoyed our final month on the beach. On our last weekend there, we were pregaming before a big party, dancing around the house barefoot to The Cranberries' new album. As we headed to the car to drive to a beach party, a gnat flew into my ear. It felt like the thing was buzzing inside my brain. This time, we did go to the emergency room. Katy drove while I screamed the whole time. We pulled up to the ER entrance and ran in. The nurses looked at us like we were crazy. Our teeth were purple from wine and we were barefoot. I was freaking out and Katy was yelling over me, explaining that I had a bug in my ear.

And right as we were standing there talking about it, the gnat flew out.

Katy and the nurses and I all watched silently while it floated away. Katy and I said, "Thank you so much," turned around, walked out, and we laughed the entire drive home.

Unfortunately, because I thought I was moving in with George, I'd given notice at my apartment on East Fourth Street with the Mary Richards–style sunken floor. It had already been rented out, so I had only weeks to find a new place to live. Katy and Andy enjoyed living in a loft, and I thought it'd be fun to try it myself. I asked a broker to show me some in my price range. I couldn't afford SoHo, my first choice, so he took me to a sketchier part of Manhattan to see a loft space on West Thirty-Ninth Street, near Bryant Park. Nowadays, Bryant Park is a green respite in Midtown, with a popular ice-skating rink and bustling crafts market at Christmastime, fancy restaurants, gardens, a fountain (and the across-the-street neighbor of the Frances Valentine showroom and offices). But back then, it was fairly run-down, with a cast of unsavory characters with lots of drug business going on. The previous tenant of the loft had been forced to vacate by the landlords when they found out he had been using it as a brothel. When I first saw the place, I wondered why it was divided into seven tiny bedrooms, each door labeled A, B, C, D, E, F and G. It had been cleaned up and hopefully sterilized by the time I went to see it. The broker said, "You can move in immediately, but it's zoned for commercial use."

I said, "Can I live here, too?" I really needed to nail this lease down right away.

"You can live here as long as the primary use is for a business."

The first thing I did was rip out the fake wood paneling and drywall to get rid of bedrooms A through G and turned the open space into a comfortable bedroom/office/living area for myself. The only downside was that for a year, former clients of the previous owner buzzed my door at four in the morning, and with slurred speech asked into the intercom, "Are you open?"

I was given some short notice by the landlord that bank inspectors were going to come to the loft to make sure that it was being used for commercial purposes. So I brought several boxes of handbags home and set up shelves to make the apartment look like a Kate Spade showroom. I was able to squeak by once, but I wasn't sure that would work again.

At that time, Eleni was looking for a factory for her new custom-ized cookie business, so I rented out the back half of the loft where my kitchen was to her. She arrived at five every day—she was an even earlier riser than me—and started baking. My apartment smelled like a delicious bakery day and night. If I didn't have anything for dinner, there were always cookies around.

* * *

While I was moving apartments, the business was moving ever forward in leaps and bounds. We needed more capital to increase production and hire more people. At first, we couldn't get credit from any bank because none of the four founders had long credit histories or assets. We needed help, so we called in a finance whiz: Rodney Bell, Pamela's father, a big, boisterous Southern businessman originally from Zebulon, North Carolina. Though he had lived in New York City for thirty years, he was dedicated to maintaining his heavy-duty accent. He had a funny phrase or Southern witticism up his sleeve for any occasion and kept us entertained while he put us on the road to good financial footing. Rodney had his own consulting company and was working with some of the biggest food businesses in the city. We contracted with him to work with us for two days a week. He called us "kids" even though we were in our thirties. (Pamela was his actual kid, so I guess that made sense.) We called him Foghorn Leghorn after the man-size cartoon rooster character, and he added yet another eccentric note to our existing grab bag of big personalities in our office gang. He had answers for everything related to finance, and since that was my domain, I was thrilled to have an expert on board to help and to learn from.

As our consultant, he reached out to Republic Bank. They'd shown some interest in working with us before, but Katy was resistant to adding on more financial risk with any kind of personal signature. We met the bankers for lunch, and with the documents that Rodney prepared, came to an agreement and opened a line of credit without personal guarantees. The bank execs really supported us and wound up being our bankers forever.

We needed a professional full-charge bookkeeper at that point. Katy's contact recommended a guy to come in full-time, and we hired him. A big part of my job was to meet with him weekly to go over paperwork and keep track of invoices and inventory. I had to work closely with him, but I never really warmed up to the guy. He was good with numbers but struck me as kind of creepy.

One day, I walked with him out of my office after an accounts payable meeting. As he went to leave and walk by me, he slapped me hard on my bottom. I'd worked with men my whole life. As a cocktail waitress at the China Club, I dodged man paws nightly. But I was this guy's boss, and he still felt like he could do that to me. I quietly fumed.

The next time Rodney came to the office, I told him about the slap. He said in his Southern accent, "You gotta fire that guy and you go right on and tell him why!"

We made a point of trying to hire only kind, competent, positive people who enjoyed working with us, so I rarely had to let anyone go. But when I did, I had learned not to give outgoing employees a deep explanation of why, because then they would try to argue their case. With the the handsy bookkeeper, I intended to tell him my thoughts.

"It was inappropriate and disrespectful when you slapped me," I said bluntly. "That was out of line."

"I was just being friendly!" he said with palms up in the air like *Whaddya mean? So what?* No apology, no shame. Certainly no guilt. He felt entitled.

"You're a professional, and you shouldn't have done that."

Believe it or not, he was furious and stormed out, slamming the door. Letting someone go has always filled me with dread, and I loathe having to do it, almost no matter what they did to warrant an action so drastic. But I have to admit, that time it felt pretty good.

* * *

A watershed moment for us came in May 1995. *Vogue* came to the office to photograph and interview the four of us for an article about the company. We were so excited about it. Andy was still working at his advertising day job, but he came to the office for the shoot. We all got ready together at the office and had a professional makeup person do our faces. We each wore our signature style: A striped top and a pink cotton vintage skirt for Katy; a crisp light-blue oxford paired with his signature worn-in khakis and desert boots for Andy; Pamela went elegant professional with a sexy blowout and navy suit with pearls; and I wore black cigarette pants with the top and jacket Katy had on at her wedding. We were giggling throughout, in awe that the revered magazine that we'd grown up reading was going to feature a story about little old us. We jokingly told Pamela Lopez, the reporter, that Katy, Pamela and I called ourselves "Charlie's Angels" because we'd often talk to Andy on speakerphone from his office at Chiat\Day. The *Vogue* photographer Eric Huang shot us all over the office, in front of the showroom display, in the warehouse. He was there most of the day, and the entire experience felt surreal. We were wise enough by this point to leave the dogs at home, given our learning experience with *People*.

With our consistent reorders from specialty and department

stores and ongoing requests from the press, we seemed to be gaining real traction within the fashion industry. The time felt right to apply for a nomination for what was like the Academy Awards of fashion, the Council of Fashion Designers of America (CFDA) Awards. Our category would be the Perry Ellis Award for New Fashion Talent in accessories design. The process was secretive and byzantine, but we followed the rules and got all the required material together—press clippings, promotions, sales stats. Everything had to be precise, no typos, nothing out of their prescribed order. Making piles of colored copies was time-consuming and expensive, and we wondered if we were spinning our wheels. But we put our package together and sent it in.

Katy didn't think we had a shot, but it was worth trying. We didn't hear anything for a couple of months, and we basically forgot about our application in the everyday chaos of trying to fill orders and keep it all together. Then our good friend Carlos Falchi, a Brazilian-born handbag designer who was a member of the awards council, told us on the sly, "I think you guys are going to get nominated. And if you win, your business is really going to take off." The sheer amount of media attention after you won a CFDA award was enormous. If Carlos was right and we did get the award, it could change our business overnight.

Sure enough, six weeks later the three of us were in the office when the call came. They asked to speak with Katy and told her she had been nominated. She politely thanked them, gently hung up the phone, then looked up at Pamela and me with a deer-in-headlights expression on her face.

"We're nominated," she said, wide-eyed.

Pamela and I held hands and twirled in a circle while we screamed, "Yes, yes!"

Katy was excited but already had some trepidation about the prospect of having to make any type of acceptance speech. She picked up the phone and called Andy. We immediately bought a table for eight to attend the black-tie awards gala. Of course, the four founders would go, along with Pamela's husband, Alex; Marybeth; David Spade and our hardworking office assistant, Anna.

In the weeks leading up to the CDFA gala, Katy was nerved up about having to make a speech if she won. She decided that she wouldn't drink at all for the entire night until her award was announced.

The day started at my former-brothel loft where we meticulously styled and accessorized the outfits that had taken us weeks to pick out. Katy wore a long white Dosa silk shantung balmacaan coat with matching Susan Lazar cigarette pants and a lightweight ivory merino short-sleeved sweater. I wore a full-length black silk body-hugging sleeveless dress by James Purcell. Pamela wore a long, slinky navy Dosa silk dress with a cropped bolero sweater. We popped some champagne and had our hair styled and blown out by our local stylist, then had our makeup done professionally by our model connection Molly Russell's favorite makeup artist, Carmen. We headed out to the first event of several that day, a pre-gala cocktail party at the Boathouse in Central Park for nominees.

Next, we all limo-ed to Lincoln Center for the main event and posed on the red carpet along with fashion royalty Donna Karan, Ralph Lauren, Calvin Klein, Michael Kors and Marc Jacobs. It was hard to comprehend that we were all standing there with these giants of our industry. I felt like we were impostors and at any moment, security would come by with a big hook on a pole and say, "Hey! Who are those punks?! Get 'em outta here!"

Katy was being especially quiet. Her anxiety level increased as the awards ceremony approached. I know she was secretly hoping we wouldn't win just so she could avoid the short acceptance speech she was ready with. To make matters exponentially worse, that year the guest of honor was Princess Diana, who was there to present a special award to Elizabeth Tilberis, the editor in chief of *Harper's Bazaar*. There were a thousand fans standing outside the white granite steps leading up to Lincoln Center, cheering and waving, hoping to catch a glimpse of Diana. My poor friend. She disliked being in the spotlight in the first place, and here we were with a crowd of luminaries including Lauren Hutton, Sigourney Weaver, Joan Rivers and hundreds of others. We were at the epicenter of everything. And to top it off, the world's greatest designers were watching, along with Princess Di.

The ceremony began and awards were given out. The crowd applauded Ralph Lauren and Tommy Hilfiger along with the other winners. When it was time for the Perry Ellis Award for New Fashion Talent, Katy was clutching both mine and Andy's hands under the table. I could feel the nervousness coursing through her body as she squeezed my hand even harder—she was petite but had a mighty grip. Her face looked a bit pale as the blood drained out of it. She smiled and looked collected while she waited to hear the winner. When the winner was announced—KATE SPADE!—I thought I would burst with jubilation at that moment and let out a triumphant squeal. Our whole table erupted in cheers as we all stood up and clapped. After a pause, Katy smiled more broadly, and then that little champ strode up to the mic over thunderous applause and killed it with the short and sweet thank-you speech she had prepared just in case:

"Thank you to my husband, my partners, all the retailers, and most importantly, thank you to the CFDA." Big authentic smile and wave. She did great.

Photographers swarmed around her after she accepted the award. At first, they asked to take photos of the four partners together. Then they'd say, "Okay, how about one with just Kate, Pamela and Elyce?" Then, "How about just Kate and Andy?" And finally, it was, "How about one with just Kate?" Pamela, Andy and I stood awkwardly to the side as they took multiple photos of Katy. When the pictures were published in the *New York Times*, the *New York Post*, and *WWD*, they chose the solo shot. This became a familiar pattern. Photographers gamely took our picture, and then peeled us off so they could capture Katy alone.

A lot of rock bands start out as a cohesive unit and later one person emerges as the star. The other bandmates think, *We created this together, and now he's getting all the credit. This isn't fair!* Before long, the band starts telling their ugly breakup story on MTV's *Behind the Music*. Our band started as equals. We had equal voting power and nearly equal shares in the company. But none of us, including Katy, were angling to be the lead singer as such. Katy never wanted to be the public face of anything. On the contrary, she was apprehensive of fame. But by creating the brand's aesthetic, she was the designer. And, despite her shyness, Katy had charisma, authenticity, the look and the X factor that made her the front person and face of the brand. Her name was on the label. We were happy with it for the most part. The only caveat was our worry for her sake about how reluctant she was to carry our torch.

Once the accessories award was announced, we could relax and just have a ball at the after-party. Katy made up for lost champagne time. The highlight of the evening for her came toward the end. An editor from *Harper's Bazaar* walked her over and introduced her to Princess Diana. She congratulated the starstruck Katy, held Katy's hand in both of hers while smiling her lovely Princess Di smile that the whole world remembers.

Linda Wells, editor in chief of *Allure* magazine wrote a piece we loved for the CFDA Awards Journal that year:

"Not often does a fashion phenomenon emerge whose price tag is in inverse relationship to its style quotient—but that's the case with Kate Spade, who has almost single-handedly proven to an industry known for thinking otherwise that a chic handbag need not cost upwards of $2,000. The little Kate Spade label has come to stand not only for a young, sprightly urban style, but a certain spontaneity, the kind of easy, irreverent fun that seems never to go out of style. If her bags to riches story has a certain sweet Judy-Garland-and-Mickey-Rooney charm, that's fine with the designer, who, with her husband and partner Andy, espouses more a style of life than a life of style. As her handbags dabble in fashion—never going so far as to leap headlong into trends—so do the Spades live and work. And with her other business partners, some of whom have been 'best friends since we were little,' as she says, the Kansas City native brings to her company an old-fashioned spirit that is more about growing a good business than business growth—a wholesome American entrepreneurial ethic that over the last 30 years had seemed on the verge of extinction. Thanks to the success of Spade and her colleagues, it can be taken off the endangered species list."

We didn't realize until years later that some brands had to wait decades for the CFDA to recognize their work. We'd won it after just three years in existence. It was comparable to winning an Oscar for your first movie. But that night, we weren't contemplating how rare our win was or what our long-term plan might be. We just toasted and enjoyed each other's company, barely ate the dinner and had a sparkling evening. The entire fashion industry swirled around us, but we were in our own little bubble. I did have a sense that the award was a turning point. I remember thinking, *This is going to change everything*. And soon it did.

CHAPTER 16

The *Vogue* article came out in February 1996, shortly
after we won the CFDA Award. It was an incredible
piece with great photos of the four of us in our office. Our phone
was ringing off the hook for press interviews and sample requests
while more stores were calling to set up appointments to see the
line. Twelve months earlier we were fighting to keep things going,
and now we were on top of the world. We were receiving large
orders from all over the US, manufacturing nearly everything in
our building with Hernan's team, and working with a handful of
other factories in the city. Our staff shortly grew to more than fifty
people, including my sister Willow, who was put in charge of our
shipping and warehouse group.

Around this time, we started getting calls from the Japanese fashion companies Itochu Fashion Systems (IFS) and Mitsukoshi and

others asking for appointments to talk about partnerships. Japan was booming, and anything American was in demand. Kate Spade was the new kid on the block, and our designs with their classic American style would be attractive for the Japanese consumer. I fielded the calls and set up preliminary meetings in New York.

By any metric, Kate Spade was going through an explosive expansion. Pamela and I saw the train coming and went to look for more room. We were already bursting at the seams on Twenty-Ninth Street. We found the ideal spot on West Twenty-Fifth Street, right next to the Chelsea Flea Market in the Flower District, where Katy and I had shopped away those lazy Saturday afternoons years before. Eventually, we took over three more floors in the building, bringing the offices to forty thousand square feet. The building itself was beautiful, with north- and south-facing windows. Hernan moved in and leased from us an additional area that he would use as factory space. The rest of it was divided between warehousing, shipping and offices. Our workforce soon blossomed to over a hundred employees. We had to rent additional floors in the building next door, move shipping over there and build out more offices.

Despite the building's location and benefits, Katy didn't want to sign the lease at first. "It's too expensive. What if we don't need all this space?" she asked. Her cautious nature was always tapping on the breaks while Pamela and I were stepping on the gas. Katy's worries subsided when the offices filled up fast, and it became obvious that we needed everyone to meet our new demands. Pamela hired dozens of development and production people. Katy hired design assistants. We needed more salespeople, HR associates and warehouse clerks.

Soon after, in 1996, much to my delight, IFS invited us to Tokyo for final talks about a licensing partnership. Katy couldn't go because she had a scheduled personal appearance at Neiman Marcus in Beverly Hills. So Pamela held down the fort while Andy and I went to Tokyo for a week. We flew on ANA to Tokyo in business class for the fourteen-hour flight. The formality of the flight attendants in their manner and dress was our first exposure to the culture of the country. We were so excited we didn't sleep a wink on the entire journey.

One funny memory from that trip occurred early on when we had arrived in Japan and I was waiting in the immigration line. I was fumbling around in my handbag for my passport, ready to give it to the officer and have it stamped. Like most women, I can stick my hand in my bag and identify every single item in there by shape. I was curious when I felt a mysterious roundish rough shape. I tentatively grabbed whatever it was, so surprised when I pulled out a medium sized Idaho potato. Of course I knew that this was a classic weirdo Katy prank. She had snuck it in there in the office the day before to make me chuckle when I discovered it. The immigration officer was glaring at me holding the thing. It occurred to me instantly that I couldn't possibly explain to him why I would be carrying around a raw potato, so hoping I wasn't breaking any agricultural laws, I kept a straight face and quietly placed it back in my bag. I handed him my passport which he eventually stamped. He sat in his booth staring after me as I walked away. I'm sure I gave him a good story to take home to his family that night.

Our hosts from IFS wined and dined us. The first night, they took us to a tiny off-the-beaten-path six-seat yakitori bar. We were being so overly polite that we didn't dare ask about the menu or if we were supposed to order. When the petite first course came to the table. It was a little bowl of . . . well, we had no idea. Fish?

Andy leaned over and asked one of our hosts, "What is it?"

The answer: raw chicken. We eventually figured out that the multicourse meal of various preparations of chicken began with raw poultry and progressed to fully cooked.

Andy pushed his bowl toward me and whispered, "I can't do it. You have to eat it." Otherwise, we feared our hosts would think we were rude. I didn't want to eat his bowl of raw chicken, but I felt we had to keep up the good relationship. Who knew what might happen if we insulted the chef in this foreign-to-us culture? I downed his first two courses, and mine. It was not pleasant, but by the third course the meat was cooked enough for Andy to eat his own portion. We had no clue how many more were coming, and after the seventh, I was full to bursting, and asked our translator, "How many courses are there?"

The server said, "Kyū." We found out that meant nine in English.

The last course was teriyaki chicken that looked really good, but I was way too full to take a bite. After dinner, our hosts took us to a karaoke bar, and we had an absolute ball singing until one in the morning. Because of the thirteen-hour time difference, when Andy and I returned to the hotel, we were wide awake. We had meetings in the morning and needed rest, so we unwisely started drinking every miniature bottle of alcohol in our mini bars to make ourselves pass out. We hadn't heard of melatonin or Ambien yet.

The next morning, I woke up to my alarm, still tipsy and exhausted. We had meetings at IFS and needed to get moving. I called Andy's room to make sure he was awake. No answer. I banged on his door as hard as I could, and he finally woke up. We arrived at the meeting on time but reeked of booze. The Japanese hosts chain smoked throughout the meeting. Andy and I could barely keep our eyes open.

I felt much better when we went outside to tour Tokyo's major department stores, including Isetan in the Shinjuku area, and learned about how they're organized. In the US, much of the first floor is reserved for fragrance. In most stores in Tokyo, there are handkerchiefs, display after display of beautiful pocket squares. We observed so many fascinating cultural nuances in Tokyo that were vastly different from the US. Outside those major department stores in the city there were hundreds of bicycles parked against bike stands. The biggest difference from the US? *None of them were locked.* It was extremely rare that bikes were ever stolen in Japan. Also, the quality of the taxis was another big difference. The headrests of the cabs—usually Mercedes—are draped with lace, and the drivers wear white gloves. The taxi doors open automatically with a gentle *ping*. The interiors of the taxis are immaculate. Even the men in neat uniforms painting lines on the street were meticulous. Japanese culture turned every gesture and action into an art form.

We were very excited to partner with IFS/Sanei to import our handbags, and to license our name for apparel for the Japanese market. Their teams would work with our design group on the concept and production of clothing, and we'd have creative approval over every garment and all the retail spaces. I loved the idea of us creating a clothing collection. They were already working with American designer Anna Sui, and we admired what they'd done with that brand in opening retail stores throughout Asia and licensing products for her. Andy and I set up a conference call with Pamela and Katy back in New York, where we agreed to move forward with contracts.

Giddy, having brokered a great deal and eager to share our Tokyo stories with everyone at the office, Andy and I boarded the plane to fly back to New York. Just as we were about to land at JFK, the flight attendant said over the loudspeaker, "When the plane comes to a halt, will Elyce Cox and Andy Spade please come to the front cabin? We need to get you off the plane immediately. Everyone else, please remain seated."

Of course, we assumed some huge personal emergency had taken place. For ten minutes, we sat there, increasingly panicked, waiting for the plane to stop. Finally, two attendants rushed us off the plane into the terminal. We were met by an airline representative.

"What happened?" we asked.

The guy said, "Your office called and said that there was an emergency, and that we had to pull you off the plane as quickly as possible."

"But what's the emergency?" Andy asked.

"You've had a major flood at your office," he said. "Your partners want you to get back there right now."

You could do that kind of thing back then, just call the airline and have people pulled off the plane. A flood was bad news, but thank goodness no one had been injured or died. Still, Andy and I raced to the office by taxi and beheld the deluge. Due to a water pipe burst on the floor above us, water had soaked the whole office, including the warehouse. Seventy-five percent of our product was drenched. Willow, in charge of the warehouse, had cleaned out every drugstore in Manhattan of blow-dryers. The entire staff was intently focused on blow-drying the bags. In the center of it all stood Pamela, ever the cornerstone of competence, in knee-high rubber Wellington boots, directing the clean-up operation. Our staff was like a hive of bees with Pamela the Queen, all just getting it done. We spent the next three days hauling out wet cardboard boxes and cleaning everything.

We saved what we could, but we lost about 40 percent of our inventory. We had to call all our customers and tell them that shipments were going to be delayed. Insurance covered some of the losses and repairs, but it was an ordeal to take care of it.

By the third night, we had mostly repaired the damage, dried out what we could and reset the shipping to fill the open missing orders. Andy and I were still jet-lagged; we had barely slept. The four of us left some staffers at the office to straighten up the last of the mess. We were all exhausted, but headed to Ecco, a cozy bar and restaurant near Katy and Andy's place. The four of us sat at the bar. The bartender served up our drinks, and Katy proposed a toast: "Here's to me, who single-handedly took care of that disaster!" In reality, she had provided some emotional support during that mess, but mostly she was in charge of fretting. We all cracked up. She knew how to make us laugh.

CHAPTER 17

Months after the deluge, business was really booming. We were comfortable in our roles and too busy to second-guess one another. As we sold more bags, our profit margin was vastly improving, what I came to call the "magic volume wand." As our sales volume increased, our purchases were higher, so we were getting better pricing on the cost of goods like the massive amount of satin nylon material we were buying. We were able to pay our bills faster, so we were enjoying a discount from some vendors for quick payment. I felt that things were really going well. Around this time in the summer of 1996, I received a call that month that made me pinch myself to see if I was awake or dreaming.

My extension rang and I answered, as always, with, "Hello, Kate Spade. How can I help you?"

The woman said, "Hello. I'm Mary Tyler Moore's manager. She'd like to see your bags."

My heart skipped a few beats before I could pull myself together. "Great!" I said. "They're sold at several different stores in town, so she can find them at Barneys or Saks."

"No, she wants to see everything you've got at your office."

A few days later, Mary Tyler Moore, the legend, walked in the front door of our office just after 11:00 am. Her assistant had called that morning to see if the day would be "convenient" for us to meet with Mary. I could hardly speak because this icon, our idol, our inspiration, was standing in front of me. She was even more beautiful than she looked on TV.

She held out her hand and said, "Hi, I'm Mary."

"I can't believe you're standing here!" I blurted, shaking her hand. I proceeded to gush and babble about how much I loved her show growing up, how she'd inspired us, that our mutual admiration for her and the show was the first thing Katy and I had bonded over. She was so friendly and kind and didn't seem to mind my rambling.

Mary said, "Wasn't that the best show?"

"Yes!" I said, dazzled. I was blown away by her sincerity and calm. Right away it was like talking to a family member. She had that quality.

She said, "It had so many good values, but it was funny. Back then, women weren't really able to go out and get a job."

"Exactly," I said. "You inspired us to do this."

"Well, that makes me so happy. I love what you're doing."

Katy had been out of the office at a meeting when Mary arrived, but she rushed back to meet her. We told Mary the story of how we got started and showed off linen and nylon totes, satin evening bags and some fun new designs that we were working on. Mary said one of the reasons she appreciated our brand was because we didn't use leather. We didn't know it at the time, but she was a committed animal-rights activist. We were using only fabric rather than leather to keep our retail price point down to make our bags accessible to most women, but we both instinctively kept that info to ourselves. We didn't want to spoil that memorable moment with our childhood hero. Katy and I enjoyed our time with her and had a wonderful afternoon. We were both glowing for a month.

Pretty soon it seemed like Mary wasn't the only celebrity who carried our bags. Kate Spade handbags started to pop up in paparazzi photos, on the red carpet at premieres and on the forearms of television and movie stars who either had stylists or had purchased them at Barneys, Charivari or their local specialty store. Gwyneth Paltrow, Winona Ryder and Sandra Bullock were a few of our favorite celebs who were photographed with our bags. Sandra Bullock came to our showroom several times to meet with us and personally select her handbags. She was so friendly, funny and down-to-earth.

Our success was confounding to many people in the fashion industry. They wanted to know, "Who are these four new people running this thing?" None of us came from a major fashion brand. Our company wasn't bankrolled by a conglomerate or a bank. We really did start the company with a dollar and a dream, which was hard to believe. Because of our atypical quirky beginnings, some industry insiders continued to write us off with comments in business fashion-trade articles that we were a flash in the pan. Eventually, when our bags were selling really well nationally and placed among the legacy brands in the best department stores, we were accepted, and the insiders knew we were here to stay.

* * *

We'd always talked about having our own retail location, and in October 1996, we opened a charming storefront on Thompson Street, a quiet block on the western edge of SoHo. The store was tiny, only about three hundred square feet, with an Italian pottery shop on one side, and the office of a security alarm company on the other. Right away *New York* magazine gave us a small mention in their Best Bets column, and Kate Spade customers from around the city came to take a look. It was definitely going to be a destination point for people seeking the brand or sightseers in SoHo checking out the side streets.

Foghorn Leghorn Rodney thought it was a risky move because our business at that point was selling to retail stores, not running our own. "You kids have no business opening a retail store," he said.

While that was true, we were excited to try showcasing our wares in a space we could control.

The store itself had an open square-display window in front. Andy took over decorating it, and his love of art and sculpture came out to play. He thought it would be funny to make a pair of cigarette pants out of real cigarettes for the front window, so we did. The quirky faux pants drew people's attention; it was one of many Andy touches that would differentiate us from any other fashion company. We took time to organize the space and make it our own. Because the store was so small, we displayed only the most popular items from our various collections. We would hang a few bags on the main side wall and use the thick wooden bench along the north side of the space to showcase various handbag groups. Andy added interesting books and personal tchotchkes throughout. You might find a used John Cheever or Slim Aarons photo book or a teak squirrel sculpture from India. The store was so quaint and charming, it became a location for photo shoots, and a destination for fashion fans who'd seen our bags in magazines or on the arms of famous people. The rent was $1,850 per month. Our goal for the store was to break even, which we did right away.

* * *

As we were growing the company, we knew that finding the right people for our team was critical. I was overseeing the HR effort, where I mostly used temp agencies to place manufacturing and warehouse jobs. For creative, corporate and administrative roles, Rachel and Jennifer, trusted employees and HR associates, and I sorted through mountains of résumés weekly. We interviewed every person who walked through the door. If the candidates were good, we passed them along to Pamela, Katy or Andy. We brought people in by consensus.

I also found staffers by chance. One night, I was having a glass of wine at Le Gamin in the West Village, and a stylish young woman with a funky bob-style haircut was seated next to me. We started talking. She'd graduated from college a year before and was working in PR. But she said ideally she'd like to find a job in fashion where she could make a difference and have fun while she did it. I thought about the time that Andy Spade landed his first advertising job when a random stranger asked to see his portfolio in the middle of Grand Central.

I asked, "Would you like to come in to interview at my company?"

"Where do you work?" she asked. I just pointed at the Kate Spade tote hanging from the back of her chair.

Her face lit up immediately. "Yes, please."

I wound up hiring her, and Vanessa worked at the company for many years in our public relations department.

While we were dead serious about the business aspects of running Kate Spade, we also set out to make our office a fun place to work. Our goal was to make sure everyone felt supported and had an opportunity to work hard and be productive every day. We started the tradition of Beer Cart Fridays. Starting at four in the afternoon, a staffer would push the cart around with a boom box playing music, offering soda, beer and wine to kick off the weekend. We made a tradition of throwing employee parties every summer and during the holidays. Katy enjoyed those parties and always wanted to make sure everyone was having a great evening. She'd dance with the guys from the shipping department and always made time to sit at every table and spend a few minutes with each person.

At our holiday party in December for the first two years, we rented out Rolf's on Third Avenue and East Twenty-Second Street for beer and schnitzel. Rolf's is a famous German restaurant with year-round extravagant decorations. At Christmas, they hang thousands of colored glass balls from the ceiling, wrap a forest of pine boughs in red and gold ribbon, and drape miles of string lights throughout the dining room. The effect was as if a giant Christmas tree had exploded. We had to stop our holiday parties at Rolf's when the company grew too big for the space. We moved up to the Rainbow Room at the top floor of Rockefeller Center with 360-degree views overlooking the entire city. For an extra kick, we hired six Rockettes to perform. Another year, we threw the holiday party in an empty warehouse building on Twenty-Fourth Street and brought in professional dancers to get our employees onto the dance floor. Everyone dressed to the nines. We had many people in our employ from Ghana and other West African countries, and they wore their traditional colorful African prints. It was just an amazing time for all of us.

And gifts! One year, we gave handmade ponchos to everyone. Another year, it was monogrammed handbags. Everyone received a turkey at Thanksgiving. A hundred frozen birds arrived on a pallet in the warehouse, and each staffer grabbed one on the way home.

The memories of those days are the ones that are closest to my heart. Our criteria for hiring people were fairly simple. We looked for people who seemed intelligent, enthusiastic and hardworking, and had a sparkle of humor in their eyes. Almost everyone stayed with us for many years. They were always there when we needed them most, as we were for them.

Up until then, Andy was still at Chiat\Day but was always with us in spirit. He spent much of his workweek on and off the phone with Katy, Pamela or me, but he still enjoyed being a top talent in the ad game and working with the national and international clients. Katy really wanted him to come full-time and help us run the company. He had invested so much energy and much of his salary for years to get it up and running. Katy understood even more than Pamela or I did that his brilliance would take us to the next level. She often tried to coax him to jump in, but she recognized that to do so, he would be sacrificing his own ambition in the advertising field.

After year three, Andy finally acquiesced and joined the team as CEO. Now that Kate Spade, the company, had his full attention, a new phase of the business would begin. We were off to an incredible start, but with Andy on board, our challenge was to evolve from an upstart accessories company to an internationally recognized brand.

CHAPTER 18

It felt right having the four of us—Katy, Andy, Pamela and me—working under the same roof. The pressure was on to keep creating fresh and exciting ideas that were in line with the spirit of the company. We also needed to shift from the reactive mode of being the new kids on the block to become a professional business with all of the responsibility that entailed. It's almost like the story of the dog that chases cars and finally catches one. What next? We had grown the company, increased our overhead for rents and built out our infrastructure for ordering and accounting. In addition, we were now responsible for the well-being of many other people who worked for the company, and, by extension, their families. While it was an exciting time, we were each feeling the burden of needing to continue the growth and evolution of the company, not just for ourselves, but for the team we had created. Having my three closest friends in offices just a few feet from one another made the challenge a positive experience. We all felt the same.

Aside from the personal appearances Katy was making, most of the time we four were working together in the office. Although Pamela and I were typically there early in the morning and would leave by six thirty, Katy and Andy would arrive in the morning by ten or eleven and stay until later in the evening. We would usually congregate in Katy's office with coffees in hand once we had all arrived, to discuss everything we had going on that day or mull over the activities of the previous night out. Katy's and my offices were on the same floor just down the hall from each other, and Andy and Pamela's were one floor down with the same layout. All of them were large and comfortable, with big windows and lots of light. Katy's office was the bustling one with colorful swatches hanging on the wallboard and loads of samples of every size and shape. A bright red lacquered desk was the centerpiece of her office space with a banquette-style bench along the opposite wall. The bold, colorful cushions on that bench were so overstuffed that they were impossible to sit on—if you tried to, you would literally roll off them. Despite our complaints, she refused to change them; she loved the way they looked. We often teased her about those, then pulled up chairs or sat on the windowsill.

* * *

On a typical day, Katy would be reviewing her schedule of press appointments and appearances for the week, or preparing for a design meeting with her team by reviewing swatches and tear sheets she had pulled from magazines. Pamela would be working with the product development and production departments, reviewing the samples for quality, or meeting with one of our suppliers to select new materials and negotiate prices. Andy could often be found in the design services office working on his plan to launch a men's line of products (eventually Jack Spade), talking with the designers and marketing manager about ideas for products and campaign ideas. My days consisted of prospective new employee interviews in the morning, a finance meeting just before lunch, and sales, retail and licensing updates with all our department heads in the afternoons.

Pamela, Katy and I always ordered lunch in and ate together, and Andy would often join us. We would favor one restaurant or another for a month or two and order from there every day until we had grown tired of it and then find a new favorite the following month. Some of our typical lunch orders were pizza and salads from Mangia on Twenty-Third Street and sandwiches from the corner deli across from our office—usually Reubens for Andy and me, turkey and Swiss for Pamela, and a BLT (hold the T!) for Katy. We placed the orders under the name Kate Spade. Andy and I ordered those Reubens so many times that the deli ended up naming it the Kate Spade on the lunch menu above the deli counter! Katy hated having those over-stuffed monster Reuben sandwiches with her name on them—she didn't even like them—but she was too polite to ask the deli guys to take the name off the menu, so it stayed up there for years.

* * *

With our expansion we were under the gun to keep sales and profitability moving in the right direction. Help came from an unexpected silent partner. That ally was the City of New York in the late nineties. The national drop in crime back then resulted in more young people and families streaming into all of the major cities, particularly New York. They arrived to take advantage of all the social and cultural advantages, along with a big increase in career opportunities. People are skeptical when I say this, but I think Sarah Jessica Parker and *Sex and the City* was responsible for a huge part of that growth in the later part of the decade. Those episodes showed the world a New York City that was an exciting place to live and a new way for women to take charge of their lives. Though I can't tell you the exact demographic shift of that time, I can tell you anecdotally there seemed to be a lot of young women who came to the city in droves, and they wanted to look dazzling.

The good news was that we thought of those women flooding into New York and other big cities as Kate Spade customers. They were just like us: transplants to the urban areas, working hard, aspiring to do something they'd dreamed about as girls. Our bags were suddenly everywhere, and we watched our sales grow nationally to other urban and suburban markets. The key for us was to remain as true to the original vision and stay as authentic as possible. Having Andy in the office full-time was a great advantage. He was a master of distilling the essence of a brand and using that to create an identity he could communicate to the world. He had honed that skill for years now in his advertising career.

The four of us were a tight team in that era. We each brought a different perspective to the effort. Andy had his valuable advertising experience and had become an expert storyteller. Though Pamela was the get-it-done production expert, she had a real interest in architecture and art, which came in handy for our store build-outs and all our design decisions. Katy had her wonderful sense of style and that uncanny ability to identify the good and choose the excellent. While I was generally in charge of the business elements of the company, my personal interest lay in the ready-to-wear apparel side of the business with Japan.

As our Japanese business expanded, I spent more time on the apparel design because it was as popular in Japan as our handbags. The style of our apparel wasn't retro per se, but it referenced timeless classics, and we would imprint those pieces with a modern, pragmatic sensibility. Customer favorites were pleated schoolgirl skirts in bright pink poplin, sky blue or the perfect shade of grass green. Our feminine Peter Pan–collared, pleated white top was another favorite. At that time, we had reached the point of having more than a dozen freestanding stores along with built out Kate Spade–branded areas called "shop-in-shops" in big department stores throughout Japan, with others on the drawing board.

In the late nineties, much of the direction of the industry tended toward a darker vision: cool and cerebral. It was a very sophisticated look and highly successful for many of the international luxury brands. We differentiated our brand by being colorful and playful, as well as stylish. These elements were appealing to women who were attracted to the affordable luxury price point. The bags were still aspirational but communicated an authenticity that spoke to generations of women who may have felt outside the target market of the famous luxury brands.

We created handbags for every time of year in seasonal fabrics with special details that felt personal, like a colorful floral-printed lining mostly visible to only the wearer of the handbag. In the spring we used bright linen and poplin, and in the fall it would be corduroy or wool tweed. We incorporated special touches reminiscent of a vintage handbag: tiny mirrors in an interior pocket; an attached coin bag inside; a thoughtful, special printed lining. Bags would seem familiar from growing up watching your mother dress for an evening out or leaving for church or a family get together. They evoked a style harkening back to that of Katharine Hepburn, Tippi Hedren or Ali MacGraw.

Andy was able to drill down on our message as a company, and I credit his effort with much of our success at that time. His branding emphasized a sense of optimism and a lightness that made us stand out in the marketplace. We tied little hang tags on our bags with messages to our customers, like "A Peter Pan collar is sexier than go-go boots" or "Whistling is encouraged." Our print ads were often shot in grainy focus to look like magazine photography of the seventies. They would show nostalgic scenes, such as a mother preparing to take her kids to school, the image of her driving off with her handbag where she left it—on the roof of the car. They were generally fleeting glimpses of our shared American youth, at once familiar and relatable to so many.

On the design side, we would start all ideas with a focus on function. A handbag served a real purpose. A woman carried her whole life inside one, so we gave her pockets and sturdy handles and plenty of space. Katy had fun with the details of her designs, but it didn't matter to us how beautiful a bag was if it didn't make sense for a woman's life. By prioritizing function, Kate Spade stood out in the marketplace.

* * *

In the meantime, Katy's star was continually rising, though as a slightly introverted person, she remained uncomfortable in that role. She persevered and did become an expert at being the company face and voice, well versed in articulating everything that had to do with Kate Spade. Katy's persona spoke to our customers; she embodied all the positives of our brand.

The more we were represented in the media, the more attention Katy was getting. It sounds like fun to be famous, and it's true that it comes with some terrific perks. At first we thought that Katy's level of celebrity was just right. Her name was the brand that was growing like crazy, but not many people knew Katy the person by sight.

In the late nineties, that started to change. I remember one night, Katy and I were at a Spanish place we liked called El Quijote in the Hotel Chelsea near our office. We were sitting at the bar after work, having a serious discussion of what licenses for new products we wanted to pursue. An attractive young woman in her twenties approached Katy and said, "Excuse me, are you Kate Spade?"

"Yes, I am," Katy said and smiled back.

"Would you mind coming to sing 'Happy Birthday' to my girl-friend? She loves your bags and it would make her night so special."

Oh boy, I thought. *Exactly what Katy wouldn't want to do.* It was a really packed restaurant, and Katy was just not the kind of person that would stand up and sing anything, anywhere. We turned her down in the politest way possible. The girl was persistent and would not take no for an answer. She was also very sweet. And a customer.

Katy looked at me. "C'mon, let's go."

"You don't want to do this," I said.

"Yes, I do, and you will, too. Get off your ass and get over here and help."

So we did it. We went to the back room and visited the birthday table of ten young women, all very nice. Out came the cake, and Katy and I smiled and sang the "Happy Birthday" song. The entire restaurant went silent and enjoyed our rendition, then applauded. We thought we were finished and really wanted to crawl away some-where, but after, the birthday girl wanted to take some photos with Katy. She went around the table with Katy and introduced all her guests by name so she could shake their hands. They asked us to sit with them, but we politely declined, finished our cocktails at the bar and skedaddled. Really, it was no big deal, but that type of scenario started playing itself out at least half of the times we went anywhere socially. I learned to be grateful to remain anonymous and really ap-preciated Katy's taking on that role.

Fueling the rise in Katy's public recognition and the expansion of Kate Spade was the seismic shift in everything due to the internet. It had been relevant already for a decade or so. But in the nineties, we went through the dot-com bubble. Huge fortunes were made then lost as technology began to grow into its own. By the end of the decade, e-commerce was finding its footing, and the real change was the universal availability of information. It supercharged everyone's ability to know what was happening in every corner of American society. If one had an interest in fashion, there was a daily tidal wave of information about who was making what and who was wearing what. It was a period of great democratization of the fashion industry, and a shift from the old analog magazine-driven style platform to the new digital online form. It was a boon for the great design houses and for the smaller ones like us.

Many of our colleagues were in a similar growth mode and really expanded in that era. We had become good friends with Cynthia Rowley years before, and her business was thriving. Later, at a sales call that Katy and I made to Bergdorf Goodman, we saw Bobbi Brown at a small sample table introducing customers to her brand much as we had done countless times. Katy had worked with her in the *Mademoiselle* days. We renewed our relationship, bought a lot of lipstick and were delighted to see her brand take off in the years that followed.

*   *   *

As our business grew and our cash flow improved, we weren't struggling every day with worrying about how to pay the bills. We had passed that stage and were able to more clearly focus on growing the company and putting ourselves in the shoes of the many women who supported us. What else would they like to see? The new categories we were adding to create a full lifestyle brand were a source of constant conversation, and we spent non-office hours together working through those decisions in an exciting way.

We started considering a number of licensing agreements with other companies to expand the Kate Spade brand. Stationery was the first because Katy was a habitual sender of handwritten notes. She felt that there would be a market for something new in that category with our signature whimsical imprint. We found the best manufacturer and contracted with them to make a line of Kate Spade stationery and paper goods that we would design and take to market. It was a huge success right out of the gate. Much of that was due to the extraordinary creative services department Andy had created, headed up by Julia Leach, a former advertising colleague and seasoned creative director. They brought together a group of experienced designers who would work with Katy and our team to come up with pages of ideas of colors, shapes and sizes of all of the new stationery items.

We generally had a particular stripe, print or detail of color that would create a thread tying new designs to the brand. Katy would spend days refining and editing the ideas, and ultimately we would receive samples that she would edit to make a full collection. I always knew when her work was finished—she would excitedly invite us up to the showroom to show us. Our interoffice lines would ring, and no matter what we were doing, Katy would be bubbling with enthusiasm, saying something to the effect of "You've got to come and see the new samples right now. You won't believe it!" In all of those years we worked together, she still maintained her passion for the design; we were as excited as she was and never disappointed.

Then Andy's branding team would brainstorm marketing, advertising and packaging. It was a ton of work, and our favorite part of the business. In the months and years that followed, we would launch Kate Spade stationery, eyewear, shoes, tabletop, bedding, fragrance and other lines using the same business model.

If the company's first few years were about moving up, our next phase was about branching out. Doors were flinging open for us, and we did our best to walk through as many of them as possible. We literally opened the door at our brand-new, much-larger retail store on Broome Street and Mercer in SoHo, to replace our tiny Thompson Street location. A nearby antiques shop was moving, and we jumped to take over the gorgeous corner store lease.

The new store was just as unique as our first store on Thompson Street, designed as if the decor might have come out of our own apartments. If we were successful enough to open multiple stores, we wanted each one to feel like a boutique and have its own personality. Ideally, our locations would be slightly off the beaten path, next door to a precious little bookstore or a favorite neighborhood bistro. The idea was to sell our accessible, functional—and beautiful—handbags where our customers really *lived*, apart from the typical retail centers. We wanted to create destination shopping locations in neighborhoods that reflected the aesthetic of our brand.

* * *

Even though we were working hard to expand, we recognized that we already had a lot to be thankful for. Our business lives were changing, and our personal lives as well. When Pamela's second daughter, Anabel, arrived in April 1997, Katy, Andy and I spent the entire day in that hospital room, eating Chinese food and toasting to another baby in the Kate Spade family. Pamela brought tears to my eyes when she asked me to be Anabel's godmother. I remember that joy-filled day when we had time to appreciate one another and take a break to enjoy our friendships. It was all about Pamela and her adorable new baby. Katy and I were so happy for her and wondered aloud when our time would come to be mothers. Who would our children be, what would their voices sound like? We looked at Pamela holding Anabel and smiled at each other knowing someday we would have the answer to our questions. Now was time for the business, but we both looked forward to our future and the children we would come to know and love.

Me at our first real offices, on Twenty-Ninth Street and Seventh Avenue, in 1995.

Katy at our offices, 1995.

Katy inspecting bags at our offices, 1995.

Me with Edna and Katy with Henry, in our offices, 1995.

Katy and her Maltese, Henry, 1995.

Seamstress and sewer Lourdes Porra in Hernan's factory, in the same building as our Twenty-Ninth Street offices, 1995.

Scenes from the *Vogue* photo shoot at our office,
May 1995, clockwise from top left: me (wearing
the top Katy wore at her wedding); Pamela,
Katy and me; and the three of us with Andy,
surrounded by boxes of our merchandise.

François Dischinger/Trunk Archive

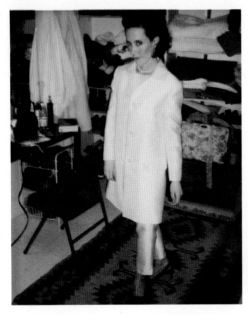

Katy preparing for
the CFDA Awards,
1995.

Andy and David Spade
at the CFDA Awards
pre-party, 1995.

Intern-turned-office
assistant Anna
Blinken, Katy and me
in 1995 at our Twenty-
Ninth Street offices.

Hernan and me in 1995 at our
Twenty-Ninth Street offices.

Edna and Henry at the summer beach house in 1996.

Kate at the Plaza Hotel, 1996.

Marybeth, me and Katy, Cabo San Lucas, circa 1997.

Me, Katy, Andy and Pamela preparing for the opening of our first store, located on Thompson Street in SoHo, in October 1996.

Katy, me and Pamela at our West Twenty-Fifth Street offices, 1997.

Pamela and me, circa 1997.

Pamela, Rachel Adams (an office assistant) and Katy at our larger West Twenty-Fifth Street offices, 1998.

Hernan, our longtime
production partner, in 1997.

Our architect, Jonathan
Marvel, walking us through
the plans for our Broome
Street store, circa 1997.

Katy and me in
Mexico at the Twin
Dolphin, 1997.

Marybeth, Katy
and me, Cabo San
Lucas, circa 1997.

Shutters LA, 1998:
Me, Katy, Pamela
and Andy Spade.

Katy's surprise thirty-fifth birthday party at the
Union League Club, December 1997.

In the Hamptons, 1998.

Me in Celine and
Katy in Bill Blass at
the 1999 Accessories
Council Excellence
(ACE) Awards.

Arons Bridgehampton house, 1998.

Me and Andy Arons,
Bridgehampton,
August 1998.

Dinner parties in
our dining tent,
Bridgehampton, 1998.
Gentl and Hyers

Katy and Andy at a boat party, 1999.

Katy at the Kate Spade employee summer party, 1998.

Katy and me in Kyoto, 1999.

Katy and Andy in Kyoto, 1999.

Andy and me in one of the
Scuttlehole tents, August 1999.

Andy Arons and me at the dinner party in
March 1999 where he proposed to me.

My dad, Dana Cox,
walking me to the
altar on Andy and
my wedding day,
Bridgehampton, 1999.
John Dolan

My and Andy's wedding day, September 1999, at the
Channing Daughters Winery in Bridgehampton.
John Dolan

From left to right:
Andy Arons, me,
Andy Spade and Katy
toast at our wedding
in September 1999.
John Dolan

Scene from the
wedding; Katy
is in the bright
dress. *John Dolan*

From left to
right: Jon Pozgay;
Missy Pozgay;
Katy's brother,
Earl Brosnahan;
and Katy at
our wedding in
September 1999.

Eleni, Katy and
Missy Pozgay at
Channing Daughters
Winery, the day
after our wedding in
September 1999.

Gibson Beach,
Sagaponack, the
bonfire after Andy
and my wedding.

Katy, Andy Spade,
Andy Arons and
me at Round Hill,
Jamaica, 2000.

October 1999 on our
honeymoon in Capri,
Italy. Andy, me and
Marybeth.

Andy with baby
Katy, circa 2001.

Katy Holiday Arons in 2002,
in a Kate Spade bag.

Katy with Little Katy and Marybeth
in August 2001 at our Bank Street
home in the West Village.

At my fortieth birthday in 2003.

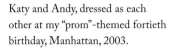

Katy and Andy, dressed as each
other at my "prom"-themed fortieth
birthday, Manhattan, 2003.

Pregnant Katy and Cynthia Rowley at the Arons' 2004 Christmas party at our Bank Street home.

Katy celebrating the sale of Kate Spade by hitting a piñata while in Cabo San Lucas, December 2006.

On our way to Grace Church School, circa 2010.

Our family in Bridgehampton, August 2008.
Sue Barr Photo

Surrounded by Little Katy and Big Katy on vacation in Napa, 2011.

Me, Chief Operating Officer Zonda Sochorow and Katy at the Frances Valentine office by Bryant Park, 2016.

Me and Katy inspecting Frances Valentine designs, 2016.
Allison Michael Orenstein/Getty Images

CHAPTER 19

Throughout 1997, we had a long string of lunches with investor types who wanted to buy into the company. We weren't interested in selling after barely five years in business but thought it worth hearing what they had to say. It was helpful to learn the basics of how an acquisition or merger would work. John Howard, the founder of Irving Place Capital, a major investor in the fashion sector, was a potential suitor. John impressed us as a very bright guy with a great sense of humor. When he came to our office on Twenty-Fifth Street to discuss his interest in buying a minority interest of Kate Spade, we sat on boxes because we didn't have enough chairs. I remember being embarrassed about it, but then I thought, *You know what? This is where we are. Our company is still small and independent, and that's an important part of our identity.* As we met with various investment groups, we mutually agreed that it didn't feel like the right time to sell. It was too early in our journey. We felt that we had more goals to achieve on our own.

With the success of the business, we were finally able to pay ourselves better salaries and invest in our personal lives. Katy and Andy bought a little house off North Main Street in Southampton and their first car, a zippy new Saab. I bought my first apartment across from the massive apartment complex London Terrace on West Twenty-Third Street in Chelsea, where there is a row of brownstones called the Fitzroy Townhouses. It was a third-floor, two-bedroom apartment with a south-facing terrace and two working fireplaces. It was the most beautiful place I had ever lived, the first large purchase of my adult life. And it was all mine.

Shortly after I moved to Chelsea, I met a guy through a mutual friend. Ben was a talented musician, and he worked writing jingles and musical scores for TV. He was an interesting person, I liked him a lot and I was hopeful that our relationship would grow into something more. Eventually, after a year of dating, he moved in with me.

Because of the proximity to our office and the cozy, crackling fireplace, my Chelsea apartment became the new salon for our gang. Katy, Andy and I were together all the time, not just at work, but after work, too. (Pamela joined when she could, but she now had two young children and needed to be home as much as possible after work.) Night after night, we usually went to my place to hang out. I ordered wine from the liquor store on the ground floor so often that they knew my voice on the phone. They'd say, "Hello, Cox. The usual?" Both the Spades and I were huge fans of California cabs and often we'd order a mixed case of Coppola, which was a great price, and Stags' Leap, which was our favorite. Our friends would bring over the vodka or tequila of their choice. We played great music and drank cocktails on my little terrace with the people who would pop by knowing we would be there. Ben didn't mix with our band all that much. I noticed that he'd often go into the bedroom and close the door, or when we were all squished onto the sofa together, he'd sit far away at the dining room table. Ben and Katy hardly ever spoke to each other. I never discussed it with her, hoping that over time she'd come around and start to warm up to him.

* * *

I always went home to the family farm in Kansas for Christmas. Traditionally, we gave each other modest gifts, but that year, now that I finally had some money to spend, I wanted to give my parents something special. Besides the tractor and other farming vehicles, my dad drove an ancient diesel-fueled Mercedes. It was maroon with tan leather seats and shiny wood paneling, really beautiful. Dad loved that car, which was why he still drove it despite the fact that it sputtered and choked as soon as the ignition turned over. It had more than two hundred thousand miles on it. Mom said the best gift to the family would be for Dad to stop driving that car. She was so worried something was going to happen.

On Christmas Eve, I went to the Volvo dealer in Wichita. I bought a station wagon on the spot, filled out the paperwork and got the insurance stuff settled. I drove it home to the farm at five that night, an hour and a half before our Christmas Eve party started and parked in the carport next to the house. It was partially hidden, so even if he'd casually looked out the window, he wouldn't have noticed it.

Once the party was underway, I said, "Dad, there's a surprise for you in the carport."

He went over to the window and saw the shiny new white Volvo.

"Merry Christmas, Dad."

He was astonished. When he recovered his ability to speak, he thanked me so sincerely that some of the people around us cried.

He was a stoic farmer born in the Depression. I know he had to try not to cry, too.

I would have given my parents whatever they needed without a backward glance. Since childhood, I dreamed of being able to pay off the farm debt so that my parents could relax. Their financial stress was always tied up with my sister Holiday's illness. My parents had spent everything on traveling to clinics around the country for her cancer treatment. Long after my sister's death, their pain and money anxiety lingered. I felt it my whole life. Now, I was in a position to help them, which in itself felt like the greatest gift I could ever receive.

* * *

While things at work were thriving, my personal life was less than wonderful. Ben and I were just not getting along—we had been together for only two years and we seemed to be on each other's bad side constantly. When Eleni and Randall asked me out to dinner in February 1998—and even though it was the fourteenth, I didn't know it was Valentine's Day. I never much cared about Hallmark holidays, and Ben wasn't big on flowers and chocolate. So of course I was free for a romantic dinner with my married friends at the Old Homestead—a steakhouse on West Fourteenth Street that specialized in Fred Flintstone–portioned porterhouses drenched in butter. All was served by slightly cranky waiters in ties with white aprons around their waists. Very old-school in a great way.

Eleni said, "Elyce, I've been thinking about talking to you about Ben for a long time. He's not very nice to you. He's rude to your friends. Have you thought about ending things with him?"

I was inching closer to agreeing with them. But I was avoiding that confrontation, it was easy to put off what with the challenge of keeping up with things at the office.

The very next day, on February 15, Katy, Andy, Pamela and I flew to Los Angeles for the opening of our new store in Beverly Hills, on South Robertson Boulevard. It was the first time that the four of us had all been on a trip together that was low-stress and just fun. We stayed at Shutters on the Beach in Santa Monica and lazed by the pool most of the day. Some of Katy's family came in from Arizona, and it was great to see all of them. We had the best few days, just like old times. Being with my friends and 2,500 miles away from Ben gave me the distance and perspective I needed. I told Katy that I was thinking about breaking up with him. She frowned, almost seeming disappointed in my decision.

"I thought you'd be happy," I said. "I know you don't like him."

"You're right about that," she admitted. "But I just don't want you to be alone."

I didn't want to be alone, either, but that was the issue. Be alone or stay in an unhappy relationship? I knew I wasn't the first person to face that choice. In the end I didn't want fear to guide my decision. Katy had been awfully silent about Ben, and I couldn't quite figure out why. She'd always provided her opinion freely about anyone new I brought into the group or dated. Why the silence now? Katy told me that she was conflicted about giving me the wrong advice. She was not a fan of Ben's, but she also did not want to hurt me by pointing out the fact that I was thirty-four and breaking up with yet another boyfriend. She really didn't want me to feel single again at an age when most people we knew were married.

After returning from California, I broke up with Ben. As I thought might happen, he made it messy by refusing to move out of the apartment right away. It was a New York real estate nightmare split.

For weeks, I asked him, "Did you find a place? When are you going?"

He perpetually delayed, always with some excuse. It was a difficult position for me to be in; I'd ended the relationship but really didn't want to further the pain by harping on him to get out. Fortunately I was able to escape on a business trip to Tokyo.

Our sales in Japan were growing and had turned into such a big operation that I had made five separate trips to Japan in 1998 alone. In the spring, Pamela, Andy, Katy and I went on one trip to Tokyo together with our architects from Rogers Marvel Architects to work on some Kate Spade store models. Being in Tokyo with the whole team was one of my favorite business trips ever. Our Japanese partners were excellent entertainers, as always. Every night, it was dinner and karaoke. They would do their Japanese songs and we would do our American songs. My go-to was Janis Joplin's "Me and Bobby McGee." Katy loved music, but she was too self-conscious to sing alone, so she joined in on group songs. Katy liked to sing the wrong words, or substitute in phrases she'd make up to some of our favorite songs—when "Bohemian Rapsody" by Queen was playing, instead of "gotta leave you all behind and face the truth" she would sing "gonna leave you all behind this faded room" loudly in my ear just to make me laugh. All in all, it was a good trip with fun friends and colleagues, and a lucrative partnership all around.

* * *

In April 1998, a month prior to that memorable trip, I had gone to a get-to-know-you dinner party on West Seventieth Street near Central Park. It was a kickoff dinner for the dozen or so people who'd be sharing a summer house in Bridgehampton on Scuttle Hole Road, next to the Channing Daughters Winery. I only knew two of the housemates—my friend Lee Ann, who brought me in as her roommate, and the dinner host, a guy named Andy Arons. A few years before, I had met Andy at an opening at our mutual artist friend Norm Magnuson's studio on Little West Twelfth Street. We talked for two hours, mainly about being business owners—he founded and co-owned Gourmet Garage, a specialty grocery store chain in Manhattan. Our paths crossed again when we opened our

Broome Street Kate Spade store. The SoHo location of Gourmet Garage was right across the street. He very generously offered to cater our grand opening party, and we accepted.

At this summer share dinner party, I wasn't thinking about meeting a new guy. Ben and I were in a miserable state of limbo, broken up but living together. Dating was the furthest thing from my mind. Besides which, Andy seemed almost too good to be true. He was a single, straight, thirty-nine-year-old, good-looking foodie with a great apartment. Like our previous meeting, we gravitated toward each other and talked for hours that night. I was one of the last people to leave. I didn't tell him anything about my personal life, but he knew from Lee Ann about Ben. What I remember most about that dinner party was not wanting to leave Andy's. And I got the feeling he would have liked me to stay, too.

Memorial Day was the first weekend at the house in Bridgehampton, and it was also when Ben finally said he was going to move out. I was thrilled not to be in town for that. I drove my butterscotch Volvo with Lee Ann to the Hamptons and arrived to find a full house of friends and soon-to-be friends. We rumbled down the long stone and dirt driveway, and as soon as I stepped out of the car, I was hit by the fragrance of freshly cut grass, blooming honeysuckles, salt water and hot sand. It all smelled like summer. The house was rustic, simple and beautiful. The acres around it were green and lush open fields set between the Channing vineyard and a horse farm. As we left for the beach, I saw my new housemates out by our pool kicking back, throwing Frisbees and drinking beer. It was a world away from the tension back home, and I soaked up the fun and sun for a blissful three days. I felt gratitude for being at this place in my life: young, single, financially independent and having a blast with my friends. It felt like college again, minus the penniless part.

Lee Ann and Andy Arons rode back to the city with me on

Monday night and came up to my place for a quick drink. I opened the door, and half the apartment had been cleared out. Even though I'd been anticipating it, the sudden starkness shocked me. I'd been begging Ben to go for months, but it felt strange now that he finally had.

But only for a few minutes. Slowly, I started to feel thrilled that I was now alone in my own apartment for the first time in nearly two years.

Until that moment, Andy thought I was still with Ben. If he was happy to learn that we'd broken up, he kept it to himself. I didn't know him well enough yet to read him. But I felt myself drawn to him increasingly as the summer wore on. If he missed a weekend at the house, it was like the music stopped playing. He made everything more fun. Andy and another housemate, Robert Lighton, would set up large canvas tents held up with mahogany posts on the property, all made by Robert's fine furniture company, British Khaki. Robert set the scene with teak and mahogany tables, and an abundance of candles inside the huge canvas tents. Andy supplied the fresh food from his store, the best of everything. All the housemates spent the afternoon and early evenings cooking together in the kitchen. It was like we were a new family, bound together by the long summer days and the breezy nights. We would dine together under the tents by candlelight along with all the people we had invited, sometimes numbering up to twenty or twenty-five.

At one of these tent parties, Andy asked me, "Can you pretend to be my girlfriend tonight? A group of people are coming and I think one of the women is being set up to meet me. Can you sit next to me and hold my hand a little so I look like I'm taken and off the market?"

I was happy to do so, but he told me later he just made that whole thing up, that little schemer. As much as I liked Andy, and looked forward to seeing him each weekend, I was reluctant to get involved with him. I thought I needed more time to recover from my last relationship and be alone for a while.

Sometime in June, Pamela, Katy, Andy Spade and I were all at Raoul's having a business dinner when Andy Arons walked in. It was coincidentally his favorite restaurant in New York for years as well as our gang's. He came over to our table and sat on the edge of a planter to chat with us for a bit. He was personable and easy to talk to, and he was sitting right next to Katy. Although I couldn't hear what they were saying, I could see that they were talking and making each other laugh. I felt a twinge of regret when he left to join his own group.

As soon as he was out of earshot, Katy said, "Oh my God, Elyce, you have to go out with him. He's great and he really likes you!" She didn't say a word about Ben for years, but after meeting Andy for five minutes, she was gushing. That was really important to me. I valued Katy's opinion and so wanted to be with someone Katy and Andy loved, too.

Andy Arons and I spent more time together out east at the beach house. We would sneak away from the rest of the gang and head to our favorite place, Gibson Beach with Andy's guitar and crack a bottle of rosé. We could talk for hours about dogs, horses, music, business and our families. We shared our early days of trying to make it in New York, which felt oddly similar. Mostly Andy made me laugh constantly. His quick mind was always one step ahead of me and he would smile waiting for me to finally get the punch line of a joke. The thing that I adored immediately was his love for animals. He had taken in many rescue pets over the years, cared for them and either found them a new home or kept them himself.

Several weeks later back in the city, Andy asked me out to dinner at Raoul's—I thought just as house buddies. He called me that day to confirm, and I said, "Okay, I'll meet you there at eight."

He replied, "Nope, I'll pick you up at seven thirty. This is a date."

"This is a date?" I said.

Eleni and Randall came over for a drink before I left for Raoul's and made sure I put on a nice outfit and not the sweater and jeans I'd worn to work. They liked Andy, as did everyone else.

Andy and I had a delicious and romantic dinner that night. One funny wrinkle was that one of us seemed to know every other person who walked through the door. We were sitting at a table near the entrance, and every ten minutes or so someone would come in, say hello or sit down at our table. It seemed really funny to me, but I could see Andy getting slightly perturbed. When our mutual friend Talmage entered and looked like he was about to join us for dinner, Andy said, "Talmage, buddy, we're on a date, can you move to the bar?"

Talmage was surprised, extremely gracious and moved right along. Andy asked the host, Raoul's manager, Eddie Hudson, to hustle along any other visitors who tried to invade our first date. We had a wonderful evening and ended up closing the restaurant. I got to sleep at three in the morning. A few days later, Andy started sending weekly cases of ripe, delicious fruit to my office, the most amazing nectarines and peaches I ever tasted, to share with the whole staff. He later told me that was his plan all along, to get the girls in the office to tell me how great he was.

Meanwhile at work, we began having high-level talks with Estée Lauder, the international beauty company, to launch a Kate Spade fragrance line. We had yet to meet with Leonard Lauder, the legendary New York socialite and philanthropist who, with his brother, Ronald, ran the business. The executive team was telling us that Leonard wanted to meet Katy, and she was slightly nervous about it. The invitation didn't seem to extend to the rest of us, but we had a good time teasing her about "meeting her new friend," which only served to make her even more anxious about the meeting.

That summer, Katy and Andy had rented out their tiny Southampton cottage and bought a modest but beautifully renovated farmhouse on Sagg Main Street near us in Bridgehampton. They purchased it from their interior designer friend Michael Bruno, a gifted decorator who would go on to found the successful e-commerce business 1stDibs. It was a beautiful home on a picturesque piece of property near the beach. Katy filled it with antiques that she and Andy handpicked from shops in the Hamptons and the city. Andy populated the walls with his eclectic art collection.

Often that summer, Andy Arons and I would spend days being lazy, picking up wine and stopping at the farmstand for cheese, bread and appetizers and picnicking with the Spades in the fields around their place. A number of huge old-growth trees surrounded the house. One late Saturday night after a long dinner, the four of us were sitting outside under a big oak by the side of their house. Katy was scheduled to meet Leonard Lauder early Monday morning. It was such a big deal for her. Leonard was a legend in our industry and a New York City business icon. She was excited for the meeting, but the prospect of having to do it solo was freaking her out a bit. We were having a fabulous time, and Katy started to tell us about her tree-climbing expertise as a kid. Andy Arons dared her to climb the big oak next to us. Although it was huge, it had plenty of branches and a swing hung on it that she could step on to pull herself up. To her credit, Katy jumped right up, stepped on the swing, and scrambled up that oak pretty high. We were applauding and impressed until, on her way down, she bumped into the swing, and knocked a crown off one of her incisors. It didn't hurt, but the look wasn't great.

"How bad is it?" She looked at us with a weak smile.

"Uh, not so good," said Andy Spade.

"Oh no! I have the Leonard meeting the day after tomorrow. I can't cancel, I can't go like this!" she said.

"Well, technically that meeting is tomorrow," I said. "It's one in the morning, so it's already Sunday." I was not being helpful.

"I'm so sorry," said Andy Arons. "It's my fault for daring you. Wait! Let's find that crown. We can get dental adhesive glue at the drugstore in the morning and glue it back on!"

"You can do that?" asked Katy.

"Yes, I'm pretty sure you can," said Andy. "And we're going to find that crown right now. Get some flashlights."

We all looked and looked for an hour. It was as impossible as you would think to find a tiny piece of porcelain tooth on a grassy sandy hill. By 2:00 a.m. we were ready to throw in the towel.

"We're not going to find it," said Katy. "What if I just go to the meeting with Leonard and explain the situation? Maybe he'll think I'm a really scrappy, down-to-earth, tough businessperson."

"Let me see," I said. "Smile."

I saw that pretty face and her sweet smile, but she was basically missing a front tooth. Seriously not good.

"No," I said. "You definitely can't do that."

She was flustered. "Okay, I'm not going to panic. I'm going to get up early and find that damn crown!"

And don't you know she actually did that? The next morning she found the crown somehow, and then called her dentist at home who agreed to meet at his office at seven Monday morning. He was able to give her a brand-new temporary crown on the spot, and she made it to Leonard Lauder's office by eight thirty. I was on my way to Japan that day, so I never heard all the details of the meeting, but within a month we were at the Estée Lauder research and development office testing a thousand different notes (essences) for our new Kate Spade fragrance, which we would launch that following spring. When I returned home from Japan, Katy couldn't wait to show me her shiny new tooth and the smile that charmed the beauty billionaire.

CHAPTER 20

We were manufacturing thousands of bags per month in 1998. Inevitably, some would be slightly imperfect—a stitch would be out of place, the lining wasn't the right shade, or the label wasn't centered. The bags were still usable, but if they had any defect—even imperfections that only we would notice—we would not ship them in stores.

But we would sell them steeply discounted at sample sales. If a flawless bag cost $250 at Barneys, we'd price a defective one for $125 directly to consumers. In New York in the late nineties, designer sample sales were for fashion insiders and magazine editors who were plugged into a somewhat secretive pipeline. You couldn't Google "Prada sample sale" to get the date and location. You had to be in the know and on the list.

Even for seasoned insiders, the prospect of buying designer goods for a fraction of the retail cost turned people into maniacs. Some sample sales were like feeding frenzies. Shoppers fought over garments and hoarded piles of dresses they hadn't even tried on (dressing rooms were rarely available). More often than not, you'd wind up dropping a ton on clothes that didn't fit, flatter or match your personal style.

Having engaged in those battles personally many times, we tried to make the Kate Spade sample sales easy, enjoyable and civilized. You know at a glance if a handbag is right for you, or your mom, sisters, friends or your kids' teachers. You didn't have to worry about sizing. The same thing with stationery, wallets and Filofax covers, which we also sold at our sales. At first, we held those events at our office, but they became untenable. People would line up around the block.

We decided to move the operation to a large venue. Our first giant sample sale was at the Metropolitan Pavilion, a 25,000-square-foot space with beautiful oak floors and sixteen-foot ceilings with retractable walls so you could alter the size of the room. It was a relatively easy setup, and customers lined up around the block there just as they had at our office. Literally thousands of women came because we'd made the process pleasant and inclusive. If someone called to ask about our sample sales, we put them on our mailing list. For years, that list was handwritten and added to by all of us. James, our IT genius, turned it into a database in the early 2000s.

En masse, our sales and accounting departments trooped over to the Pavilion to help out. The salespeople fanned out to work with customers, and the accounting people set up checkout credit card and cash stations. Rodney hired a private company to handle security. We also used gold and silver Sharpies to mark each bag with an S inside the interior pocket. The customer would never even notice it. But if anyone tried to return the bag to one of our retailers, the cashiers knew to check the pocket for that telltale S, meaning "sample."

Though Katy never liked spending any time at the sales (the imperfections going out on the bags were really distressing to her), Pamela, Willow and I spent all day at the Pavilion overseeing the operation. Rodney Bell and Reepal Shah, our controller, came to oversee the accounting crew. Other staffers from the warehouse, production and product development teams took shifts. It was an all-hands-on-deck situation.

If we ran out of product, I'd call the office and say, "Send more boxes."

A guy with a cart would show up twenty minutes later.

If two women fought over a bag, I'd say, "Let me see if I can go find another one of those for you."

Our sales weren't wild stampedes, but they were wildly busy. By the end of the day, our legs were just shot. My back ached, but I didn't care. Those sales were amazing. We were able to interact with our customers directly, and everyone said, "I adore your stuff," and "You guys are so nice." We would see the appreciation of our products firsthand, which was so gratifying.

After those three intense sample sale days, Pamela and I would usually leave the load-out responsibilities to our staffers and reward ourselves with a great dinner somewhere. On one of those nights we swung by the office, picked up Katy then headed downtown to Ecco, Katy's neighborhood Italian place on Chambers Street. The warm ambience, red banquettes, tin ceiling and old-fashioned Italian fare were just what we needed. I remember it being a fun dinner despite Katy purposefully irking the two of us a bit. Pamela and I always gave her a hall pass on working those sample sales; we understood being around all those imperfect bags made her really unhappy. In Katy's world, she would have rather tossed them all than sold them at a discount.

That night, out of guilt, Katy was teasing us about her not helping at all with that multi-day effort. She would say, "Well good thing I was back at the office to hold down the fort." Or "Well, the brains of the operation needs to stay behind to run things." That sort of kidding. Funny, yes, but Pamela and I were so bone weary we weren't really in the mood. Towards the end of the meal, Pamela and Katy left together to use the lady's room. It seemed like the perfect opportunity for a little fun at Katy's expense.

I walked back to the restrooms and caught Pamela on her way out. "Hiya," I said.

"Hey, you!" she replied, smiling as she walked past me.

I walked into the ladies' room and Katy was still in one of the two stalls. I gingerly grabbed the top of one of the stalls and shook it.

"Hey, no, no, no, I'm in here!" she said.

"Yes, yes, yes!" I replied, shaking the flimsy antique stall door hard again. I lowered my tone and put some Queens in the accent to disguise my voice.

"No, no, no!" she cried.

"Yes, yes, yes!" I said again. I rattled the door even harder a second time.

I went a little overboard on the shaking, and the old latch holding the door closed gave way and it swung open. I was about to say something jokey until I realized that it wasn't Katy sitting inside the stall. A middle-aged woman was glaring at me with her handbag clutched to her chest trying to cover herself up. Her face looked fearful, like a *what kind of nut is this*–type of expression.

I was staring at her for a frozen second and all I could think to say was, "I thought you were my friend!" That made it even weirder. She yelled back at me, "But I don't even know you!"

I could do nothing but say I was so sorry, turn tail and run away. I got back to our table, and there was Pamela sitting with Katy, who somehow already made it back there. Luckily they were paying the check. I met them outside and dragged them up the avenue towards Katy's loft. When I told them what happened, they had to stop and lean on a building while they both convulsed with laughter. I was pushing us along, sure that the poor woman would have called the police by now. I made sure to steer clear of Ecco for a while after that.

* * *

On the wholesale side of the business, increasingly large orders flowed in from Neiman Marcus, Saks, Nordstrom and Bloomingdale's. We had to add manufacturers and shift some of our manufacturing to additional production facilities. During that growth period, our longtime corporate attorney and confidant Ken Cera had been working on a project with the legacy luxury retailer Neiman Marcus. That spring, Ken let us know that the Neiman Marcus executive team would like to meet with us to discuss a possible partnership. We were extremely interested in what they had to say. They were a great customer, and the company had a sterling reputation. We had numerous meetings with them to get to know each other and eventually started discussing various ways our small company could work together with them.

By the fall of 1998, things were really heating up with Neiman Marcus. The corporate executives came down for a series of visits. They were interested in putting together a group of five or six fashion and beauty brands (cosmetics brand Laura Mercier had already signed on) that were doing well at Neiman Marcus stores. They saw our growth and our potential, and they wanted us to be their second acquisition.

One of our meetings with the Neiman Marcus owners and execs was on the top floor of Bergdorf Goodman. We were in the middle of a very serious discussion about the future of Kate Spade. Someone brought up the recent purchase of a competitor—a massive investment for the financial firm that bought in—and Katy said, "Why would anybody want to shoot their whole wad on that?"

The entire room got quiet. The execs looked down at the table. Katy glanced around. "What?!" she asked.

Technically, you can say that phrase in a business discussion and everyone will know what you're talking about. In this case, it was a slightly out-of-context remark that hung in the air as our team was trying not to crack up at the double entendre. Pamela and I looked at each other with *Holy shit* expressions. We were dying inside and could not wait to get out of that room. The second we did, we explained to Katy that "shoot their wad" had sexual connotations. In the car back to the office, she was mortified, but we cried laughing the whole way. For a while, that story became part of our everyday teasing of Katy.

In the past, we'd rebuffed all previous partnership inquiries, but our thinking started to shift when Neiman Marcus entered the picture. We thought we could really grow with them. They already knew our business and understood the brand. We could open more retail stores with them as partners, and it wasn't just an investment for them, it was part of a strategy. As far as I was concerned, Neiman Marcus was the best department store in the world, and they had no intention of limiting our sales to just their stores. The chairman and executive team of the company were all professional, polite and conservative but excited about the path of partnering with smaller brands.

Unlike Katy, Andy and me, Pamela did not want to sell any part of the company. She thought we could grow the business on our own. She took each of us aside to give us her point of view on the benefits of staying independent. The tagline of her pitch was, "Once you sell the majority, you're not in control anymore." She was absolutely right about that. We tried not to sell the majority, but that was a nonstarter with Neimans. They insisted on buying 56 percent. We were already far down the road, making plans for that influx and feeling good about the partnership. Pamela had to go along in the end.

* * *

On the home front, Andy Arons was busy rolling out the red carpet for me. Several times per week we would go out to fancy dinners. Prior to his starting the Gourmet Garage stores, Andy had come to New York City directly from undergrad at UMass Amherst with his roommate Walter Martin. In the early eighties, they started an importing and distribution company called Flying Foods to fly in and sell fresh European products like Dover sole, caviar, truffles and radicchio lettuce, and sell them to restaurant chefs in the city. They opened offices in other cities, and eventually sold the company to Kraft Foods in the late eighties. Andy kept in touch with all the chef customers who had become mentors and friends—André Soltner from Lutèce, Daniel Boulud from Restaurant Daniel, Sirio Maccioni of Le Cirque and many others had helped him get started, and he remained close with them.

I stepped into that world, and it was amazing. When we dined at one of their restaurants, the owner or chef would always send out extra courses and little treats to our table that didn't show up on the bill. I wasn't used to eating all that rich food, but it was mind-blowingly delicious. We invited Katy and Andy most nights, and always had incredible dinners and a great time. I was glad Andy Arons got on so well with my dear friends. It was the thing I had been waiting for a long time.

The four of us went to the opening week of BondSt, an upscale sushi and Japanese-inspired restaurant on Bond and Broadway in the up-and-coming Nolita section of Manhattan. The food was extraordinary and really creative. Andy A. was buddies with the owner, Jonathan Morr, who sent out lots of little extras. As we were heading out, we all approached an adjacent table. Andy S. knew one of the four people dining there. We made some friendly talk, when I realized I knew one of the guys at the table. He was eating, but I had to say hello.

"Hey, how are you?" I said. He had a mouthful of food and politely smiled and nodded like a *I'm good, thank you* sign.

"I'm sorry, I just can't place you. Are you from Kansas?" I babbled. I knew him, but it seemed like we had not seen each other in a long time.

He was still eating, but he just shook his head a little at me.

"C'mon, we have to figure this out. It's going to really bug me," I persisted.

I felt Katy claw at my back, dragging me away. We said our goodbyes. I said to her, "Hey, that's a little rude, Katy." I thought she was just in a hurry to go.

"You don't know that guy, you kook. That's Gabriel Byrne, the actor."

"Oh dammit. I have to stop doing that, or at least learn to give up when they say they don't know me," I said as we walked home together up bustling Broadway.

"You're just a kook, face it," Katy said.

"No, you are! You're the kook" was my not-clever reply.

It went on like that for a while on the stroll back to my place. It was a truly silly exchange, but for whatever reason, for years after that, we often called each other "Kook" in general conversation. As in *Hey, Kook, what are you doing tonight?* I don't know why, it just stuck.

* * *

While we were in talks with Neimans, we opened our first Boston store, right on Newbury Street, a space in a beautiful old building we rented from the Junior League. I flew into Boston from another business trip, and Andy A. met me there. We'd been dating for four months and had been apart for only a few days, but those few days of being apart felt like forever. We were staying at the Ritz-Carlton in Boston's Back Bay area.

That night, when we were cozying up by the fireplace in the beautiful oak paneled bar with some cocktails, I said to him, "Let's not see anyone else."

He looked at me and smiled. "I haven't been seeing anyone else for a long time."

"I haven't been, either."

"That sounds good to me," he said. "I didn't want to push you at all with you just getting out of another relationship."

I met Andy's family on that trip, too. He'd grown up outside of Boston, and his parents; his older brother, Jim; and Jim's wife, Martha, came to town to get a look at his new girlfriend. Andy's brother was a terrific, kind guy, the chief of cardiology at Tufts Medical Center. We hit it off right away. I liked them all very much, and I guess I got the seal of approval. I was really happy.

* * *

Our Kate Spade holiday party that year was at the Russian Tea Room, the legendary tsarist restaurant that had a giant bear-shaped aquarium in the center of the dining room. We invited our manufacturing partners, our UPS delivery guys and anyone with whom we worked on a daily basis.

Our head of product development, Zonda Sochorow, after seeing the beautiful over-the-top restaurant decked out in its Christmas best, said, "I love our company. I'm never leaving!"

I smiled and thought, *Me too.*

Side note: The Icelandic singer Björk came to that party! A design team called As Four had done some work with us and become good friends. They were a wacky, cutting-edge foursome who lived together, created together, and were an avant-garde team in the fashion world. What was most surprising to me at the time was that for all their eccentricities they were such disarmingly *nice* people. They had done a lot of design work and become friends with Björk and brought her along to the party. Of course, we had to quiz her about her famous swan dress she wore to the Oscars. I'm sure everyone asked about that back then, but she was a good sport and happy to answer Katy's and my questions.

* * *

That gave me plenty to talk about when I flew out to Kansas a few weeks later. Just as doors were opening for me with my new relationship and the possibility of the Neiman Marcus sale, they were opening for my parents, too.

After forty years of hard work, with no one to take over from the next generation, my parents were selling their farm and moving east to be closer to Willow and me in New York. The house and farm had been in my family for four generations. Along with the property, they were auctioning off pretty much everything they owned. The land was being sold to our neighbors, who had been farming their own land nearly as long as my family had, and it felt good to keep it among local farmers. I think mostly my parents were ecstatic to be moving on with their lives and starting a new chapter. Shon, Willow and I went home to help. I got up at six in the morning to begin packing things up and got looks of disdain from everyone in my family because they had been at it since four.

"About time you got up," said Dad, smiling.

The job took us all working nonstop from predawn to dusk. We found jars of canned peaches from the 1930s in the basement cold cellar. We sorted everything into categories: stuff someone in our family wanted to take; items to be auctioned; things Mom and Dad wanted to keep; junk. I kept a couple of things, mostly family photographs of my grandmother with her first car, other family shots with all four sisters together, and photos of my older sister Holiday. I especially cherish the pictures where we are lined up together, all four of us dressed in the same outfits my mother had designed and sewn. I loved the ones with my sister with her thick black hair, hugging a dog or steer before she got sick. With time, her image had started to blur in my mind; I wanted as many photos of her as I could get.

After the auction, we threw a big party, inviting our extended family, all of our friends and our neighbors from Sedgwick. We had a band, and everybody got up and sang songs, kind of like karaoke with dancing.

I expected to be emotional about saying goodbye to my childhood home. I was prepared to cry. But seeing the joy on my parents' faces made it all okay. The entire time they were singing and dancing, exuberant to be free of the burden of the farm. I don't know if I'd ever seen them so happy. The farm was our last strong connection to Holiday. She had been so attentive to me and taught me much when I was little. My memory of her beautiful smiling face when she was patiently teaching me to ride a horse when I was four, will be with me forever. I realized then that I didn't need a physical place to remember my big sister. Her permanent place would always be in my heart. I knew she'd be happy to see how each one of us was starting a new chapter of our own.

CHAPTER 21

The year 1999 was a time of mergers and acquisitions, both personally and professionally. Like most part-nerships, they all started out with best of intentions, with some working out wonderfully, and others not so much.

We had been working with Neimans on the due diligence for their purchase of over half the business. It took months of work on the part of lawyers, financial advisers and accountants, but we were getting close to the finish line by the end of 1998.

We thought we would get the deal closed before Christmas, but there were snags. A big part of the holdup was the legal language around the use of Katy's name. There is an inherent complexity to the process when the name of the company is the same as the name of one of the principals. Our lawyers had to work hard to get it right, but Katy wasn't present to sign off on it during those final days. The delay had cut into a vacation that she and Andy had been planning for months. They were at the Hotel Twin Dolphin in Cabo San Lucas that didn't have any telephones in the room, and those earlier cell phones did not work in areas of Mexico. The only way to reach them was the fax machine the resort used for reservations. I just kept faxing every modification in the legal language. Katy would call from the rickety front desk and try to talk to us, but the lines were full of static. It wasn't optimal, but we finally got it done, and closed on February 4, 1999. We sold 56 percent of the company to Neiman Marcus.

That same day, Pamela and I called the staff into our largest showroom and announced what was happening. We wanted to inform them before the newspapers covered it, and we had only a small window of time. Most of the staff already knew about the potential sale because our meetings with Neimans had been going on for months, and each department had to help prepare information for them. The team was excited by our new partnership and the bright future ahead and had a lot of questions, though, like any change, there seemed to be an element of concern in many of our colleagues' minds. The fact that we were all staying on board with them did a lot to assuage their worries.

After months of negotiating and very long days meeting with our attorneys for several weeks, I was relieved, exhausted and exuberant all at once. I asked a bunch of friends over to my apartment that Friday night, fireplace roaring, and much wine was consumed celebrating the deal being finally closed. I was sad that Katy and Andy were not there to enjoy this moment with Pamela and me. The Spades called as soon as they returned home from their Mexico trip. Like Pamela and I, they felt relieved the deal had closed and were excited to begin a fresh chapter with a new partner.

People asked, "Why sell?" Running the company and keeping it growing had been exhilarating and all-consuming for us, and we had worked hard. The next phase of our business expansion would benefit from a great strategic partnership. We felt that working with a legacy retailer with their expertise in running stores coupled with their financial investment was a good fit. The partners split the purchase price according to our share of the business. Katy and Andy received 30 percent each; Pamela and I, 20 percent each, per our original agreement. The price that Neimans paid for their portion of the company was substantial. The new structure also removed all the risk that we had signed on to. One big example was when Neimans became the majority owner, it took all our personal signatures off every lease.

Katy, Andy and I had all grown up under financial strain. I didn't fully realize how much my sister's cancer diagnosis and treatment cost the family while it was happening, and it wasn't until years later that I began to understand how my parents shielded me from their money anxiety and our debt. I only clued in when I had to apply for student loans for college, unlike many of my high school classmates. Katy had undergone a similar downturn. After her parents split, life was harder. We both had experienced a loss of lifestyle and were always so careful as businesspeople about limiting our debt. With the sale, we now had a sense of security and we could really focus on taking the business to the next level.

How did we adjust to our newfound financial freedom? Happily. The windfall from the sale was life-changing for all of us personally and professionally. Everyone who has ever sweated looking at a pile of bills at the end of the month knowing that you were spending more than you were making knows that feeling of creeping dread. To have that lifelong stressor suddenly removed was like a dream come true.

* * *

During off-work hours, while I was circulating in the foodie scene with Andy Arons, Katy and Andy Spade were getting more involved in the New York art world. They started going to a bunch of black-tie galas at museums. One of these events was held at the Whitney Museum while it was still in its prior location uptown. Katy left a breathless message on my answering machine saying the most embarrassing thing happened. The next morning at the office, she recounted the story.

She and Andy were seated at a table next to the famous large-scale portrait artist Chuck Close and his wife, Leslie Rose. About ten years prior, Chuck had a seizure that left him paralyzed and a wheelchair user. He bravely developed a system to keep painting despite his disability, in which brushes were strapped to his wrists. The tablemates chatted for a while and got along well.

Leslie Rose then said to Katy, "No matter what, don't let Chuck smoke." Apparently, Chuck was no longer allowed to smoke for medical reasons, but he was always on the lookout for a sympathetic fellow smoker to give him a cigarette or a few drags of their lit one. He was a giant in the art world; I'm sure it was hard to say no to him about anything.

As she'd been warned he would, Chuck whispered to Katy during dinner, "Can you please just give me a cigarette?" She was torn. Should she listen to his wife or give in to the artist?

"He looked so desperate for a smoke and he kept asking! I held off for a long time, and then I just caved," she told me the morning after. "I lit one and let him have a puff, and you wouldn't believe what happened next."

Uh-oh, I thought.

"As Chuck was inhaling," said Katy, "the red-hot tip of the cigarette broke off and landed on his thigh. I had to pat it out without making a scene. Smoke was drifting off from his pants as I slapped at it. His wife looked over at me like I was crazy, patting her husband's leg, until she figured out what happened. I think she was furious with me for giving him a lit cigarette."

"Oh no," I said. "You really should have listened to his wife."

"Really? What would you have done?"

"I have no idea," I said.

"You would have given him a whole cigarette!" she said.

That was true. I was a soft touch. It would have been worse.

Around this time, Andy Spade made his first short film, *Paperboys*. The director was Mike Mills, a friend of Andy's. The forty-minute documentary was about the shift of a classic American first job—being a paperboy—from teens to adults. The movie was shot in Minnesota. Mike Mills went into three or four of the boys' homes and talked to them and their parents about their paper routes. It was really a poignant Americana piece, looking back nostalgically at an aspect of boyhood that no longer exists. Andy was very proud of the film, and it got great accolades at the time. He would go on to make more short films, but this one marked the beginning of his broadening interest in other mediums.

Andy had a concept that he could distill those nascent memories and the nostalgic longing that American men had by creating a men's line of products that related to the Kate Spade ethos. He called the brand Jack Spade, not wanting to use his own name in the way that Katy's had evolved but liking the Spade connection and the sound of "Jack," which also was the name of his favorite uncle. Andy had the idea to sell the bags to a hardware store in SoHo. They were a huge hit with workmen and the hip downtown set alike. Soon after we launched the Jack Spade brand with messenger bags, masculine totes, and dopp kits to men's wholesale accounts like the boutique Ad Hoc in SoHo, Barneys, and to Apple stores (we were the first non-Apple item for sale in those stores) in 1998. They were designed by Andy and his four-man Jack Spade design team, with the thread of functional style. He hit a home run with his version of men's canvas and wax-wear messenger bags. Pamela worked closely with

Andy to develop all the products and spent the majority of her time during that period helping launch the new addition to the Kate Spade family. The bags were stylish yet masculine and ultra-durable and shortly developed a cult following across the US. The first Jack Spade store opened in autumn 1999 and was just around the corner from the Kate Spade location in SoHo. While in one sense, the Jack Spade venues were homages to male Americana, everything in the store had a style that spoke to quality, individuality and simplicity. Clothes and accessories were the kind of stuff a top architect, a law professor or a film student would wear. They brought other legacy brands into the store like Mackintosh raincoats and Seavees boat shoes to expand on the scope of the Jack Spade items they designed.

The build-out and the decor of the Jack Spade store was also unique. There were tall oak-paneled wall cabinets with hundreds of tiny drawers among the displays for the customers to explore. You might open a drawer in a cabinet and find a Slinky or a Wham-O Superball with its swirly colored design. A battalion of little green army guys stormed a shelf. Vintage motorcycle helmets from the 1960s perched on an adjacent table. Something in Andy's psychological makeup pulled him toward this era of his life. He challenged himself to re-create that sense of adventure and wonder, a style reminiscent of a childhood in the heartland but with a hefty slice of downtown New York City sensibility blended in.

* * *

My non-handbag focus at the time was Andy Arons. We'd been together for nearly a year, had met each other's families and friends, and were a committed couple. My friends got him. They respected what he did and his taste level, and the feeling was mutual. We would work the rounds of our favorite restaurants and bars—Indochine, Nobu, Balthazar, MercBar and many more. We socialized with big groups or small ones, but at the end of the night, I always went home with my Andy. My friendship with Katy was my foundation, but I was building a new life with Andy on top of that base.

For my thirty-fifth birthday, Andy offered to host a big dinner party at his apartment on the Upper West Side the night before I left for a ten-day business trip to Japan with Katy and Andy Spade. He was going to handle it all: the invites, the menu and the food. I arrived at his apartment about an hour or two before the guests to help him set things up, and Andy asked if I'd like a glass of champagne. It was a bit early for me, so I passed, but he got a glass of Scotch for himself. He left the room to prepare his drink and came back with an unusually big goblet of Scotch and wearing a different shirt.

What's all this? I thought.

I asked, "Why'd you change?"

He said, "This is my lucky shirt."

O-kay. Why is he so nervous? It's just a party.

"I wanted to wish you a happy birthday. I'm so glad you're here spending it with me," he said.

"Well, I'm so glad to be here spending it with you. Ah . . . why would I be anywhere else?"

Before I could figure out what was going on, Andy dropped to one knee in front of me and said, "Elyce, I want to spend all your birthdays with you. I want us to be together for the rest of our lives." He held up a ring box and opened it up. I found out later that months before, Katy had helped him select the gleaming diamond ring in front of me, though the timing of the proposal would still be a mystery to her. It's a sparkling classic round Tiffany style–cut engagement ring, and I instantly loved it. Katy was a great keeper of secrets, but I'm sure she was bursting to tell me a hundred times.

I sat there really surprised. Stunned, I would say.

"Well, are you going to answer?" he asked.

"You didn't ask *the question*." I'd been waiting a long time to hear it.

He smiled and said, "Oh, right! Will you marry me?"

I said, "Yes, of course I will!"

We called our families first, and they were thrilled. Our closest friends were on their way over to Andy's place at that very moment. I said, "It'd be kind of fun to surprise them with the news."

We concocted a plan. I turned the ring around so only the band was visible on my finger. We had cocktails and an amazing dinner. Andy had flown some fresh Alaskan spot prawns in for the event (one of the many perks of dating a gourmet grocer!). Toward the end of the meal, we did a semiregular ritual of going around the table and talking about the people there, and what the speaker found so special about any one person. We had a variety of after-dinner conversation kickers that we had developed over many dinner parties. Although this sounds kind of corny, it always degenerated immediately into hilarity and a merciless heckling roast of sorts.

When it was Andy Arons's turn, he stood up and said, "It's been a long time since I've had a real home. I loved the feeling of being home when I was a kid. I want to say, 'Happy birthday' to Elyce because being with her has always given me that feeling of home."

Everyone said, "Aww."

Andy held up his glass for a toast. "And one more thing," he added, "I'm happy to tell all of you, the people who we care about the most, that earlier tonight, Elyce agreed to marry me and be my wife."

I turned the band on my finger around and held my hand up with that shiny rock for all to see. There was a brief stunned silence while our guests tried to evaluate if this was a prank or not, then suddenly the table erupted with cheers. No one was more excited than Katy. I was more interested to see her reaction than anyone's. We had talked about this moment nearly our entire lives. She sat there with her mouth open and eyes wide, clapping and cheering with everyone, and discreetly wiped the tears from her eyes. Though she knew the proposal was in the works, her joy in seeing me finally finding the right person was a really emotional moment for both of us.

The very next morning, Katy, Andy Spade and I flew to Tokyo to meet with our Japanese partners. My airplane seat was a couple of rows back from theirs. The poor Japanese businessman who sat next to me had to listen to me talk about my engagement the entire trip. I showed him my ring at least ten times. He smiled and nodded politely (though I'm not sure if he understood a word of what I was saying). I was that annoying girl, but I couldn't stop beaming. I was so happy.

We spent five days in meetings, and then, to my delight, Andy Arons arrived in Tokyo to join us for the second half of the trip. We made a quick stop in Kobe to open a new store and have some of the famous beef, and then on to Kyoto for another opening. The four of us spent three days at Tawaraya, a Kyoto ryokan (a traditional Japanese inn) that dated back to 1709. It was like living in a Kurosawa film, with all the otherworldliness of those historical locations. We wore robes and sandals, ate multicourse kaiseki dinners, got shiatsu massages together on futons and had huge Japanese breakfasts. I was giddy the entire time, grinning ear to ear, enraptured with my fiancé, and overjoyed that my dearest friends liked him so much.

When the four of us weren't luxuriating at the ryokan, we wandered Kyoto at night, paper lantern light bouncing off the shiny black cobblestone streets and red teahouse doors, a magical cinematic experience. It's a very romantic city, and certainly that was my mood. We walked those streets of Kyoto, and Katy would disappear for a few minutes into various Japanese stores that interested her. There were tiny vintage collectible shops where she found miniature figurines of Japanese objects, as well as antique brightly painted small bowls and sake cups all in startling, lacquered colors. The figurines, we came to learn, were carved ivory objects called netsuke. They were used as decorative attachments to kimonos and could be centuries old. She bought a bunch of these types of pieces, attracted to their uniqueness and gorgeous colors.

From there, as planned, Andy Arons and I flew to Bali for nine days. We stayed for a few days at each of the three Aman Resort locations on the island: one by the beach, one in the mountains and one in the jungle. Every day, I pinched myself. The fact alone that I was able to have these experiences was incredible to me. The most astonishing thing was that now I had a life partner to share them with. Being newly engaged on that trip had me asking, *Do I deserve this?* I had often asked myself that question, but this time, I didn't have to convince myself that I'd earned my happiness. I felt at peace and hopeful for our future.

While lying in our hotel room in the jungle, looking out of the floor-to-ceiling window into lush greenery and a waterfall, Andy and I decided to have the wedding in September, our mutual favorite month. Andy said, "Let's do it at Channing Daughters Winery," right next to the beach house we'd shared the summer before.

We had to move quickly. Planning a big wedding the right way could take a year or more, and we had less than six months. It would be a challenge, but I was all in. Katy and Andy's wedding had been small and special with close friends, but we were all broke then. That was no longer the case. I could spend as much as I wanted on my wedding, and I decided to go for it. Traditionally, the bride's family paid. But I was going to cover it myself, not my parents, not Andy or his parents. It meant so much to me to be able to do this for us. No one but me would ever see a bill. I know Andy had in mind a small, intimate ceremony with our closest friends and family present. I let him cling to that false dream for a few weeks until we returned home.

CHAPTER 22

In some ways our lives had become far less stressful. Our new situation with the company, however, created an entirely different set of challenges. I came back from that fantasy trip to Bali to the reality of working with a corporate partner. Before the sale, we were four partners who made this crazy thing work, created a nurturing culture for our employees and had a great time doing it, all on our own terms. Now we were being encouraged by the board at Neimans to bring in a veteran industry insider as president to help us continue to grow. We'd tried that in the past for short periods of time, with no luck finding a fashion industry pro who fit into our culture. This time, we intended to find someone roughly our age we could relate to. The four of us interviewed a long line of candidates but we couldn't agree on anyone. After months of searching, we finally hired a person whom I'll call Janet

McDonald, a former high-ranking executive at several major fashion companies.

Janet spoke our language in board meetings with Neimans. We were confident enough to leave the brass tacks business stuff to her while we handled the culture, strategic planning, design and creative. Within weeks, she brought in a fantastic controller who became our CFO, and a bunch of senior executives, VPs of retail, licensing, and international sales. We approved, and we liked all of these people. They appreciated how we'd built the business to get to where it was.

But at the same time, the company started to feel less focused. We were called to attend senior-level meetings that would last for hours. Katy called them "butt burners" (and she would always skip them). Our feeling was that any one of us could have achieved more in a morning than the room full of people did after hours of discussion. We understood the need for the team to be informed, but our style was very different. Those meetings were one of the first indications of the chasm that would eventually grow between our entrepreneurial culture and the new more corporate model. Pamela and I sat through them and shared anything necessary with Katy and Andy, who now focused solely on design and marketing. This freedom did separate them from the nuts and bolts of running the company. I was fine with all the rapid changes, but when without our prior knowledge Janet brought in a VP of production, that tread on Pamela's turf. Pamela was not thrilled about that and neither was I.

About two months into Janet's tenure, we had an off-site strategy meeting on Nantucket. Pamela, Katy, Andy and I stayed up late one night, sitting on Adirondack chairs on a patio, gazing at the sea, drinking wine and talking. In that setting, Pamela and I felt it important to discuss with Katy and Andy that we'd noticed some red flags about Janet. We both worked more closely with her than they did, and we thought she was often overextending her authority. We both noticed that she'd been dismissive of and unkind to some of our longtime employees. Little did we know that our circle of chairs was right under Janet's room, and her windows were open. Unfortunately, she'd probably overheard every word we said.

Janet never let on, but I did notice that our interactions became five degrees chillier after that weekend. I chalked it up to predictable tension during a transitional period. I had high hopes that we'd all work together well and that one day soon, Janet would be sitting with us in a tight circle of Adirondack chairs.

As it turned out, that was wishful thinking.

* * *

At home, I was working hard on another important milestone: my wedding. My first appointment after we got back from Bali was at Vera Wang, as I was an avid fan of her fabulous wedding dresses. I was able to get an appointment at the designer's showroom so fast because we had a friend who worked for the brand. I rarely used my fashion world connections for personal reasons, but this time, it really helped. Katy went with me to the boutique. I was looking for something simple and slender, no frills, nothing poofy. I only had time to try on three dresses that day and fell half in love with all of them. I went back with my mom and my sister Shon when they came to New York for a visit and modeled a few more. In the end, I bought the first dress I tried on, a slim strapless gown with a dark green velvet ribbon around the waist and a bow in front. Katy agreed with my choice, saying, "It's perfect. Simple but sophisticated." Her approval meant so much, and I knew that if she didn't like it, she would have told me.

After hosting half a dozen engagement parties between us in the last decade, it was now our turn to be feted by our friends. Lee Ann and Frank and Eleni and Randall threw parties for us at their homes.

Katy was dying to plan one for us, but given her schedule and all the celebrations we had in the works, I convinced her not to. Andy's summer housemate Robert Lighton hosted us at his British Khaki store and at his Upper East Side apartment. Pamela threw a huge sit-down dinner for us at her loft in SoHo. At one of these gatherings, Andy A. and I, Katy, Andy Spade, Marybeth and Rob (her boyfriend at the time) were talking about honeymoon destinations. Capri was at the top of our list because we'd never been there before.

Katy said, "Wouldn't it be fun if we all met you there after a few days? Why don't we all go?"

Although it was our honeymoon, Andy and I both felt that it could only be more fun if our close friends joined us for some of it. And so that night, the six of us planned to meet up in Capri for part of our honeymoon.

Word spread in our extended circles about our upcoming celebration. Darcy Miller, an old friend and the editorial director of *Martha Stewart Weddings*, called and asked, "Can we cover your wedding for the magazine? I can help you get a fantastic photographer and a great florist." Whenever Darcy needed handbags for a wedding photoshoot, we'd just make one exactly as she described and send it to her. Sometimes, those wedding designs became part of our line.

I took her up on her offer and used Darcy's recommendations. She was a godsend. She knew everyone in the business and introduced me to the talented photographer John Dolan, who shot our wedding and dispatched a writer to cover the ceremony. With *Martha Stewart Weddings* covering our event, the pressure was turned up by a thousand.

We proceeded to take meetings with the various caterers and planners. At one point, Andy tagged along to Channing Daughters Vineyard when I was meeting with our flower design crew that Darcy had introduced me to. David Stark and Avi Adler were the top of the pyramid in the wedding floral stratosphere. They arrived precisely on time to the vineyard, driving up in a pair of matching black Mercedes with their crew of handsome young guys all dressed head-to-toe in black. Andy looked on anxiously as Avi described the twelve fifteen-foot-high sunflower towers that they intended to build to ring the perimeter of the outdoor wedding ceremony. They had a sketch and it was breathtakingly beautiful.

After they left, Andy said, "Geez, do you think we really need all this stuff? It's nice, but how much is all this going to cost?"

Then and there I had to introduce my beloved fiancé to a side of myself that I had yet to share with him. It was a facet of my persona forged by a decade of arguing out manufacturing contracts with gruff New York City male factory owners and for scolding lying shipping managers who had lost our inventory.

I glared at Andy with a steely look, pointed at his chest and said slowly through gritted teeth, "Don't even think of discussing any of these plans with me. I'm running this wedding. You just show up in your tux and look good."

"Whoa! Okay . . . got the message, ma'am!" he said, a combination of amusement and alarm on his face.

After that, he kept his opinions of the wedding plans to himself, and I've hardly ever had to use that voice on him again.

* * *

In the midst of wedding planning, I got a call from Michelle Kessler, the market editor at *Vogue*, who told me counterfeiters were selling faux Kate Spade bags on blankets right in front of the Condé Nast building. She bought five of them to show us.

Unlike the other three of us, Andy Spade was unfazed by the knockoffs at first. He declared it the highest form of flattery and thought there had to be a way to market the fact that fake Kate

Spade bags were being sold on a blanket in Times Square alongside faux Gucci, Prada and Louis Vuitton.

He said, "We've hit the big time! Pop the champagne!" He proposed an ad campaign that featured the sidewalk sellers. Though it was very clever and out there, the three of us killed that idea early on.

Pamela, Katy and I were incensed by the counterfeits. Selling them was a violation of trademark law, and we were infuriated that no one in the city government would do anything to stop it. Selling fakes might seem like a victimless crime, but we knew from law enforcement that the fake bags were made in overseas sweatshops utilizing child labor. The cheap prices affected the knocked-off luxury brands and hurt legitimate businesses that played by the rules and employed thousands of people.

We got serious about cracking down on it. Katy and I approached a counterfeit hawker on the street one day with the intention of asking him politely not to sell his Kate Spade bags. The man had no idea what we were talking about. He just kept saying, "These are my bags."

Katy said, "No, these are *my* bags. You can't sell them." She was getting more and more upset. The guy looked frightened. He rolled up his blanket and took off. I was wearing Ray-Bans and a trench coat; he might have thought I was an FBI agent. In all likelihood, he went two or three blocks, unrolled the blanket and sold the counterfeit bags there. Trying to control this was like playing an endless game of Whac-A-Mole. You knock down one seller, but a truckload of goods would arrive the next day with enough product for ten other street vendors. We were getting calls from California, Florida and Texas about the proliferation of fakes.

It was hard not to take it personally, after the years we had put in. Katy and Andy happened to be walking by Barneys one day, and someone was selling knockoffs right outside on Madison Avenue. A woman and her ten-year-old daughter were looking at all the fake Kate Spades, and Katy said to the older woman, "Those aren't real."

The mother said, "How do *you* know?"

Katy said, "Well, I'm Kate Spade. These are fake bags. You can go into this store and buy a real one right now."

The woman didn't seem to understand that this was actually Kate Spade, the person. She said, "The real ones are more expensive and the fake ones look the same."

Katy badly wanted to engage the woman and explain that most of the fakes were made in sweatshops overseas with no oversight and with cheap materials, but she thought better of it and walked away flustered.

I resolved to fix this problem myself, though I realized I would have to learn how to do so working with New York City law enforcement. Through the mayor's office, I started to visit NYPD precincts, training officers about the practice and teaching them to spot fakes by how they were stitched and structured. I brought in private detectives and assembled our own counter-counterfeit task force. I was spending less time in the office while Janet continued to assert her new authority and hire people to take on responsibilities that had always been mine. I welcomed moving some of those jobs off my plate, but it was somewhat disconcerting when I would walk through the office and see so many unfamiliar faces. The vibe at work was decidedly less fun.

* * *

As stressful as work was becoming, at home I was having a great time ramping up to our wedding. After months of planning, our big weekend finally arrived in late September.

While my dad hosted a guys' pizza and beer party for Andy and his buddies, I hosted a women's-only bridal luncheon at the Bridgehampton Café (now the Almond Restaurant). Katy gave a speech and was so emotional that she cried through the whole thing. I felt bad for her, I got up and hugged her in the middle of it.

"Are you okay?" I asked. "Do you want me to read your speech for you?"

"No! This is for you. I'm fine, let me finish." Then she burst into tears again. She stumbled through it and was just adorable as her voice hitched and she sniffled from allergies and crying. That evening, we had the rehearsal dinner at the restaurant Alison by the Beach in Sagaponack. There were more toasts, and Andy's college buddies played and sang a funny song they wrote about how he finally found the right girl, and how unworthy he was of his bride.

The wedding was held in the late afternoon behind the vineyard adjacent to the share house where Andy and I fell for each other (we would eventually buy the place for ourselves years later). It was a dry crisp fall day with abundant sunshine and the scent of hay in the air. The ceremony was in a broad, open field between the grapevines. Our planner had arranged all 220 guests to sit in a huge circle around us. We decided to keep the wedding party small—Willow was my maid of honor, Andy's brother, Jim, was his best man. My mother was escorted to her seat by our good friend Robert Lighton, and my father walked me down the long corridor through the vines into the middle of the circle where the ceremony was held. The service was officiated by Dr. Robert Kauffman, a nondenominational pastor affiliated with the New York Society for Ethical Culture, who had married Frank and Lee Ann the prior year.

Several of our friends spoke during the ceremony. Andy asked his pals Agnes and Charlie to speak. I didn't ask Katy to prepare a speech because she would be nervous about it and would likely sob uncontrollably, so I asked Lee Ann and Andy Spade to say a few words. Unbeknownst to me at the time, Andy Spade lost his stack of index cards with his speech on the way to the wedding. So during the ceremony, he furiously wrote on a piece of crumpled paper to re-create his notes. In the end, he gave a heartfelt speech. As part of the ceremony, Andy Arons's friend, musician/producer Dennis D'Amico, performed a song he wrote for us, "The Best Thing." Many happy tears were shed on that beautiful autumn afternoon.

I remember being so touched that all our families were there, including my nieces Anna and Ashley, my sister Shon's teenage daughters. Shon, with her powerful voice, sang "The First Time Ever I Saw Your Face" by Roberta Flack during the reception to a standing ovation. Most of Katy's family came, too, which made sense since the Brosnahans had been my second family for nearly twenty years. At the party, we basked in the ocean breeze and candlelight, and everyone danced and toasted until 2:00 a.m. Still wide awake, Andy and I went into our "bridal suite" bedroom at the summer share house next door. Much to our surprise, we found the toilet covered in cellophane and the bed short-sheeted—camp pranks for the newlyweds pulled on us by Robert Lighton. I absolutely loved it. Live by the prank, die by the prank.

In our group, when we celebrate, we keep the party going as long as possible. The day after the wedding, about a third of our guests had left. For those who stuck around, we had an afternoon clambake at Channing Daughters on Sunday with a band, then a giant bonfire on Gibson Beach with singing, guitar playing and cold beer. The hugest orange harvest moon I have ever seen shone over the ocean. If I could repeat one day of my life, it would be the day after our wedding.

We left for our honeymoon in Capri that Monday. It was a trek to get there, but all worth it when we arrived at the honeymoon suite on the top floor of the Grand Hotel Quisisana, a seaside resort overflowing with charm, Italian marble statues, bougainvillea and umbrellaed chaises by the green-bottomed round pool. We put on the fluffy terrycloth robes and sat on our room's private terrace under the bluest sky.

We'd been there a half an hour when the phone rang. I had no idea who could be calling us. The restaurant to check on our reservation?

I answered and said, "Hello?"

A female voice said, "I'm here!"

Huh? "Who is this?"

"It's Marybeth!"

Marybeth had been in Europe for the last three weeks going to fashion shows in Milan, Paris and London. She'd missed our wedding because she had to work. At first, I had no idea why she was in Capri, but then I remembered the half-baked plan we'd made months ago at our engagement party. We'd discussed Katy, Andy, Marybeth and Rob coming along on our honeymoon. Not too long after, Katy and Andy canceled, saying things were just too busy. Rob had dropped out weeks before. But apparently, no one, including her own boyfriend, had told Marybeth they weren't coming!

Suddenly, we were on a honeymoon for three.

While it was a little unusual having three of us there on our honeymoon, Marybeth was (and is) excellent company and it was fun having her there with us. She was at a different hotel, and she gave us plenty of alone time for a romantic day trip to Positano, some private dinners and walks around Capri. Looking back at the photos is hilarious—I'm sure we're some of the only honeymooners ever to have three people in every shot.

One afternoon, Andy and I were out on the terrace of our top-floor suite having coffee, when several bees started buzzing around our plate of pastries. Andy instinctively jumped up and closed the terrace door so the bees would not get into our hotel room. The thick glass door closed with an ominous click. We were completely locked out of the room. We yelled down from our terrace to the empty courtyard below, but because of the height and a loud conference near the pool area, no one could hear us. We tried screaming and waving. It didn't work.

I started panicking a little. I said, "We could try stepping over the railing and jumping onto the terrace next door."

He said, "We're seven stories up. Who are you, Batgirl?"

"I know I can do it!"

"I'd hate for you to die on our honeymoon," he said calmly. "Worst-case scenario, we're stuck out here all night long. House-keeping will see us in the morning. We have champagne."

We were in bathing suits, and it was October. We'd be freezing overnight.

Finally, after what felt like hours (but was probably only forty-five minutes), a waiter walking across the lawn heard us yelling and sent somebody up to finally let us back in. It was a very memorable honeymoon in one of the world's loveliest places.

* * *

Now that we were married, Andy stayed at my apartment. He kept his stuff at his place until we could find and move into a home we bought together. He was hesitant to get rid of his great apartment on West Seventieth Street where he had lived for so long. He was obsessed with the Upper West Side, as I had been years ago. It still had that historic connection with the performing arts, and Andy loved being surrounded by all of those creative personalities. His next-door neighbor was the virtuoso violin star Itzhak Perlman. Itzhak and Andy shared a love of corny borscht belt jokes which they would trade when they bumped into each other. I favored Chelsea, so we decided to compromise and move to a completely new neighborhood together. We agreed our new home would be somewhere we both had always dreamed of living. By a unanimous vote of two, we chose the West Village.

While we started shopping for a new home, Katy and Andy Spade were renovating and eventually moving into theirs, a three-bedroom apartment at 850 Park Avenue. It took them a year to fix it up into their dream space.

Their apartment opened into a very large foyer decorated with Andy's art collection. The whole house was filled with gorgeous pieces. Beyond the foyer, there was a gracious living room with a huge fireplace. To the left was a beautiful dining room, a kitchen, laundry and a guest room. To the right of the living room was a library, TV room and two bedrooms. Katy made every room homey with mostly black-and-white photos of family in antique silver frames. If I couldn't figure out a gift to give her, I could always find a silver frame. She also collected silver cigarette boxes from vintage shops, inspired by her mom, who also had a collection. Their place was unique and beautiful, posh in a classic Upper East Side kind of way with their combined whimsical design sense running through the artwork and furnishings.

Katy and Andy had been downtown for so long. All of our friends, our work and our favorite places for dinner and drinks were all below Twenty-Fifth Street. I guess I thought of them as downtown people, so their move to the Upper East Side surprised me. Downtown was artsy, a little gritty and, in my opinion, the center of the action. At this point, Katy wanted a simpler, calmer, cleaner, more civilized life in a doorman building uptown, away from the chaos.

I admit, their move saddened me. I didn't feel as if they were trying to put literal and figurative distance between us, but as an inevitable result of their move, we spent less time together. We still saw each other in the office daily. We all showed up for large gatherings and business events. It wasn't like I suddenly never hung out with my best friend. We were on the phone constantly, even from office to office in the same building. But it wasn't the same as living within a dozen blocks of each other. I could feel a shift coming in our friendship.

At the same time, my life was full and taking on a new shape. Andy Arons and I were a two-person unit now. He brought a whole new world of his accomplished and funny friends and family into the mix. I still had all my old downtown pals, including Frank and Lee Ann, who bought an apartment half a block from mine in Chelsea. Andy and I hung out with them often.

I never thought that my friendship with Katy would stay exactly the same forever. It'd already evolved from being carefree college BFFs to young adults supporting each other through the struggling years to business partners. It was miraculous that our friendship stayed rock-solid through personal and circumstantial changes and working so closely together. Even though our lives had been entwined for so long, we talked and saw each other every day, and we retained our individuality. With my marriage, my life was moving in a different direction. Not away from Katy per se, but toward something else. I knew it was natural and healthy to reprioritize things over time, to meet new people and gravitate toward discovery. That said, I also knew that my friendship with Katy would endure through the ebbs and flows of life. No matter which direction we were pulled in—even if it was in different directions—we would remain each other's emotional home base.

I also needed an actual home base to live in with my husband. And our dogs (plural).

Andy, like me, was a dog lover. On the sidewalk in front of the SoHo Gourmet Garage, the downtown-based pet adoption group Animal Haven agreed with Andy to park one of their adoption vans next to the store each weekend. Passersby could go inside the vehicle, meet some dogs and cats, and hopefully adopt them. Andy visited the van every time they came, just to lend his support and give the animals some attention. He got to know the volunteers, exchanging numbers and telling them that he might be available in an emergency foster situation. During the summer, a volunteer called Andy and said, "We have an amazing year-old yellow Lab, but she's big and we can't house her right now. Can you take her for the weekend?"

We had plans to go to Katy and Andy's house in Sagaponack that weekend, and they were not very into large dogs. But still, we loaded up Edna, my six-year-old naughty Yorkie, and the one-year-old Lab named Sandy and drove out to Long Island. Well, Sandy tore through their house; she jumped on the furniture and slobbered all over everything. Katy clutched her shaking Maltese, Henry, protectively to her chest and said, "Elyce, I don't think you want to keep that dog."

Of course, we kept the dog.

Andy walked our new vivacious Lab three or four times a day. We both realized that Sandy would need a lot of room to move around, hopefully with some outside area. A brownstone with a backyard started to seem like a good idea. With a real estate broker we knew, we found one in the West Village. It was light-filled and lovely. The owner was a former nun, very kind but very specific about who she wanted to sell the house to. "I want this house filled with kids," she said. We could do that eventually. But first, we'd fill it with dogs. We went back to see the house three times and put in an offer. A day later, we learned she accepted a *lower* bid from another couple. They already had children.

Flash forward to several years later. Andy and I were having cocktails at a party with our neighbors Oliver Platt and Camilla Campbell, the owners of that house we had tried to buy in the West Village. We asked them how they got the owner to accept their lower bid.

Oliver explained, "We knew she had a thing about the house being filled with kids, so I had one of ours bouncing on my shoulders.

Camilla had one in her arms. Another kid was running around. We played that one just right."

All we had were dogs—a tiny one with tummy issues and a big one that slobbered.

I said to Oliver and Camilla, "Well done. You won that fair and square."

We lost that house, but we were determined to get the next one.

Our broker friend told us about the perfect place on Bank Street, a storied street in the heart of the West Village: "I know the owners, an elderly couple, but they're not ready to move. They're both turning eighty this week, and they can't maintain the place for much longer. They know they need to sell soon. What I want to do is just bring you in and introduce them to you as my friends. Very low pressure."

And that was how we met Jean Dubinsky and Shelley Appleton, two fascinating and adorable people. Shelley was the nattiest dresser—when we went to their brownstone for that first meeting, he wore a Harris tweed jacket, bow tie and gabardine trousers. Jean was a "force to be reckoned with" type, also very stylish, in cat-eye glasses and with her hair and nails perfectly done. They were the quintessential Greenwich Village intellectuals, fascinating people with incredible back stories. The house was loaded with artwork that covered its many walls. As we walked in, I saw a huge Chagall oil painting leaning against a wall. "Is that real?" I said.

"Of course it's real, don't ask that," scolded Jean whom I had just met. "I bought it from Chagall personally in Paris right after the war"—I guessed WWII? —"and he charged me way too much for it." She paused for a beat. "So, what would you like to drink? All we have is vodka."

Andy and I glanced at each other, and I said, "In that case, we'll take vodka."

The bottle was dusty, like it'd been sitting in their cupboard for thirty years. She put a silver dish of almonds on the coffee table, poured the vodka neat, and, as we sipped our drinks, she said, "Just so you know, our house isn't for sale."

We said, "Okay."

"But do you want to see it?"

Jean and Shelley gave us a tour of the house that lasted a solid hour. The place was fantastic, built in 1851, and they were only the third owners. They'd lived in that house for fifty years and gave us a history lesson on Bank Street's famous former and current residents, including writer Willa Cather, Yoko Ono and John Lennon, Graydon Carter, Courtney Love, and Sylvia Plath. The previous owner of their brownstone in the early 1900s was Virginia Kirkus, founder of the illustrious book-centric publication *Kirkus Reviews*. Ms. Kirkus had painted the front door glossy tulip red, we believe at the behest of her good friend, designer Dorothy Draper, whose book she had reviewed. That front door is still bright red eighty-five years later.

We stayed for two hours and appreciated every minute of their company. When we left, we said to each other, "Well, they don't want to sell their house. But we just met two amazing people. Let's keep in touch with them."

The next day, Jean called us and asked, "Do you want to buy our house or what?"

They needed to find the right people to trust with their beloved home. They knew that we'd care for it, appreciate it and cherish it, as we have for the last twenty-five years (and hopefully twenty-five years to come).

We brought the Spades to meet the Appletons and see the house before we closed. They adored both, as well as our charming street. Of course Andy Spade was more taken with the extensive art collection above all else.

We signed the closing papers for the house in April 2000. As soon as we got the keys, Andy and I ran up the front stoop holding hands, opened the door, dashed in and started jumping up and down in the air screaming. We realized that in your own house, you can make all the noise you want. In my earliest New York years, I used to walk through the West Village, thinking, *Who gets to live on these tree-lined streets in these town houses?* It was another one of those moments when I could hardly believe how my life was playing out. I smiled at Andy and knew that this was going to be the happiest of homes.

CHAPTER 23

Not all was right in paradise. In the summer of 2000, workers at a domestic factory we used were trying to unionize, and they had some issues with the factory owner. It was only a small supplier of ours, but the organizers chose to protest outside the Kate Spade store for the publicity, using the sidewalk out front as their podium to air their grievances. Our company had nothing to do with the conflict. Our legal advisers told us to just stay back and let the workers negotiate with the factory owner.

Nonetheless, the news got out about something happening in front of the Kate Spade store in SoHo. Suddenly, Broome Street was crammed with photographers and picket signs. The signs were not anti–Kate Spade at all; they were protesting the factory. We mostly kept out of it, apart from asking the factory owner to work things out with his workers as soon as possible.

Andy Spade had hired my father—now living in New Jersey—to work for him at the new Jack Spade store on Greene Street, around the corner from Kate Spade on Broome Street. Andy liked the idea of a seventy-year-old Midwestern gentleman working there. When the picketers amassed, Dad felt a surge of protectiveness and thought telling them to leave would be a good idea. Things didn't go as planned. They surrounded him and started shouting. A photographer pushed a camera into my father's face. Dad grabbed it and pushed it back, bonking the guy in the nose. Luckily Andy Arons's partner at Gourmet Garage, Adam Hartman, a very large, strong fellow, happened to witness the incident and stepped in to rush my dad out of there before it got very ugly. When Adam walked through a crowd, most people instinctively moved out of the way. He basically picked up my dad by his shoulders and hustled through the crowd with him. Dad was fine, but when he moved east for some excitement in his golden years, crossing a picket line probably wasn't what he had in mind.

I hoped he would be excited about becoming a grandfather again. Almost immediately after we finally moved into Bank Street that fall, I was pregnant at thirty-six with our first child. Having a baby was a big change on the horizon, and with our new partnership at work, it was a lot to take in. But we were all excited about the prospect of Kate Spade making it to the big league, and I was thrilled at the idea of being a mom.

When our sale to Neimans was first announced, it generated an avalanche of coverage in the business press, which we expected. A pleasant surprise came a year later when students at Harvard Business School contacted us for more information about it. They wanted to prepare a case study on the sale, focusing on the factors that went into our decision to go with Neiman Marcus over the other suitors vying for our company. We were fully on board with the project and very curious what they'd write about us, so we agreed to sit for interviews with the students and provide them with documentation on the different offers.

The case study didn't editorialize. It was mainly a history of the company. Reading it was like going back in time and reliving the last seven years. We stumbled along, made decisions as they came up, and wrote the rules as we progressed. We had never drafted a business plan or model, and it was kind of surreal to become one.

In November 2000, Pamela, Andy Spade and I went to Harvard to speak to the graduate students who'd written the case study. It was one of the best experiences I've ever had. The students asked such astute questions, and we all felt validated in our choices as we answered them. Andy lightened up the proceedings with his speech introducing us both as graduates of Arizona State University, which, he said, "you all know is generally referred to as the 'Harvard of the West.'" Big group chuckle from the Harvard B-School gang.

Their big question was, "Why would you sell the majority when the trajectory of your company was going up?"

Pamela got her moment to say, "I didn't want to sell!" (In the final study, she was referred to as "the dissenting partner.")

I said, "When you're in it, it feels very different from looking from the outside. We felt the trajectory was going in the right direction, but that with a strong strategic partner we could accomplish more and faster." That was true, and we were fortunate that we found a partner willing to offer us an excellent valuation and let us keep such a large amount of stock. Taking some money and risk off the table was a life-changing moment for all of us, but that was a little hard to translate to those ambitious and hungry young students who were about to start their careers. They were just like we used to be.

What we didn't tell the students was that we were starting to experience some speed bumps in our new partnership. But we remained optimistic about the future, still sure we had made the right call on the sale and determined to make it work.

We went to the CFDA gala every year (along with Katy's first award, she won again in 1998 for Accessory Designer of the Year). We attended the Costume Institute Ball, a.k.a. the Met Gala, every year as well. Back then the Met Gala wasn't the celebrity extravaganza it is today. It was, however, an elegant and magical evening for the top folks in fashion and entertainment. During my pregnancy year, the theme was Jackie Kennedy.

I asked Katy, "What the hell am I going to wear?" I had gowns in my closet, but I wouldn't come close to fitting into any of them.

Katy had a eureka glow in her eye and said, "Diane von Furstenberg just came out with a black-tie maternity wrap dress. You have to go check it out."

I went to Bergdorf Goodman, tried it on, and bought it. It was a black, classic, hyperfeminine V-neck wrap dress, a Von Furstenberg signature silhouette with a little extra material in the right place. I wore it to the party, feeling pretty good about myself. For once, thanks to being pregnant, I had some cleavage to show off. Diane Von Furstenberg herself came over to me at our table and purred, "My dress looks fantastic on you. That is mine?"

I said, "Yes, it is yours."

Katy leaned over and piped in, "I told her to buy it."

We gossiped and chatted with Diane and had a glittery evening, probably my favorite of those events.

Another black-tie event during my pregnancy—this one a fundraiser at Lincoln Center for the New York City Ballet—was called Arabian Nights with the theme "Dance with the Dancers." Katy, Pamela and I arrived at the party in gorgeous drapes of beaded silk. I felt glamorous that night, too. At the other black-tie events we had attended as my pregnancy wore on, I started to feel unwieldy. We all felt pressure to show up for these functions to stay in the mix and support the company. It seemed like stepping off the carousel, even for one spin, might make it all disappear.

* * *

I was a week past my due date in June 2001 and finally started to get labor pains. Nobody can really describe to you what they will feel like. I didn't know what was happening and thought something was wrong. Then I realized, *Okay, I must be in labor.* I ran into the shower, washed my hair, blow-dried it and curled it. I put on makeup and did my nails. I know it sounds ridiculous, but I was not going to look messy in all the photos that we were sure to take.

Our little girl was born tiny—five pounds, thirteen ounces—and healthy. My parents arrived first and Katy, Andy, Pamela and Marybeth came up to the room immediately after. Andy Arons had focused his charm beam on the floor nurses and brought them doughnuts, coffee and snacks all night—and they gave us a huge corner room. We were glad, because we needed the space as more friends and family came by.

Andy Spade and Katy were the last to leave that night. My Andy was perched leaning on the radiator smiling, while the Spades sat on the edge of my bed and marveled at our beautiful little girl. Like me, they were amazed that we had come so far.

"Can I hold her now?" Katy said.

"Of course! You need to get to know her if you're going to be her godparents." I handed that beautiful little package to my best friend. Katy gently pulled our tiny baby to her shoulder and gently hugged her.

"Really, we're her godparents?" Andy Spade said. They were both smiling ear to ear.

"Oh, and we've decided on her name. Want to know?"

"Oh my God, yes, what's her name?" Katy asked.

I smiled. "Her name is Katy. Katy Holiday."

Little Katy looked up with newborn blue eyes at her godmother. Big Katy looked back, smiled at her, brought her close and gently stroked her cheek for a long time. That moment is one of my happiest memories.

CHAPTER 24

The turn of the twenty-first century in downtown Manhattan was a period of general calm and prosperity. The crime rate in the city had plummeted and businesses of all sorts were thriving despite the burst of the dot-com bubble in the previous years. Much of Manhattan had undergone a period of great gentrification, a mixed blessing that would result in higher living costs and would continue to drive many of the creative class to decamp to Brooklyn. For Katy and my purposes, both business and personal, it was a great time to live in the city and raise families.

That peaceful and productive time was shattered on a crisp blue autumn morning. I was just getting our three-month-old daughter Katy out of her crib and ready for the day when the landline rang. It was Andy's mother telling us about the initial plane strike on the World Trade Center. We ran to our third-floor window, where we could view the North Tower a mile away, smoke pouring from the top of the building. I know everyone in America has similar feelings as I do about those minutes. We watched it in real time and on the news. It's hard to put into words the distress we felt for the people trapped in those buildings, or our pain when we knew the extent of the loss of the first responders. We felt the aftershock of that day for months and months on our walk to work, a sadness shared by our community for the brave officers and firefighters we lost from the precinct and stations in our neighborhood.

My takeaway was that I promised myself to live every day as if it was precious. I had a family now, and I understood that it would always be my priority. Time passed and the city slowly recovered, but that dreadful period left a heaviness in all our hearts. There was some comfort in New Yorkers and all Americans coming together to grieve in our different ways. I wish we could tap into that sense of unity again.

That experience helped us put our work challenges into perspective, but we had to deal with them, nonetheless. I returned to the office that October after my maternity leave, and there were even more new faces that I didn't recognize. Some of the people Janet had brought in seemed terrific, like our new financial controller and merchandise planner who were doing necessary jobs we had never filled; others, it was hard to tell with the reorganization that was going on. Many of the new hires were brought in as VPs at high salaries and put in charge of business functions like production, domestic sales, retail and legal affairs, areas that Pamela and I had been managing prior to the partnership. Almost all these positions had to do with our core business of handbag wholesale and retail sales, which were the most essential areas of the company. The staff appeared to me to be getting very top-heavy, and Pamela and I were concerned there were too many cooks in the kitchen. But we did not want to make any waves, assuming the more corporate direction the company was taking was a positioning for future growth. We trusted Janet knew something we didn't know about expanding the business, and we tried to step back and hope for the best. Andy and Katy's area of design and marketing were pretty much left alone. In hindsight, that should have been a clue as to what would soon transpire.

The company continued to grow as we opened more retail locations—now totaling six—and increased our international business, so we were all busy. I was happy to have some help from the new in-house counsel we hired. It saved me a lot of time with the reading of contracts and the wrangling of attorneys for the redlining of the leases, licensing agreements and dealing with counterfeiting issues. Same with having a professional CFO like Reepal Shah. I worked together with him regularly to review the financial structure of those various agreements.

The licensing of our brand had become a big business and was one part of the company that would pull in the original four founders to decide what would be our next products and how they best fit into the Kate Spade brand. Before the purchase by Neimans, the four of us had developed a game plan for rolling out multiple product lines. We had started with stationery, which was a small but successful foray into something new that we all liked but knew very little about. We then moved to add a shoe license, which Katy was thrilled to work on. Our Kate Spade eyewear launch was next. We reached out to three eyewear companies: Essilor, Luxottica and Safilo. They were all eager to work with Kate Spade, and each would come to our office and present a plan in a bid for our business. We ended up partnering with Safilo, a well-known luxury Italian manufacturer. They had great quality, manufactured everything in Italy and had produced Ray-Ban, Persol and other brands we admired. As in most of the license relationships, after the initial agreements were inked, the project would move through the design phase with Katy and her team, then to Andy's marketing crew, who would plan and eventually execute the launch with the licensor. The eyewear was a great success, and a good example of how all the new licensed product lines would work within our brand aesthetic. We received a percentage of sales from the manufacturers who were happy to be working with us, both companies enjoying the benefits of strong profits.

Despite what we perceived as potential issues with Janet's top-loading executives at the company, Kate Spade New York continued to grow. New opportunities kept coming up to showcase the brand to a wider audience. We were especially excited about our upcoming fragrance launch with Estée Lauder.

* * *

David Spade had left *SNL* in 1996 to star in films and other TV shows. In 1997, he got a big break, being cast along with actors Wendie Malick, Laura San Giacomo and George Segal in the NBC sitcom *Just Shoot Me!* The show was set in a fictional New York–based fashion magazine named *Blush*. David played Finch, the acerbic assistant to George Segal as the owner of the magazine. We'd all been fans since its debut and never missed an episode. David was hilarious as always, stealing the show (we thought) from his veteran costars.

In the series' sixth season, in an episode called "*Blush* Gets Some Therapy," Katy made an appearance as herself. The producers of the show knew Katy was David's sister-in-law and offered her a cameo in an episode. We thought it'd be a great opportunity for Katy to talk about the fragrance launch. I'm sure David helped, and it seems that the producers were happy to include our fragrance in the segment. Katy flew to Los Angeles and went to a soundstage at Universal Studios to film her scene. She called me after the taping, anxious about how she did and looked. "I have no idea how I came off," she said.

"I know you did great, Kook," I said. "You're always worried, but you end up knocking it out of the park every time. You'll see: It will be fantastic and good for the fragrance." I really knew that to be true.

We had to wait a couple of months to see that episode air on TV in April 2002. Everyone on staff was excited to watch it, none more amped up than me. Katy, not as much. She was full of dread about possibly making a fool of herself. It was one thing to be photographed on the red carpet or for someone to take video at a lunch, panel or gala. Those cameras loved her. But for *Just Shoot Me!*, Katy had to deliver lines of dialogue and react to the other actors. Professionals made it look easy, but it was incredibly hard to act natural in front of a camera.

We decided to watch the show together at our house on Bank Street. Katy, Andy A., Andy S. and I ordered pizza and beer, piled onto the big stuffed sofa in our second-floor "family room" and turned on NBC. We recorded it so we could rewind it and watch her cameo a few times.

The show started, and in its opening scene, there she was. Katy was escorted into the fictional *Blush* office by George Segal. She wore a black dress with a red pendant necklace and carried a lime-green Boxxy bag. The handbag was a sample of one of our new Italian leather designs that Katy flipped for when she first saw it in our factory in Florence, and they were due to launch in the next month.

As soon as she saw herself on-screen, Katy gave a little shriek and ran out of our room. The rest of us watched her scene unblinkingly. Segal explained to the cast that *the* Kate Spade had come by to talk about partnering with *Blush* to promote our real-life fragrance. Wendie Malick, the magazine's editor, greeted her, "Kate Spade, you old bag hag!" followed by a triple air-kiss. Laura, David and Wendie started trading insults while Katy reacted (very well!) with amusement at their bickering. At one point, David meant to step on Wendie's toes but stomped on Katy's instead. She said, "Ouch! I'm going to go. I'll be in touch," and made her dramatic exit.

Her entire scene lasted one minute and ten seconds—and we were blown away! We hooted and jumped up and down at her amazing line deliveries and how professional she looked. Andy Spade cajoled her back into the room to watch herself on rewind. In truth, she came off as very relaxed and natural, and interacted well with the others on-screen who were all experienced comedic actors. She couldn't have done any better. We played it over and over, analyzing her every facial expression, and cheered loudly for her. Katy was trying not to shrink into a ball with embarrassment, but in the end she said, "I don't hate it."

She'd done hundreds of personal appearances and media interviews by then. But appearing on network television was something else entirely. This was the next level of exposure, which, as always, she was ambivalent about. Now *Just Shoot Me!* viewers were aware of our fragrance launch and saw Katy model the Boxxy. Back in the mid-nineties, our bags were on the arms of celebrities like the Olsen twins, Tina Fey and Amy Poehler, and appeared in paparazzi photos constantly, but this was a new and welcome level of exposure for the brand. The fact that she was on the show at all was further proof to us that Kate Spade—the company and the person—was continuing to capture the imagination of the public.

* * *

A few months before, in that spring of 2002, things had taken a downward turn for Pamela and me back at the office. Layers of our responsibility and those of some of our long-term staffers were being peeled away. Janet would tell us it wasn't necessary for us to be doing certain jobs anymore that were the more hands-on type of busywork, but which we knew were essential. For example, we let go of reviewing the weekly warehouse inventory, assuming it would be watched closely. When it was just the four of us running things, we'd never had to play office politics. I'd dealt with it in past jobs, but I didn't think I'd ever have to contend with it at Kate Spade. Soon I started to hear whispers among the veteran staffers that Janet was subtly discrediting their work in favor of the people she brought in, and was not-so-subtly disparaging Pamela and me. Veteran staffers would tell me they were upset when Janet would say something like, "If we had a proper head of product development, we wouldn't have this or that issue. If we had a proper head of legal, HR, retail, sales . . ."

Pamela and I felt that the office was slowly becoming an unhealthy business environment. It was a tricky situation for us because we were no longer the majority shareholders of the company and were therefore hesitant to create a situation where there was a confrontation. We really wanted to be cooperative, but we were concerned that some things were falling by the wayside or just not being done correctly, and that Janet's direction was too often wrong either in execution or for our brand's identity. She was pushing to open more stores in mall locations where the rents were too high for our business. Those leases would come back to bite us later.

Pamela challenged Janet on some of her decisions—for example, that she was taking large orders from department stores that Pamela didn't think would be able to sell in such quantities. Instead of listening to her, Janet brought in people who agreed with her without consulting us. I'd walk past a conference room and see that a meeting was taking place that I should have been invited to but wasn't. Not only did it make me feel demoralized, but based

on recent experience I was afraid that they would be making decisions that would impact the company in negative ways. The new
people Janet had hired lacked the history with the brand to make
informed decisions.

Later, Katy told me that Janet went into her office to complain
about Pamela and me, comments like, "I don't feel like I can talk to
them." She would say that she needed to hire other people. Katy and
Andy were uncomfortable with Janet's whisper campaign and the
rising tensions and were busy with their own responsibilities. But I
felt they were ignoring what she was doing to Pamela and me and
not taking it seriously. Janet had carved them out from making many
of the day-to-day office decisions that we used to all handle together,
and she had not yet brought new people into their areas of marketing and design. It appeared to me that she was hoping to drive a
wedge between the original partners to consolidate her position with
the company. From her perspective, that made sense. Tension was
mounting at work, and the worst part of it was that my relationship
with Katy was beginning to fray over that and other issues.

Though Katy and I still saw each other almost daily and spoke
often on the phone, we had drifted to some degree from our decades-
long sister-level closeness. I was wrapped up in being a wife and
mother. Andy and I were hanging out with our old crowd downtown,
and I had also developed new friendships with some of his female
friends and his close buddies' wives. Katy was doing the same in
the uptown circles she and Andy were now involved with. We had
some cross-pollination, and I enjoyed Katy's new friend group, as
she did mine. But she and Andy were still able to keep up the pace
with going to nightly parties and events. As new parents, Andy and
I just didn't have that freedom any longer.

Her fame was another factor in our drift. At this point Katy
had profiles and interviews written about her in scores of national

magazines—*Vanity Fair*, *Vogue* and most of the other blue-chip publications. She and Andy had dozens of invitations weekly to every conceivable event. Each night they had a choice of many things to do with a growing roster of people, most of whom I didn't know. I can remember one night in particular when my Andy and I had reservations with Katy and her Andy for dinner downtown. The plan was to meet at our house for some cocktails, just the four of us, then head out to Pastis in the Meatpacking District, one of our frequent dinner spots. We dressed up our little fourteen-month-old Katy in an adorable outfit to visit with her godparents and put out a spread of appetizers. Katy and Andy showed up two hours late with a handful of people we didn't know. This had happened before and was becoming the new normal. We had put our Katy to bed an hour earlier, and we were disappointed not to spend the evening catching up with them and hanging out at one of our favorite places.

They would never have done anything to hurt our feelings, but that experience was emblematic of the change in our relationship. Part of the fame game is that you have a thousand people vying for your attention, and it's hard to maintain close friendships. Your old friends can only be left on the back burner so many times before they will eventually drift off. I still loved them, but I had a new life with caring, interesting people who highly valued my time and friendship. There would always be a place for Katy, but I chose the path of least resistance. I would find out later that there was another side to that story of hurt feelings, and it would make me wish that I hadn't let my ego rule my actions.

Katy had her own very legitimate perspective on our drift, which would not become clear until much later. We continued to see Andy and Katy socially, celebrate big events together and occasionally slipped into our old camaraderie. But not often, and it wasn't the same. There was usually a strained element to our conversation that had never been there before.

* * *

Many things at the company were still going our way. Oprah Winfrey, then at the height of her popularity with her TV show, was considering a few Kate Spade handbags for her annual list of her favorite things. Our wares appeared in *Oprah* magazine regularly since its inception in 2000. We had a great relationship with the accessories editor there. But being included in Oprah's annual favorites list was special. We were over the moon when we got that news.

A few days later, somebody from *The Oprah Winfrey Show* contacted our office and upped the ante. Now they wanted to have Katy come on the show as Oprah's guest, sit on the couch to chat with her for about fifteen minutes and gift Kate Spade bags to every member of the studio audience. It would be hard to overstate Oprah's stratospheric status at the time. She was *it*. Her talk show was watched by twelve million people every single day—and her fans stampeded to stores to buy anything she endorsed, from apparel to books to wellness and beauty products. If Oprah had Katy on the show, we would benefit immensely, possibly connecting with millions of potential customers. All we had to do was wrap 150 of our black nylon shoulder hobo bags named Marybeth (after our co-honeymooner) into tiny pouches that could be hidden underneath the audience seats and ship them to Oprah's studio in Chicago for the taping. Katy had to fly to Chicago and contend with her anxiety all by herself. For one reason or another, none of us could join her on that trip.

She called me to help steady her nerves before she went on. She called again as soon as the taping was over. As always, she thought she did okay, but it went by so fast and we wouldn't know how it turned out until it was too late anyway. They sent over a VHS of the episode a day or two before it aired. We popped it into the video player and watched it in Katy's office. Despite her preshow nerves, her interview with Oprah was a success. She came off as charming, sincere and grateful to be there. They chatted about the company and how we got started. Then Oprah said, "Okay, I want everybody to look under your chair. *You* get a Kate Spade bag, and *you* get a Kate Spade bag, and *you* get a . . ." The audience started screaming and waving their Marybeths over their heads. It was amazing to watch, a display of exuberance like I'd never seen. With Oprah's stamp of approval, we could see the stratosphere, too.

Another milestone for the company: After years of development, Kate Spade Beauty, our fragrance, finally launched in April 2002. We were all thrilled with the final product. The bottle was teardrop shaped with three colored stripes at the top. The packaging of white roses on a red background was inspired by the wallpaper in Katy and Andy's summer house. The fragrance itself smelled like magnolia and jasmine—floral, fresh, sophisticated. I was sure the fragrance would be a hit. We threw a big party in our office's beautiful showroom, and Leonard Lauder hosted a dinner at the 21 Club. I was newly pregnant again and wasn't in the right mood to chitchat with anybody, but the dinner was so elegant and enjoyable, I rallied.

For some companies, a fragrance license can become bigger than the brand. The potential sales were huge because of the wide distribution to every department store, national and international, that could carry the product. A hit fragrance could become a brand's signature, like Chanel N°5; many more women own a bottle of Chanel perfume than they do a Chanel handbag. And if one fragrance did well, you could launch as many new ones as the market would bear.

In short, it was easier and more lucrative to sell a bottle of perfume than a handbag. However, you had to promote the hell out of it. Katy—and only Katy, because the bottle bore her name—had to go on the road to do launch events all over the country. I still have a copy of her calendar from spring of 2002 that exemplifies her grueling travel schedule: On April 20, the official launch date, she was in Toronto doing events, appearances and local media for two days. Next, she flew to Dallas on the twenty-fifth, followed by Houston on the twenty-sixth. She did a personal appearance at Tyson's Corner in Washington, DC, on the twenty-ninth, on to Atlanta on the thirtieth and Chicago on May first.

Katy came home for one day to throw Andy's fortieth birthday party for eighty guests at a big loft space downtown overlooking the Hudson River. She was completely exhausted and emotionally wrung dry—not in the best shape to host a party—but she pulled it off beautifully. Andy's birthday is on May 5, Cinco de Mayo, so Katy served tacos, enchiladas and margaritas and hired a mariachi band to serenade the guests. It was a huge success and went late into the night. My best memory of that celebration was that there were a lot of toasts, and as the night wore on, they kept making less and less sense. I was pregnant so I wasn't drinking, but the tequila was flowing, and it was hilarious to watch the toastmasters from the sober perspective.

The next day, Katy flew to San Francisco for a few days of events, then on to Seattle and other West Coast cities. Those were followed by Southwest and Midwest stops. The tour just kept going and going. Day after day after day, she rose at dawn in a strange hotel room, did an hour of hair and makeup before appearing live on a local morning TV talk or news show. Then she'd sit for interviews with regional magazines, newspapers and radio. In the afternoon and evenings, she had in-store promotions, lunches and dinners with execs. She had to be "on" the entire time, shaking hands, being friendly, listening, answering questions, making sure her style and outfit were fresh and different from the previous city. With years of experience, she had learned to compensate for her introverted nature, but this much face time was a lot for anyone to take. Unlike events in New York, Katy didn't have a buffer person with her on the road. Sometimes, a PR person from Estée Lauder would accompany her, but traveling with a stranger with an agenda had its own set of challenges.

She liked to have someone close with whom she could just be herself, on tour, at events, even for her charity lunches that were so meaningful to her. Katy was enthusiastically involved with the New York Center for Children, a local clinic that treated abused kids. She started hosting annual parties for the organization at her Park Avenue home. I found it rather adorable that she would ask one of our gang to stand next to her when she made the evening speech at those events, sometimes asking one of us to speak so she didn't have to. She also supported the Make-A-Wish Foundation, often donating a private lunch with her at our offices for donors who bid on the package at gala auctions. She always wanted either Andy, Pamela or me to join her at those lunches to help fill in the conversation. One of us would be happy to back her up for these functions. It made us all proud of Katy to use her name to support a worthy organization.

On the fragrance tour, Katy called me late one night from somewhere out West. "I can't talk for long," she said. "I have to get up at five in the morning to do a show, and then it's interviews all day."

"How are you holding up?" I asked.

I knew she was wrung out, but she had enough energy to sound angry.

"Not great! And I know it's not your fault that you're not here, but I feel abandoned by you. You guys got me into this. You should be doing this tour with me."

We'd never discussed that, and Katy had never asked me to join her. It wasn't remotely feasible for both of us to be out of the office for weeks at a time. My calendar was busy, too. I had a full plate at work, was a new mom, and pregnant again on top of that. I did feel terrible that we had laid this weight all on Katy's shoulders. It was the first time she had mentioned anything about it. All I could do was try to empathize with her, as a friend and a partner. At one point earlier, I had thought, *How hard can it be to chat and smile?* I had no idea how tough it was because I'd never done it. In hindsight, I wish we had all taken turns going with her so she didn't feel like she was carrying the burden alone.

For all Katy's effort, Kate Spade Beauty sold a respectable number of bottles. The Lauder people stayed positive, but we were expecting to have a bigger hit with the fragrance than we did. No one wanted to acknowledge our disappointment, so we all acted as if it were a success. The early numbers were a further drag on Katy's attitude toward her long touring schedule, which she continued throughout the fall. She got a short break in October to accept her trophy at *Glamour* magazine's Women of the Year Awards alongside Alanis Morissette, Sigourney Weaver and Tina Fey, all people we admired. We went to the elegant awards ceremony in Midtown, where actress Julie Bowen, from *Modern Family*, gave a beautiful introduction to a nervous Katy as she stepped up to accept her award. And then she was back on the road.

* * *

Katy's fortieth birthday party was at the 21 Club in late December. My second baby was due in a month; I was massively pregnant and uncomfortable. Fortunately, the party was small, just twenty people in the restaurant's private wine cellar, a former huge bank vault. The special birthday menu for the night included some of the specialties of the house at 21: their eponymous burger on a challah bun with a homemade onion relish; Katy's favorite, the New York strip steak in sherry sauce; and an enormous steamed lobster with drawn butter. Katy preferred the old-world steakhouses and New York City institutions. Though she would gamely try anything, she was at heart a meat-and-potatoes kind of person. She also had a passion for fast foods she had grown up with like Taco Bell and Burger King. Occasionally when the spirit moved her, Katy would send her assistant out to bring back Popeyes fried chicken for the team. She often asked me to make her favorite meal for her: meatloaf, mashed potatoes and peas, finished with my mom's recipe for chocolate buttermilk cake. Looking at her, you'd think Katy was a salad person, but that wasn't the case. A great steak (medium) and a California cab were her thing.

Her fortieth party wasn't on Katy's actual birthday, December 24. Unlike most Christmas babies, Katy loved her birth date. Her middle name was Noel because of it. Growing up, her mom had a big Christmas Eve party every year, and Katy always felt like it was just for her. The holiday season was her favorite time of year. She adored over-the-top decorations and loved to hang ornaments on as tall a tree as she could fit in her living room. Every year, she tried to outdo herself with a new Christmas design around the apartment, which made her so happy.

In the final days of 2002, Katy was out of town for most of December and didn't have a chance to decorate her apartment or buy a tree. Andy was also traveling, and she told me that she was dreading coming home to find her house undecked and unadorned. Her assistants, Dallas and Jenel, knew how disheartened she was, too. They took it upon themselves to buy the fattest Christmas tree they could find, bring it to Katy's house, get out her boxes of ornaments and decorations, and do up the entire place for her. They spent the whole day trimming the tree, decking the apartment and wrapping any gifts they knew she'd bought for certain people to put under the lowest boughs. She told me the next morning that walking in and finding a beautiful tree with the apartment full of all those decorations was one of the best gifts she'd ever received.

It says a lot about the kind of boss Katy was that her assistants cared so much about her that they went out of their way to make her happy. As for me, I hated to see her miserable and was frankly relieved when the fragrance touring dwindled in early 2003 and eventually stopped. Katy was in the office more often, but I barely saw her. We were all so busy, we felt like we were constantly playing catch up, while the gap in our friendship continued to grow.

CHAPTER 25

My second daughter, Jane, arrived in January 2003. She was named after my husband Andy's best friend and prom date from high school, Jane Walsh. As was our tradition, all of our friends came to the hospital with wine and food to meet little Jane. Another girl! Andy and I were thrilled to give two-year-old Katy a sister to go through life with. I knew all too well how precious and special the sister relationship is.

Two months later, I turned forty. Our friend owned a photography studio called Studio 450 on West Forty-Fifth Street, and we rented it out to throw a giant birthday party/costume bash. It was on the top floor of a tall building in Hell's Kitchen, with huge windows on all sides that looked over a 360-degree cityscape. Our theme was "Your Prom." Everyone was supposed to dress up in the same type of outfit they wore to their own prom. We had a DJ spinning seventies tunes, heavy on classic disco and Motown. Most of us grew up in late seventies and early eighties, so the baby-blue tuxes and magenta taffeta gowns ruled the room. My dress was actually pretty happening. My high school prom theme had been "Southern Comfort," and at eighteen I had worn a white tulle top and black poufy long tulle skirt, but this night I wore a slinky light blue silky long gown. Katy and Andy surprisingly showed up dressed as each other. She showed up in a men's black tux with a top hat, and she had a five o'clock shadow penciled in. Andy had on a little organza skirt with a tulle tutu and silk poofy blouse. His lipstick was applied to perfection.

Later, my husband came out of the men's room laughing. I asked, "What's so funny?"

He said, "There were guys lined up at the urinals in tuxes, and Andy Spade was standing at one of them lifting his big skirt and tutu in one hand and trying to navigate everything else with the other hand. We were all cracking up!"

* * *

Another reason to celebrate: Marybeth joined Kate Spade in April 2003 as the head of PR. She'd been working in fashion PR since the early nineties and knew everyone and everything about it. Most importantly, she was a known quantity to the founders, so she was the right person to oversee our PR and help us with strategy. For me, it was a treat to have a friend around. She was one of us. She'd been with us in spirit—and at our after-hours gatherings—since the company's beginnings. Having Marybeth on-site was comforting, but her presence alone wasn't enough to fix our problems at work.

Pamela and I had been telling Katy and Andy about our issues with Janet as they came up, but they were absorbed in their creative roles, and since the changes had not touched their departments, they couldn't relate to what we were going through on the business and production sides. They would always listen to us, but didn't want to discuss doing anything to rein Janet in. They did not understand what we considered to be the gravity of the situation, and they shared our early feeling that they didn't want to rock the boat with our majority owners.

Pamela and I reached our tipping point in late 2003, when Janet was lobbying to relieve us of the responsibility of attending management meetings. We went to Katy and Andy's apartment one night to have it out. I said to them, "We need to have a serious conversation. Janet is making the office dysfunctional. She doesn't treat the staff well, and she's making bad decisions. We're concerned with what's going on at the company."

I went on to explain that for the first time, I was not happy showing up every day. The old energy and passion had drained out of me and the company seemed to be going in the wrong direction. It seemed clear to us that Janet was trying to drive a wedge between us and Katy and Andy to force us out. She likely saw Pamela and me as vulnerable because we had more traditional business roles at the company. Katy and Andy were difficult for Janet to control because Katy was the face of the brand and Andy was the creative force behind the brand identity. She was right to some extent. But that strategy did not take into account our experience with the business and brand, and the corporate culture the four of us had built together.

Pamela said, "We can't have her going behind our backs, undermining us so she can run the company off the rails."

Since Katy had been on the road so much, and Andy was laser focused on Jack Spade and his other interests, they didn't witness what we were seeing day-to-day. They were aware that people were unhappy and that Pamela and I had concerns about Janet's leadership. And yet that confrontation with Andy and Katy did not have any immediate results. Andy had been on our side; he always listened and agreed and understood. Katy listened and tried to understand our side, but she also considered the corporate world Janet was coming from, as we had early on. Katy's diplomacy was noble, but it also let her avoid taking a side and getting in the middle of a conflict. As Pamela and I felt months before when discussing the clash of cultures, Katy hoped we'd all just work it out. We saw Janet's power play as an existential threat to the company we founded. Katy and Andy were just not on that page. Yet.

During Katy's personal appearance bonanza for the fragrance launch, her design team was left without a leader for weeks on end. Janet convinced Katy to bring in a senior designer and additional design staff to ease the pressure in her schedule and allow more time for the other responsibilities. Katy expressed to me over the phone that she had some real concerns with sharing the design accountability with new people she did not know. But like all of us, she was trying to go with the flow. Within a few months, new handbag samples were waiting for Katy's approval. The new team proudly displayed the luxe collection they had worked on. Katy politely complimented their work, although she was not necessarily happy with what she had seen. It was not in her nature to go against her better judgment, but Janet was pushing her to go along with what she called the "fresh design direction." Janet and her new team insisted they were "on trend." Katy hoped that the new direction was what we needed to do to take the brand to new heights but had never been one to follow trends. Her sensibility was to stay outside the trends and go her own way. One of my favorite Katy quotes is "If you're not 'on trend' you can never be 'off trend.'" Katy hesitated to approve their production but, once again, she gave her go-ahead to try to be cooperative and acquiesce to the new team's experience.

The designs weren't bad. They were beautiful bags but, to us, they were clearly off-brand, definitely not Kate Spade. They had a European luxury feel and were made with the most expensive materials, such as exotic animal skins, and included lots of shiny hardware. Not our thing. The retail price for one of the new snakeskin bags was $1,200. In our history, we'd never made a bag that cost more than $500. We knew most of our customers were not going to like the drastic change in sensibility. It was so counter to our value proposition. Accessibility had always been one of our mandates, coupled with a simple, sophisticated American style.

It was no surprise to us when the bags didn't sell well and editors at fashion magazines rarely added them to photo shoots. They did not justify the cost of that big investment and subsequently we were stuck with a season's worth of expensive inventory. The new line had bombed. Some retail specialty store and department chain customers now questioned if our collections would continue to drive sales with the change in our products. When Katy realized that following the new direction was a road to failure, she finally understood what we'd been concerned about for the last few years.

As a company, we had made our fair share of mistakes in the past, but never in the design of our bags. These off-brand elitist designs cost a fortune to produce. We had far too many of them left in inventory, and on top of that, we were getting substantial returns. Janet didn't have a solution as to how we'd recoup our losses. It would be a big financial problem, and it was primarily our fault for letting it happen.

A few weeks later, Janet announced that she was leaving Kate Spade to join a major American fashion brand. I know she'd come to Kate Spade with good intentions, and I did not consider her a bad person. In fact, we got along well in the office and socially. She brought a corporate sensibility and experience with very high-end brands, which she had attempted to plug into our company. I felt it didn't work out because she failed to understand our brand on a fundamental level. As partners in the company, all of those problems were ours to own.

Around the same time Janet left, a number of her top executive hires also resigned from the company. The relief around the office seemed palpable. To me, it felt like we had unruly houseguests who'd overstayed their welcome for years and were finally gone.

But the damage was done, and we had to get to work to try to fix it. My lifelong friendship with Katy was also feeling broken. I was not sure how, or if, that would ever be fixed.

* * *

For months after Janet's departure, we were still digging our way out of the hole we had found ourselves in. Aside from the deep inventory issues, there were a host of other unpleasant issues to reckon with. One big example were leases for a number of new stores that had been negotiated with expensive rents, high escalations over the term of the leases that were structured with many giveaways to landlords. The disciplined strategy for store leases that we had adhered to for years had been abandoned for the sugar high of store openings and non-profitable sales growth. I am convinced that if Pamela and I were not left out of the decision-making process, things would have been very different.

With the two of us back in charge of our divisions, Katy overseeing all the design, and Andy focused on his marketing group, we worked long hours to get back on track. Slowly some of the magic felt like it was starting to flow again. Katy and I were still walking on eggshells with each other. It had been close to a year now since Janet's departure, and it felt like the arm's-length relationship between Katy and me had become the new normal. We were both constantly annoyed and angry with each other, and often I found myself trying to avoid her at work.

One dark and chilly March evening, when we were both working late and the floor was mostly empty, I went down the hall to Katy's office for a planned meeting to discuss upcoming trips and the schedule for our Japanese partners. Katy was at her desk on the phone when I went in, and she didn't even look up to acknowledge my entrance. She was wearing her big Oliver Goldsmith eyeglasses that had oversized lenses that I thought were so chic on her, but my Andy had told Katy that they made her look like a bug.

I waited a few minutes and sat down on the chair opposite her desk, and soon began to drum my fingers on her desk. She stayed on the phone and looked up at me with mounting fury in her eyes. She gave me the *One minute* sign with her lips pursed and her index finger up in the air. I waited another few minutes, my anger bell about to ring.

After another few minutes, I knocked on her desk, hard. When she looked up, I held the palm of my hand up and shook it with a *What the F? . . . Let's go* gesture.

That really got her goat. She barked into the phone, "I'll call you later!" and slammed down the receiver. "What the hell is your problem?" she asked.

"You're my problem. Leaving me sitting here like I don't exist for ten minutes!"

"Oh boo-hoo, poor you. It's not always all about you," she said.

"Oh my God, that's a good joke. It's clearly not all about me. It hasn't been anything about me for a long time."

Now that we were fully engaged, I had a feeling that a lot was about to come out. I was mad and so was Katy.

"What are you talking about?" she asked. "Are you crazy? *You're* feeling ignored? You're the one who left me hanging out there alone all those months on the road. How could you do that? You said you'd always be with me." She was now really visibly angry.

"Well, you were ready to let me quit when your little buddy was running the company into the ground. Why would you blow me off and side with her? Do you know how that made me feel?"

"Blow *you* off? Are you kidding me? You left me alone on those personal appearances for over a year! A year! Do you have any idea how hard that was, how lonely?" Katy was raising her voice now.

"At least I didn't treat you like you were just some asshole who happened to be working here, and feed you to the lions!" I said, my loud voice now matching hers.

"You *are* an asshole!" Now she was screaming and jabbing her pointer finger at me. The lenses on her huge glasses magnified the size of her eyes.

"No, you're the asshole," I screamed back. "And you do look like a big mad bug!"

There we were, both furious, both screaming and pointing at each other like idiots. We glared daggers for a few seconds, still hopping mad. And then suddenly, we both softened. We realized that we were two forty-year-old women, jabbing our fingers at each other and screaming like we were in a high school spat in the cafeteria.

I smiled first.

She tried her hardest not to, then she smiled, too.

We both broke down at the same time. We laughed and laughed, the deep belly-hurting kind that we used to have.

I was the first one to speak. "I'm sorry, Kook, I know it was hard for you all alone out there. I was so stressed about everything happening with the business, I should have been paying more attention to you. I'm so sorry, and I've missed you so much."

"No, no, *I'm* sorry, I was wrong not to listen to you and Pamela," she said. "I was just so busy, so tired and stressed. I felt overwhelmed and thought that you left me out to dry. The politics in the office seemed like such a nothing to me. I just didn't see it. I should have listened to both of you."

We collapsed into each other's arms and the waterworks started. We cried together, which soon turned to laughter. All of our frustration and fears about losing our friendship poured out at once. We broke out of our embrace and wiped our tears away. We hung out for a while, calming down and talking about everything else.

"Oh my God," Katy said. "Let's go get a margarita."

"I'll get my coat," I said.

I opened her door out into what I thought was the abandoned floor. When I walked out, there was Jenel, Katy's lovely longtime assistant, sitting at her desk just outside Katy's office. Her eyes were wide, and her face was drained pale. She must have heard that whole loud exchange.

"Is everything okay?" Jenel asked, her voice shaking a bit.

"Yes," I said. "We're okay."

And we were.

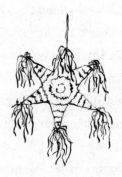

CHAPTER 26

The four of us were finally back in full productivity mode. It took us a long time to right the ship, and having done so, we were working harder than ever. To Janet's credit, during her tenure she had structured the company for growth, and many of the new hires were proving themselves very effective at their jobs. From an emotional standpoint, it felt like old times again. My sense was that harmony had returned to the relationships between the four of us, and the company had followed suit.

Katy was doing a smashing job on all the designs with her team in place. She had a full plate with our core handbag business and all the licenses we had put together.

Looking back on the advertising campaigns of that period, I think Andy was doing some of his best work, continuing to communicate the narrative of Kate Spade's brand connection to the nostalgic American experience.

Pamela and I could barely keep up with everything on our to-do lists, but we liked being too busy to kvetch at each other about anything. Best of all, Neiman Marcus, our majority owning partner, was pretty much leaving us to our own devices. We were in super-growth mode with strong profitability, so they were happy.

It's funny now thinking about that period of my life; it seemed to have flashed by in a heartbeat. Over a decade had passed since I had been sitting with Katy and Pamela, sewing labels onto the fronts of our newly minted first bags, but it felt like only yesterday. Through all our trials, a company had been created and a new brand born. As a company, we had over ninety-six department store retail locations nationally who gave us space for our Kate Spade branded "Shop in Shops." We had opened twenty freestanding Kate Spade stores in the US, with more than 260 boutique stores carrying our brand across the country. Our licenses for shoes, eyewear, stationery, tabletop (china, cutlery, crystal, etc.), bedding and beauty were all doing well. Our international business was strong and growing. Besides our thirty wholesale department store customers in Japan, our partners had opened twenty freestanding stores. The rest of Asia was growing for us, too. By then, there were Kate Spade stores in Hong Kong, Shanghai, Bangkok, Seoul, Singapore and Kuala Lumpur.

We were strictly nose to the grindstone in 2004, when during that summer, Katy shared the best news.

"I'm pregnant!" she said.

"I can't believe it! Congratulations!" I said. "Fill me in on all the details!" They'd been trying for a while, and my heart skipped a beat knowing that Katy and Andy were finally going to have their hearts' desire, a baby of their own.

Katy ran down the list of all the things that new mothers think about. She already had everything planned perfectly, from the hospital stay to the layout of the nursery, in her usual über-organized style.

"Let's go out and celebrate tonight!" she said

"Yes, yes!" I said. "But no drinks for you, Kook."

"What? Oh damn . . . I forgot about that."

"Don't worry," I said, speaking from experience. "You won't want to drink anything soon. But guess what? You can have all the cheeseburgers, milkshakes and big salads that you want."

"Baby!" she said. "Let's meet at Sant Ambroeus for dinner and order the desserts!"

Our local Italian fave on West Fourth Street in the Village had great pasta specials and ornate scrumptious desserts that changed all the time. We usually had to skip them or split one of them because they were so rich. She was loving this idea. We went over the top, ordering three desserts: a heavenly tiramisu; their selection of four gelatos, which arrived as four mini cones balanced in a little silver rack; and a slice of chocolate mousse cake—so good, and we shared everything.

Katy's pregnancy was a breeze for her. She had no issues throughout. Her style during pregnancy was to pair cardigans and cropped jackets with flowy cotton poplin tops and wear black cigarette pants or leggings underneath. Like me, she didn't want to buy too many maternity outfits (not much to choose from back then). She got creative, using pieces we had bought in Mexico on one of our many trips like our generous, flowy Mexican dresses and cute boxy voluminous tops. She also confessed in a *New York* magazine article, "It's funny—I wear high heels even more now that I'm pregnant. My legs seem shorter because I can't see much of them." Katy seemed to enjoy her pregnancy. If she felt queasy, like I often had, she never mentioned it. If she felt uncomfortably large, I didn't hear her complain even once.

* * *

Over the next few months, we all felt a sea change in the way Neimans was interacting with us. Our contact people were not reaching out to us as frequently. We had our monthly telephone financial check-ins, but any discussion of short- or long-term strategy seemed to be pushed off until the next month. Pamela and I were working on our real estate plans for the next flight of US store openings, but the feedback from my Neimans contact was minimal to nonexistent. Eventually we heard through the grapevine that the Neiman Marcus Group was potentially being acquired. When we mentioned the rumors to the execs at the monthly board meeting, they denied it. And yet, the whispers did not die down. If anything, they got louder.

Despite our good relationship with them, our partners contradicted what we had heard and said that there were no plans to sell off the company. "We are buyers, not sellers" was always the reply we received. Though that transaction would not have impacted us much in the short term, there was a big unknown about what would happen to Kate Spade should Neiman Marcus be sold. That scenario made us nervous, naturally, because we still owned almost half of our company.

In October, a front-page article appeared in *Women's Wear Daily* that reported Neiman Marcus was being acquired by private equity firms Warburg Pincus and Texas Pacific Group (TPG). We were shocked and disappointed that our partners had not informed us ahead of the announcement. I understood it happened in business. They needed to maintain silence on a transaction that big and likely had a nondisclosure agreement in place. But it felt like a bit of a betrayal nonetheless in that I had a lot of interaction with all those executives and personally like them very much. We reached out to the co-CEOs of Neimans, and they never phoned us back, which increased our angst.

We had one possible solution: In our original agreement with Neimans, we included both a "put" and a "call" option that kicked in after seven years. The "call" option gave Neimans the right to buy more of our stock at a fixed price within a set time. The "put" option, on the other hand, gave us the right to force Neimans to buy our stock at an agreed price within a certain time frame. We sent that letter to "put" our stock to them by FedEx and expected that would get their attention. Any financial buyer they were currently talking to would expect the Kate Spade arrangement to be status quo and part of the deal. The Neimans team had to recognize that we would all best be served working together.

The letter had the desired result. They called us as soon as they read it. But buying our stock while they were being sold would complicate their negotiations. They suggested a new idea: "Let's work together and sell Kate Spade separately to a different buyer, and you can pick who that new partner is going to be."

Instead of selling Kate Spade along with Neiman Marcus and the other brands they owned to the private equity groups they'd been negotiating with, they suggested we work as a team to find a suitable buyer for Kate Spade standing alone—one we would choose and that we'd be more comfortable with.

This plan wasn't quite what we wanted. In the best of all worlds, we hoped to buy the company back, not sell it to Neimans or to someone else. The obstacle was that with the high valuation placed on the Kate Spade business, we didn't have the capital to buy our shares back outright. Finding a new partner with Neimans was our best option if we didn't want to be owned by private equity firms that were unknown entities to us.

While we weren't thrilled about going through the process of vetting and dazzling potential strategic buyers, having a choice to find a new partner who understood our vision was exciting. We hired Peter Solomon Group, a well-known investment banking firm. Their role was to help us put together a detailed deck about the potential for investing in the company. It showed our historical data, an exact and accurate accounting of sales for shoes, handbags, home, fragrance, all the licensing stuff, everything we did. We made charts, graphs, and gave explanations about why our growth dipped here and exploded there. And it ended with a detailed plan for the next five years. It took months to get the deck together and was a tremendous amount of work. Peter Solomon Group sent it out to potential buyers, and we started meeting with them.

We were fortunate in that *a lot* of companies were interested. We did presentations for around twenty-five of them. In the end, we narrowed it down to the two highest bidders: the VF Corporation (Girbaud's parent company in North America) and Liz Claiborne (a strategic partner who owned close to forty fashion brands). We felt that Liz Claiborne would be a good choice for us. They had a strong executive team and lots of experience growing companies. They were super pros, but also seemed like decent, authentic people. We were particularly impressed with their star CEO, Bill McComb, a seasoned professional who respected the brand we had built and knew how to run a company.

We ended up going with Liz Claiborne, and Neiman Marcus agreed with our decision.

* * *

Back on the home front, on February 17, 2005, I got a call from Katy around 9:00 pm. I'd finally put my daughters to sleep and was ready for bed myself at the end of a long day. I thought Katy was just calling to unwind and gossip a bit or talk about work.

I said, "Hey, what's going on?"

"Andy and I are at the hospital, and . . ."

"Oh my God! Are you in labor? When did the contractions start? I can be there in half an hour!"

She chuckled a little (not the sound you'd expect from a woman in labor). "I already had the baby! A girl! It all went so quickly, I didn't have a second to call."

I just started crying. I'm not one to burst into tears. I hardly ever do. But that night, I was overwhelmed with happiness. Andy and Katy would've been thrilled with a boy, too, of course. But with a girl, Katy could put bows in her hair and dress her the way she wanted to—until her daughter had style thoughts of her own. While I tried to muffle my sobs, she told me that she and Andy rushed to New York-Presbyterian as soon as she felt contractions, and her beautiful, healthy daughter arrived just two hours later. Compared to her, I had the worst, longest, most painful labor. But for Katy, it was a snap. You don't hear many ideal childbirth stories, especially from women our age.

The next morning, I taxied uptown to the hospital with a bottle of champagne. Pamela and I arrived simultaneously. We sat in Katy's room and talked for hours. Unlike most new mothers who might be nervous about caring for a newborn, Katy was unusually calm and collected. We marveled at how this was so typical of her, to come in and ace childbirth in two hours, just like in college with those exams. I glanced at the two of them and was overcome with gratitude for our friendship. Now that we were all mothers, it was like the cosmic scales were finally balanced. If we didn't always understand each other in the past, as moms, I knew we would have an even stronger emotional shorthand moving forward.

Katy didn't have many other visitors at the hospital. She kept the news quiet. Many of Katy's family members showed up later that first week to help and meet their newest family member, who Katy and Andy named Frances.

From day one, Katy was a doting mom and occasionally would bring the baby to work. I brought my daughters to work sometimes, too, and all the women on staff loved it. Having Katy's and my daughters at work was such a pleasure. Katy's baby was serene and easy. My girls would run around the office, chatting with everyone and creating happy chaos. Their favorite time was the year we had Santa and several reindeer holding court in our showroom to present our holiday collection to store buyers.

Our office finally returned to a place that thrived in a culture of mutual support, kindness, diligence and fun. I was grateful to have the company back and run by the four of us, even if my workload tripled.

Over the past year, we had gone from presentation to presentation to find a buyer. Our fundamental questions had been, "Who will we sell to, and what will our future look like?" Now that we had our first answer, we started seriously discussing the important pathway we had considered only briefly before—whether to stay with the company or not? Andy Spade said at the time, "People write books on how to start companies. No one writes about how to get out of one."

During our protracted, monthslong negotiation with Liz Claiborne, the four of us did a lot of soul searching. We didn't start the business with a particular strategy. We didn't know what success would feel like, until we experienced it. We certainly didn't know what fame would be like for Katy or its emotional toll on her. When we reached a certain level, we thought our continued success was just a matter of adding to the foundation we'd already built, repeating the process a hundred times all over the world—more stores, more products, more licenses. We had done our job and felt creatively satisfied. We'd been reenergized to get our company back, preserve our culture and return it to the brand we had created—excellent reasons to stay. And I think we would have been swayed to carry on if we could have held onto a minority stake in the company. But none of the groups we had spoken to—including Liz Claiborne, the eventual new owners—were interested in partial ownership. It was all or nothing for all of them. We would have been more interested to find a partner to co-own the company with, but that was not an option that would work. We all started to lean toward an exit of some sort after the sale.

Katy and Andy Spade had their daughter. My Andy and I had Katy and Jane, and now I was pregnant with our third child. Pamela had her three kids, Elenore, Anabel and Will. We all felt that Kate Spade's valuation from Liz Claiborne was good and fair. The four of us discussed how we had an excellent thirteen-year run, and that we'd taken the company as far as we could. Maybe it was time for the next chapter in our lives, and for the company we'd created.

The fashion industry—the entire world—had changed since 1993 when we started, with the emergence of the internet and online shopping, viral marketing and advertising. We'd been keeping up and trying to maintain our company and culture while becoming a part of the digital revolution. But we learned a hard lesson from Neiman Marcus that when you sell a majority, you give up control. Pamela had been right. We would have no real authority after Liz Claiborne took over. And we all had different priorities now. It took a full year for us all to accept the reality that it seemed like the right time for us to go.

Over many conversations, we adjusted to the idea of leaving and moving on to the next chapters of our lives.

"But what will we do all day?" I asked Katy.

She responded exuberantly, "Are you kidding? I'll be so happy not to have a thing on my calendar. I can't wait to be bored, read magazines, go for walks in the park and shop without being in a rush. I'm not thinking about finding something to do!"

I thought about my own life, and there were a lot of things I'd like to do as well—learning to play tennis, taking cooking classes (I was married to a foodie, after all), redecorating our home and, most important, spending more time with my girls. I started warming to the idea of a new life.

Soon enough, I had another exciting reason to be happy about not working. On a clear April Friday morning, baby Marni joined our family. She was a stubborn little package. I laid in that birthing room, waiting hours on end for her. When Marni arrived, the doctor placed her on my chest, pink and wiggling from being born. Marni reached out her tiny hand and gave me a little slap across my face. *This is going to be the feisty one*, I thought. I was right about that.

* * *

Earlier that week, the four founders had been in a tense in-person discussion about deal points with the Neimans guys and Liz Claiborne team. I was very pregnant, and a week overdue. One of the Liz execs made a good-natured comment that maybe they should take it easy on the terms of the contract because, as he observed, "Elyce looks like she's going to have a baby any minute." It was well-intentioned and we all chuckled at his comment.

Marni was born on that weekend, and we had another meeting with the same group scheduled for the following Monday, so I thought I was going to miss it. But when I woke up on that Monday after giving birth to Marni, I felt really good—not like going-for-a-jog or doing-jumping-jacks good, but I was definitely okay to sit through a meeting in the office. I did my hair and makeup, picked out a flattering outfit and headed over to our banker's office where the meeting was scheduled. Andy was happy to take over with baby Marni for a few hours.

Katy and I arrived in the lobby of the building at about the same time.

"You're friggin' kidding me," she said.

"What?" I asked.

"Just what is it you're trying to prove? You had a baby two days ago. You're crazy!"

"Ah. No big deal. All in a day's work for some of us," I countered.

We entered the office and the eight men sitting there just stared at me. Ken Cera, our attorney, broke the ice. He looked at me and said, "What are you, some type of cavewoman that has a baby in the forest one day, and goes hunting the next day for dinner?"

Everyone chortled a little, but it was a weird kind of laugh like, *This is so odd*. I didn't mind at all. I always like showing the fellas what we gals are capable of. It keeps 'em guessing.

Liz Claiborne really wanted us to stay on and were generous and energized in their offers to try to keep us on board. In the end, we negotiated that we'd stay for six months and after that, we would have a two-year noncompete. By the terms of that agreement, none of us could start a competing business for two years. Katy had some additional terms that were negotiated independently, mostly to do with use of her name.

In December 2006, Kate Spade New York was sold to Liz Claiborne, Inc. Neimans and Liz Claiborne had pushed to get the papers signed before the end of the year. When I found out the closing date, I realized I had a conflict. Pamela and I were cochairing one of the biggest events at our kids' school. Grace Church School held an annual "holiday shopping" event for the children to purchase gifts for everyone in their family and have them prewrapped and tagged by loving volunteers. It was a really big deal to all of the hundreds of kids at the school. We couldn't change the date or not show up, since we were both running the event. Katy and Andy were not planning on going to the closing at all. We weren't really needed there; we'd signed power of attorney over to our lawyers, and all our required signatures were already filed. Our attendance would have been symbolic, but in the end it was an emotional journey that none of us really wanted to take.

Our priorities had already shifted. A few years back, I would have wanted to be present at such a monumental event to acknowledge it and remember how it felt. But now, chairing a school event for my kids was far more important to me. Mentally, I'd moved on, which was easier to do than I would have thought. I felt that we were walking away clean, on good terms with everybody, and happy about how it played out.

The four of us started the company on our own terms, and we left it the same way. We ended our business partnership, but our friendships continued with just as much affection and closeness as ever. Looking back, we stayed true to our roots, to being a team who respected and valued each other. Over thirteen years as business partners, we faced setbacks and problems, but we never turned on each other. We kept our friendships and sanity intact because of our mutual trust and respect. Even when we had a "dissenting partner," we always came together in the end.

More than anything else we were grateful to have had that journey, and to have taken it with the people we loved.

* * *

The Arons, Spades and Bell/Simotas families decided to celebrate the sale together. The day after Christmas in 2006, just two weeks post-sale, we all flew to Cabo San Lucas for a joint family vacation at Hotel Twin Dolphin to ring in the New Year and our new lives together.

That trip was glorious. The weight of the business was off our shoulders. We'd conceived and nurtured this wonderful thing—the company, our baby—and now we'd launched it into a future of its own. It honestly felt like taking your child to college, equal parts proud and sad, knowing it was for the best.

The Twin Dolphin was a special place for us. Katy had discovered it while working at *Mademoiselle*; she'd done a few fashion shoots there, and the Spades were there when we negotiated the deal with Neimans, checking in over the wonky phone line.

It was built by a Texas oil mogul as a private hideaway for his family and wealthy contacts. Its charming white villas with fireplaces and stunning remote location perched over crags and pristine beaches attracted the rich and famous since the 1970s. It looked like one of those exotic locations from an old James Bond movie. By the time Katy first traveled there in the nineties, the Twin Dolphin was sun and sea worn, a bit less lustrous compared to the luxury resorts that had sprouted like mushrooms all over Cabo. But it had a nostalgic and unpretentious aesthetic that Katy adored. Katy and Andy and Andy and I went back, again and again, at least once a year for a decade plus. The staff never changed and treated us like family, even remembering the names of our little kids. We talked about trying new places, but somehow always returned to the Twin Dolphin. One last time, we wanted to make memories there, as we found out the hotel was going to be torn down and replaced with a luxury resort and a huge golf course. The demolition was scheduled to begin almost as soon as we checked out. It was yet another symbol of the end of an era for us.

The kids played and laughed, stacking on each other to form a giant pyramid on floaties in the middle of the pool. We strung up a piñata for them that Katy had bought, a giant, colorful star with tissue paper fringe all over it. They whacked it to bits with an old broom handle and shrieked as they scooped up the fallen candy.

We lazed in lounges, bobbed on waves in the ocean, ate the most delicious huevos rancheros for breakfast every day and danced with margaritas on the beach at night. Along with the happiness and bond of old friends being together, we felt an underlying heaviness. The four of us knew we'd always remain close. But it would never be the same as seeing each other every day at work.

We *had* made it after all, bigger than we'd ever imagined. My personal and professional life had been intertwined with Katy, Andy and Pamela for more than a dozen years. Our closeness was, in part, due to our shared devotion to Kate Spade. We'd created this wonderful thing and now it was in the rearview mirror.

At one point during that vacation, Katy said, "This is probably the last time we'll ever do this all together." As great as that trip was—and it was so joy-filled for all of us—it had the feel of a bittersweet ending.

But it wasn't the end of Katy and me. That would never, ever happen.

Katy and I had often joked about being in our eighties, the two of us sitting somewhere warm, finally learning to play bridge, telling our stories and reminiscing. Watching Katy play with her two-year-old daughter by the pool at the Twin Dolphin expanded that vision of our distant future for me. I pictured us on the porch at Katy's house. Our grown daughters were there, and our grandkids were running around on the lawn in front of us.

The lazy week rolled by, with all of us enjoying the company of our old friends and partners. The poignancy of the moment, however, didn't stop Katy from being Katy. From the first day there, we had both been gawking at the biggest iguana we'd ever seen. It was perched on the wall next to the outdoor shower by the hotel pool, just above the knob to turn on the water. It was huge, terrifying and beautiful all at once. When you were nearby, it just stared off into the distance, its beady little lizard eyes focused on the horizon.

We asked the pool guard about it. He said that the big iguana had been there on and off for months. "Iguanas are very gentle creatures and would never hurt anybody," he said.

We took him at his word. By the end of the week, we were fairly used to having that leathery creature next to us when we showered. Katy passed on those moments, opting to shower in her room. I gave her a hard time, letting her know that when you grow up on a farm, you need to get used to animals being around you all the time. I was a bit sanctimonious, yes, but every now and then, it was still important for me to one-up her a bit.

On one of our last days, I was showering after the pool. I had brought shampoo down with me and gave my hair a good wash after a week in the sun and salt. My eyes were all soapy when I felt the scratchy claws of that hideous thing running straight up my back.

The shriek I let out startled all the guests at the pool, and I didn't let up on it for a while. I was screaming like a maniac. I feel the need to add, for accuracy's sake, that I am not at all an adorable screamer. I'm not like a damsel in distress. With my screams, think of the long, ear-splitting squeal of a steam locomotive grinding to a stop in a cowboy movie. Embarrassing.

My eyes were full of soap but I could suddenly hear people laughing all around me. When I cleared out my vision I saw sneaky Katy. She had quietly crept up behind me in the shower and was waving the very hand that she had run up my back like a creepy huge iguana.

"Gotcha!" she said with a big grin on her face.

Even with the adrenaline coursing through my body, I had to give her big bonus points on that one. It became a thing for our entire gang to try to replicate my shriek for the remainder of the trip, with even the kids giving it a try.

On our last night in Cabo, Katy and I stole away for a sunset cocktail by the beach. We left the little ones with the guys, and they welcomed a few hours of crazy with their girls. Katy and I laid on two white painted chaise lounges on the beach, which was pretty much deserted by then. We both ordered margaritas from the bar and sipped them slowly. I remember that scarlet-red sun setting behind the Pacific. There was a warm wind blowing across our bodies, which felt great. We watched the bright red flashes from the setting sun reflected off the wavelets on the ocean, and listened to the shallow surf hiss softly on the sand as the foamy seawater slid in and out. I felt completely relaxed for the first time since I could remember.

"So what's next?" I asked.

"I dunno. We get dressed for dinner?" Katy was lying back on her lounge with eyes closed, taking in the gentle breeze and the warmth of the setting sun.

"No, Kook. I mean, what's next for us?"

"Oh. Ha, sorry," Katy said. "I don't know. It doesn't matter. Whatever it is, we'll do it together."

She turned toward me with a sweet smile, still keeping her eyes closed, then laid her head back on her lounge.

I looked at that face that I knew so well. She never could control that spray of freckles across her little nose, no matter how hard she tried. In my mind, I traveled back to the first day we met at school all those years ago, standing in front of the mirror getting ready to go to our first college party. There was that same upturned nose, the same freckles, that funny smile I knew so well.

I leaned back and closed my eyes, happy to be with my best friend.

EPILOGUE

The four of us stayed on at Kate Spade for the six months to help with the transition. My last day was June 9, 2007. I wrapped up all of my meetings, packed my last box and quietly left. It felt too difficult emotionally to say goodbye to anyone. I was good with leaving, but the prospect of saying goodbye to all our wonderful colleagues was daunting. Katy, Andy and Pamela came in and out over the next two weeks and finally all left the same way I did. Despite our quiet exit, we all felt that when you have one foot out the door, you can't wait to get both out of there.

Once we had left, we kept in touch with a lot of the staff. Many of our people stayed on, and we eventually came to feel that our choice of selling to Liz Claiborne was a good one. It's been amazing to watch the company grow over the years. Today, Kate Spade New York has a global following and annual sales north of $1.4 billion. What was once our modest start-up is part of the publicly traded Tapestry company, which also includes Coach and Stuart Weitzman. They now have three hundred Kate Spade retail locations and employ more than thirty-five hundred people. Entire new generations of Kate Spade fans have been created. It feels like a great reward that what was once upon a time our little company is still creating jobs for people and bringing happiness to women around the world. I don't think Katy and I could ever really have envisioned what Kate Spade would become, but it feels good to know that our great adventure launched something that will be around for years to come.

* * *

A few days after our departure, I drove out to Long Island with my kids for the summer. Pamela had a house in Southampton. Katy and Andy had their place in Sagaponack, and we had ours in Bridgehampton. The kids played together on the beach, and there we had dinners, parties and big bonfires with all the friends we'd made over the years.

When I got back to the city in September, I left Marni, the baby, with our nanny, and walked my older daughters to Grace Church School in the Village. After drop-off, I stood there without any idea what to do with myself. I had never not had a place to go before.

I got into the habit of putting on my iPod Mini and running all the way uptown to Katy's place on Park and Seventy-Seventh. We'd walk around Central Park for hours, just talking. Then I'd head back downtown to pick up the kids when school let out. When winter came, it was too cold to be spending so much time outside, and I had some very long days indoors.

I didn't realize how much I'd miss work. I discussed it all the time with Katy, who had the same reaction to being at home. What we missed most was being part of the social fabric of the office, interacting with the people there every day, chatting with them about work and life. I love my children and adored spending time with them, but I needed more adult interaction. My solution was to get heavily involved at our kids' school. I volunteered to chair events and eventually became the parents' association president, helping to raise money for a new high school Grace was building downtown. I later joined the board of trustees and became board chair for four years while we built our new high school, which in retrospect was a tremendous learning experience. Besides that, I took cooking classes. I learned how to play tennis and hit the courts several times a week. As one does, I managed to stay busy. But it wasn't the same. On some level, I missed the intense challenge and hard work that I was used to, and I missed fashion. I had to leave Kate Spade to fully appreciate how much of my sense of self had been so wrapped up in the company.

Katy was always going to be Kate Spade, so she escaped the feeling that her identity had changed so dramatically. However, she had a different set of issues in no longer working at the company that still bore her name. People would come up to her and say, "I saw Sasha Obama wearing your purple coat at the inauguration. Congrats!" We'd sold the company three years before Barack Obama took office in January 2009, and Katy hadn't had any part in designing the beautiful coat worn by Sasha. But Katy wasn't going to stand there and explain all this to a kind well-wisher. She graciously said, "Thank you so much."

A few years after the sale, Katy walked into one of the many new Kate Spade stores to replenish her supply of the fragrance. She looked around and thought, all things considered, the new owners were doing a good job. The salesperson was being helpful and offering to show her their new line. Katy politely declined.

"At least let me put you on our mailing list?" the salesperson asked.

"Oh, no thanks," Katy said, and then left the store.

I asked her why she just didn't tell the woman who she was. Her answer, very much in character: "I thought that might embarrass her."

* * *

Andy had started a new branding and advertising company, Partners & Spade and could now work with new clients and come up with fresh, innovative campaigns, the career he always enjoyed. Another huge benefit for him was not having to talk about work stuff day and night with Katy, as they had for over a decade. Starting his own company allowed him to separate church and state.

Katy and I still talked daily, and we were as close as ever with Pamela. To celebrate Pamela's forty-fifth birthday in 2013, Katy, the two Andys, Pamela and I met for dinner at the Waverly Inn in the West Village. Even though Waverly is known as one of the top celebrity sighting spots in the city, they give everyone the red carpet treatment. It's right at the end of our block on Bank Street, and since the day they opened they've treated Andy and me, and all the locals, as if we were the famous ones.

At dinner that night, Katy and I started talking about the possibility of getting the band back together and founding a new business. Our noncompete agreements had expired more than five years before, so that was not an issue. Andy Spade had just been featured on the cover of *Inc.* magazine for Partners & Spade and was busy with new clients, so he wasn't interested in another full-time commitment. Pamela had a new company called Prinkshop that created copy and designs for bags and T-shirts to help nonprofits raise money for their missions, and she was involved in her free time with the Mental Health Coalition, so she couldn't commit.

But Katy and I kept talking and ultimately decided to launch a new accessory company with handbags and shoes. Andy Spade agreed to handle the ad campaigns and branding from his agency. We had a few hoops to jump through about handling our time commitments to other things, but we easily solved those. Before we knew it, we were off to the races.

Our first order of business was to come up with a name. As always, that process is fraught with a thousand back-and-forths of great ideas that we couldn't use for one reason or another, and bad ideas that are just dumb when you think about them. In the end, there was a tiny fraction of real goodies.

We decided to use family names. Any Spade reference was off the table, due to our contractual agreement with the new Kate Spade owners. The name Frances popped up in multiple generations in Katy's father's side of the family. Valentine was her maternal grand-father's name. We ended up using them together to create our new company name. In our minds, it would represent that special woman, Frances Valentine, who was both stylish and smart, like your favorite aunt who made you laugh harder than anybody else. She was your confidant, your best friend, your favorite person. In effect, this woman represented who we were to each other.

It took us from 2014 to 2016 to launch. It was harder than we thought it was going to be. We'd been out of the industry for nearly eight years, but the world had kept moving. Social media and e-commerce were already gaining speed when we sold Kate Spade. We had to unlearn what we knew and learn about a whole new landscape. That took some doing. When we started our first company, we were thirty years old. When we started our second, we were fifty. Katy didn't like to use the phrase "grown-up," but we were now. We were different people. Together we had a lifetime of experience in the business. We wanted different things in terms of goals for the company and for our brand's aesthetic.

We set out to create handbags and shoes that made our customers smile every time they wore them. We thought of this as the next chapter in our journey, building upon what we created before and tempered by the sensibilities of the women we had become. At the beginning of Frances Valentine, we made everything from sexy four-inch heels to bright pink and marigold-yellow ballet flats. Our first handbags were bucket bags and totes in shiny silver and gold Italian metallic leather. We made soft, tumbled organic leather boxy and cross-body bags in saturated hues of red, blue and olive with interesting but subtle hardware details. The two of us working together again felt like slipping into a much loved, well-worn set of pajamas, at once familiar and comforting. We hired a terrific staff of professionals who knew their jobs inside out, which allowed me to spend more time on the design side. We were back in business, and our creative and productive selves began firing on all pistons.

There were a host of issues early on with selling our concept to buyers. Our plan was to create great style and quality at an accessible price point, but buyers told us that now our prices were in "no man's land," somewhere between bridge and luxury. When I told buyers, "We're affordable luxury," an idea that worked brilliantly at Kate Spade, they looked at me like I was speaking a foreign language.

And we made some early mistakes. In America, the typical woman's foot is a "B" width. But our new Italian factory manufactured them all in a narrow "A" width. After our first delivery of shoes started shipping from Italy and arrived at US stores, customers returned them in droves. It cost a fortune in returns (we were self-funded, so that really hurt), and we lost two seasons because of it. We hired Zonda Sochorow (now our COO at Frances Valentine), an exceptional Kate Spade alum who has also worked at Coach, Lo & Sons and other companies, as our new head of production. She came in and within a few months straightened everything out.

We did recover. By late 2017, sales were strong. We were opening wholesale accounts with department and specialty stores across the country. Our e-commerce was doing especially well, essentially a new business for us that was ramping up beyond expectations. It was starting to look like lightning might just strike twice.

A year later, Katy was gone.

* * *

The morning I got the news I was working at my desk in my office just after nine. Katy's assistant, Dallas, called me and told me to make sure I was sitting down. Then he told me that Katy had taken her own life. I didn't believe him at first. When he finally got through to me, I let out a cry of distress from a grief so deep that I barely remember what happened next.

It had been just the day before when we were talking on the phone and Katy was laying out her plans for spending the summer in Napa, which Katy, Andy and their daughter had done for many years. In the middle of the conversation, her dad had called her, and as always she would stop what she was doing and pick up for him. She told me she would call me back. It was just inconceivable to me that we would never speak again.

A few weeks after her passing, I was interviewed on a national TV morning show. The agreement with the show was that I would be happy to talk about Katy's life, but they were not allowed to ask me questions about her death. Of course, they did. The interviewer said something like, "If you could ask Kate one question, what would it be?"

As I was sitting there with the live cameras trained on me, the question that popped into my head was: *Where's my pink skirt?* She'd borrowed it months ago.

Of course I didn't say that on live television. My answer was "I would have asked her, 'Why?'"

If I had given my honest first answer, and if Katy, from wherever she was, had heard it, she would have roared laughing. That would have made me smile. Our friendship was all about trying to get big reactions out of each other—screams, laughter, tears. And we succeeded, for nearly four decades.

Losing my best friend for life—the woman who shared my sense of humor, who'd been my constant companion at school, at work, at dinners, on the phone, in my house, on vacations—was like losing your face in a mirror. It was disconcerting, disturbing and very lonely.

I plagued myself, asking "Why?" and did a lot of looking back, trying to find things I might have missed.

I talked often with Katy about her struggle with depression, which I knew she had been dealing with those last few years. She was actively seeking help with specialists, and we understood the goal was to mitigate the times Katy was carrying that deep sadness she couldn't seem to shake, and which had weighed heavily on her in recent years. Most of the time she was herself, and we spent our days together as usual, working or socializing. We had discussed the suicides of celebrities in the past and she had said definitively to me, "I would never, ever do that."

It pains me deeply to imagine Katy sinking into a deeper depression and not talking about it with anyone. She was private about many things, even with me. Other people, some who knew her and many who didn't, wrote articles about surface-y, ready-made explanations for her actions—marriage problems, our company not being as successful as we had hoped in the first years, along with stories about her struggles with depression.

Though they were working out their marriage issues and living separately (though not legally separated), I can tell you that Katy and Andy loved each other to the ends of the earth. Katy worshipped her daughter. She'd dealt with professional and personal wobbles throughout her life. A highly sensitive person, she felt things more deeply than most. But I know for sure she was not so upset about how many pairs of shoes we sold that she would take her own life. We all have dark moments and periods. In one of those moments, she lost hope.

Like many people who have passed in that shocking way, taking their loved ones by surprise, Katy left us with many questions. We've had to learn to cope with our grief, and after seven years of trying to comprehend her actions, I'm still peering into the well and not finding answers. All of us who loved her have had to find a way to make peace with her incomprehensible choice. It's not been easy.

One outcome from our tragedy is that I've learned to never take the people I care about for granted. As I tell my closest friends: Go to your sister or your best girlfriend who's just like a sister to you. Go to her today and hug her so hard that it's like you won't ever let her go.

I will never let Katy's choice in those tragic last few minutes of her life define her. Katy is still with me every day. She is the most gracious, sweet, intelligent, funny woman I've ever known. When I miss her most, or when I've needed my friend in the years since she's passed, I've learned to simply find her.

In a quiet moment, I just close my eyes and there we are together. Laughing until we cry.

ACKNOWLEDGMENTS

First and foremost, my deepest thanks to my husband, Andy Arons, who cowrote this book with me. Working together on this project has been a wonderful experience, and I am so grateful to have you by my side.

I want to extend my sincere gratitude to Aimee Bell of Gallery for believing in this book from the very beginning. Your wisdom, guidance, enthusiasm and infectious energy have made this journey truly special. I couldn't have asked for a better editor for this project.

A heartfelt thank-you to the wonderful Jennifer Bergstrom for publishing our story and bringing it to life.

I am immensely grateful to my wonderful partners Pamela Bell and Andy Spade for taking countless strolls down memory lane with me. Thank you to my dear friend Marybeth Schmitt for your humor and stories, which have enriched this process, and I wouldn't have recalled so much without your help.

Thank you, Valerie Frankel, for your invaluable time and skills and providing the scaffolding and support I needed to shape my stories.

I want to acknowledge the fantastic team at Gallery: Sierra Fang-Horvath, Sally Marvin, Jill Siegel, Heather Waters and Pamela Cannon. Your dedication ensured everything was completed on time and with perfection.

A special thank-you to Susan White, a talented photo editor and friend, whose insights and expertise were invaluable.

I also want to express my appreciation to Dan Strone, my literary agent, for believing in this book, and to Richard Beyman, our attorney, whose guidance throughout the project was instrumental.

My gratitude goes to Maggie Cepis, Adam Ward and Lauren Klas from our creative team at Frances Valentine. Your talent in helping craft the book cover and chapter icons and assistance with photos brought everything together beautifully.

Special thanks to Jemme Aldridge for creating the beautiful peony print for the endpapers of the book.

Thank you to Dallas Sowers for his excellent memory and recounting precious moments to me.

To all of our dear friends who contributed in countless ways—your support means the world to me, and while I can't name everyone, a special shoutout to Jan Geniesse and Lynn Grossman for their unwavering friendship and honesty during this writing journey.

To the whole Kate Spade team who made all the magic come to life with us from 1993–2007 and to those who have joined us at Frances Valentine to make it happen all over again! Working with all of you wonderfully talented, creative and clever people has been the dream of a lifetime, and I am lucky to call you all friends.

Finally, I am blessed to have such a supportive family: my parents; my sisters, Willow and Shon; and my nieces, Anna and Ashley. To my beautiful daughters, Katy, Jane and Marni, you inspire me every day. Thank you for always believing in your mom and for giving me the time and space to work on this project. I adore you, my darlings.